£1.75

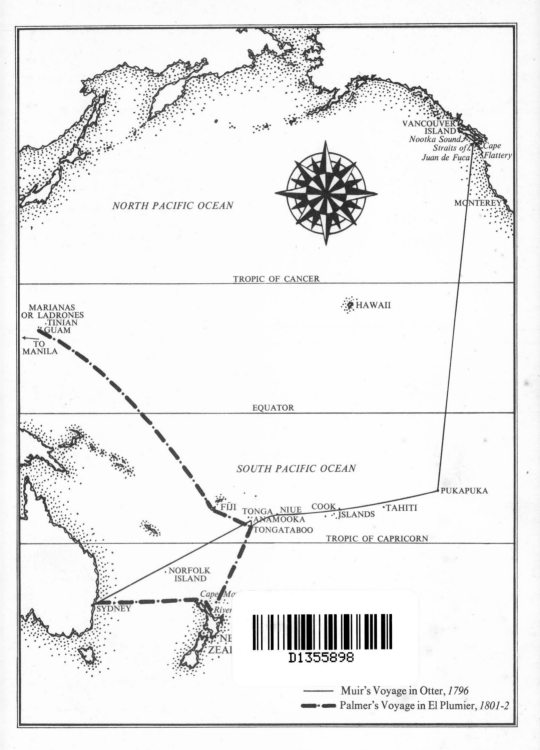

NORTH PACIFIC OCEAN

VANCOUVER
ISLAND
Nootka Sound
Straits of
Juan de Fuca
Cape
Flattery

MONTEREY

TROPIC OF CANCER

HAWAII

MARIANAS
OR LADRONES
TINIAN
GUAM
TO
MANILA

EQUATOR

SOUTH PACIFIC OCEAN

PUKAPUKA

FIJI
TONGA NIUE
ANAMOOKA
TONGATABOO
COOK
ISLANDS
TAHITI

TROPIC OF CAPRICORN

NORFOLK
ISLAND

Cape Ma
River

SYDNEY

NE
ZEAL

D1355898

———— Muir's Voyage in Otter, *1796*
▬▬▬▬ Palmer's Voyage in El Plumier, *1801-2*

THE SCOTTISH MARTYRS

By the same author

Autobiography
TRY ANYTHING ONCE
TRY NOTHING TWICE
KOREAN DIARY

History
WILD COLONIAL BOYS
THE KELLY HUNTERS
OVERLAND TELEGRAPH
SCANDALS OF SYDNEY TOWN
MURDERS OF MAUNGATAPU
JIMMY GOVERNOR
BLUE MOUNTAIN MURDERS
PIRATES OF THE BRIG "CYPRUS" (in collaboration with P. R. Stephensen)
BOUND FOR BOTANY BAY
SEARCH FOR THE GOLDEN FLEECE
SERENADE TO SYDNEY
THE NORFOLK ISLAND STORY
SCALLYWAGS OF SYDNEY COVE

Adventure Stories
THE RED HEART
THE PACIFIC PARADE
THE FORLORN HOPE
LAND OF MY BIRTH

Biography
D'AIR DEVIL (Pard Mustar)
CHINESE MORRISON
THE GREATEST LIAR ON EARTH (De Rougemont)
CAPTAIN STARLIGHT (Harry Redford)
GOLDEN GOLIATH (E. H. Hargraves)
DEEMING THE DEMON
A NOOSE FOR NED (Ned Kelly)
THE VIKING OF VAN DIEMEN'S LAND (Jorgen Jorgensen)
   (in collaboration with P. R. Stephensen)
MARTIN CASH
CAPTAIN MELVILLE

Exploration
DIG (Burke and Wills)
THE LAST OF THE EXPLORERS (Donald Mackay)

Historical Novels
DARK OUTLAW (Frank Gardiner)
BEN HALL THE BUSHRANGER

Travel
ROLLING DOWN THE LACHLAN
ROAMING ROUND THE DARLING
FREE AND EASY LAND
SKY HIGH TO SHANGHAI
TO THE ISLES OF SPICE
ALL ABOARD FOR SINGAPORE
PROWLING THROUGH PAPUA
TOBRUK TO TURKEY
SONG OF INDIA
ROAMING ROUND AUSTRALIA
HIGH-HO TO LONDON
LAND OF HOPE AND GLORY
ASHES OF HIROSHIMA
ALL ROADS LEAD TO ROME
HANDS ACROSS THE PACIFIC
SOMEWHERE IN NEW GUINEA
CASTLES IN SPAIN
FLYING DUTCHMAN
LAND OF AUSTRALIA
ROAMING ROUND EUROPE
ROAMING ROUND NEW ZEALAND
THE FORTUNE HUNTERS
A TALE OF TAHITI
FLIGHT TO FORMOSA
*JOURNEY TO CANBERRA
*ACROSS THE SNOWY MOUNTAINS
SAGA OF SYDNEY
JOURNEY TO PITCAIRN

*Revised and combined and now published as JOURNEY TO KOSCIUSKO

THE
SCOTTISH
MARTYRS

Their Trials and Transportation to Botany Bay

FRANK CLUNE

ANGUS AND ROBERTSON

First published in 1969 by
ANGUS & ROBERTSON LTD
221 George Street, Sydney
54 Bartholomew Close, London
107 Elizabeth Street, Melbourne
65 High Street, Singapore

© Frank Clune 1969

National Library of Australia
Registry Number AUS 69-2262
SBN 207 95254 X

Registered in Australia for transmission by post as a book
PRINTED IN AUSTRALIA BY J. C. STEPHENS & COMPANY, MELBOURNE

DEDICATED
TO
MY FRIEND
JOHN EARNSHAW
HIS *THOMAS MUIR*
INSPIRED AND ENCOURAGED ME
TO WRITE THIS STORY

ACKNOWLEDGMENTS

AGAIN I wish to thank the Trustees of the Public Library of New South Wales, the Trustees of the Dixson Collection, and the Trustees of the Mitchell Library for making available to me the many thousand items of Australiana that have helped me to trace this story.

And once more, my sincere thanks to the expert staff in charge of these collections for ever-willing assistance in finding the information I needed.

I thank also Jeffrey Gibian of London for the part he played in locating numerous items in the archives of the Public Records Office, London, and newspaper files in the library of the British Museum.

I also owe a debt of thanks to my trio of friends in Edinburgh—Dougal McCallum Hay, Alexander Dunbar, B. Sc., Ph.D., and Arthur Hill—for help in researching the doings of the Scottish Martyrs.

Thanks once more to my friend Noel Pearson of Randwick for his work in photographing, under difficulties, many of the old portraits reproduced in this book.

My thanks are due to Cavan Hogue, First Secretary of the Australian Embassy, Mexico City, for unearthing from the National Archives several missing links dealing with the arrival of Thomas Muir and the eleven convicts who escaped from Port Jackson to Mexico in the year 1796.

Finally, to my secretary, Mrs Chiquita Cullip, for typing this mile-long manuscript, and for translating the French diaries of Maurice Margarot.

Vaucluse, 1969   FRANK CLUNE

FOREWORD

FIVE years ago I began the arduous task of writing a history, in which I proposed to narrate stories about the senior citizens of Botany Bay — the "baddies" and the "goodies".

Daily I visited the fount of Australiana in the Mitchell Library, collecting and collating materials from century-old manuscripts, hard to decipher and tough on the eyes, dealing with those who had arrived in shackles — as well as those who arrived free — on the First Fleet in 1788, and on later vessels from England and Ireland.

Sad to relate, chronicles of good convicts and law-abiding colonists were scarce, and what little was recorded about them — with some exceptions — made dull reading. But deeds of the scallywags were more exciting. Convicts pirated ships, and sailed to the South Seas usually wrecking their vessels, and beachcombing happily with dusky damsels until the British Navy disturbed their idyllic life by hanging them from a handy yardarm. On land the "baddies" wagged it from school, stuck up the "goodies" in their carriages, and swilled firewater by the firkin. Almost all died with boots on, shot by troopers dedicated to preserving law and order, or dangling in a noose on the end of a hempen rope.

Week by week I filled pages with thousands of words about the First Fleeters and pioneers of Botany Bay. Weeks became months, and months grew into years. About three years later I browsed into the office of my publisher all ready for a yarn. Then I showed him a manuscript of 400,000 words which had spilled into nearly 1600 pages, and told him that there was more to come.

The arbiter of my literary fortunes, my lifelong friend, blanched.

"Take it away, Frank!" he advised. "You have enough material there for three books."

With bowed head and heavy heart I sadly mooched home, and with quivering fingers began the Olympian task of performing a Caesarian operation on my brain-child. From these 1600 pages, many months later, triplets emerged — *Bound for Botany Bay*, followed by *Scallywags of Sydney Cove*, and finally, last but not least, *The Scottish Martyrs*.

Before I could finish the story of these political martyrs, I prowled the archives of London, Edinburgh, and Mexico City, seeking new light on matters that had remained obscure for more than a century and a half.

So here we are with the true story of six men who were tried in Scotland in the 1790s for sedition, found guilty, and transported to Botany Bay.

Vaucluse, 1968.   FRANK CLUNE

A WORD TO THE READER

In this book, as in others that preceded it, I have discarded numerals and asterisks, with their footloose footnotes, which I consider irritating works of the devil. I cannot subscribe to the view of the intelligentsia that footnotes are necessary. They clutter the pages and delay the narrative by constantly referring the exasperated reader, who is not always *en rapport* with the author, to the bottom of the page — or worse — to hurdle scores of pages to the aftermaths, in search of the story that goes with the symbols and footnotes, usually in tiny print. I prefer to quote my authorities as the text unfolds, letting my characters tell their tale, giving the name of the book from whence the story comes, with a comment by me.

Unfortunately, some of the Scottish Martyrs — and the judiciary who convicted them — were marathon orators and lovers of redundancy. In the cause of less infuriating reading, and to save sending some of my audience round the bend, I claim an author's* privilege — without any beg-pardons — to shave the rhetorical repetitions of the Martyrs and their contemporaries. I trust readers will agree.

*FRANK CLUNE

CONTENTS

CHAPTER SIXTEEN   122

The Diary of Monterey — "Otter" Arrives — Péron Meets the Governor —
— Purchase of Provisions — Dorr Sails Away — Péron's Lawsuit in Boston
— Jane Lambert and Others Left in Monterey — Who Was Jane? — Muir
Leaves Mexico — Imprisoned in Havana — Departs in Spanish Frigate
"Ninfa" — H.M.S. "Irresistible" Captures "Ninfa" — Muir Wounded in
Battle — Loses Eye — Different Accounts — Muir in Cadiz Hospital —
Writes to Thomas Paine — Paine's Clash with Robespierre — Muir Fêted
in Bordeaux — Citizen Mazois — Muir Arrives in Paris — The Sword
Brothers of Glasgow — Muir Rides in his own Carriage — Muir and Paine
Argue on Religion — United Irishmen Seek French Help — Muir Meets
Napper Tandy — Wolfe Tone Warns Muir — Liberation Army Invades
Ireland — Wolfe Tone's Capture and Suicide — Napper Tandy Saved —
Death of Thomas Muir.

CHAPTER SEVENTEEN   131

Palmer Shares a Home — Mr and Mrs Boston — James Ellis — Mr and Mrs
Margarot — Palmer Writes to Whitbread — Martyrs Refused Permission to
Depart — Palmer Thanks Disney — Boat-building with an Encyclopaedia
— Schooner "Martha" — Captain William Reid — "Martha" Wrecked at
Little Manly — Palmer's Illness — Extortions of Officers — Wreck of the
"Sydney Cove" — Coal Discovered — Bass Looks for Survivors —
Aboriginal Farmers — Native Customs — Palmer's Last Letter from
Sydney, 1799 — Writes to Rutt — Arrival of the "Hillsborough" — Wake-
field's Pamphlet — Schemes to Survive in Sydney — Brewing and Boat-
building — Boat Disappears — Townson's Speculations — Palmer's Pains
—Biography of Rutt — Trial of George Mealmaker — Fourteen Years'
Transportation.

CHAPTER EIGHTEEN   141

Boston-Palmer-Ellis Sydnicate — Arrival of "El Plumier" — Captured by
Whalers — Governor Hunter's Report — Schooner "Martha" — William
Reid — Skipper of "Francis" — Boston and Ellis Sign Petition — William
Smith, Missionary from Tahiti — Robert Campbell Employs Smith — An
Unlucky Trader — Murder of Samuel Clode — Campbell Returns —
William Smith Jailed — Palmer and his Friends Plan to Leave Sydney —
Offer Smith a Passage on "El Plumier" — Palmer Sells Land to Ebor Bunker
— Smith Escapes — Captured — "Royal Admiral" Arrives — George Meal-
maker on Board — Jail Fever — Wilson Helps Smith — "El Plumier" and
"Royal Admiral" Depart for New Zealand — Arrive in River Thames —
Cargo of Spars — Maoris Pilfer — "Royal Admiral" Sails for Tahiti.

CHAPTER NINETEEN   148

Voyage of "El Plumier" — Captain Wilson's Letter — Prisoners of the
Spaniards at Guam — Boston, Ellis, Reid Reach Manila — Palmer Dies at
Guam — Dampier and Anson at the Ladrones — Palmer Buried in
Unhallowed Ground — Bones Taken to Boston — Haswell's Journal —
Voyage of the "Lydia" — Arrival at Guam — Journey of "El Plumier" —
Indians on Guam — John Boston at Manila — Captain Balch — Mystery

ILLUSTRATIONS

Thomas Muir
*An engraving from the bust made by Banks
from the cast taken on board the* Surprize

Silhouette
of Thomas Muir

Huntershill House, Auchinairn, home of Thomas Muir as a young man

CHAPTER ONE

"WHEN our ashes shall be scattered by the winds of heaven, the impartial voice of future time will rejudge your verdict." So said Thomas Muir at his trial in Edinburgh in 1793, when he was found guilty of sedition and sentenced to be transported to New South Wales, thus becoming one of the group known to Australian history as the Scottish Martyrs.

Of the five men usually given this title — Thomas Muir, Thomas Fyshe Palmer, William Skirving, Joseph Gerrald, and Maurice Margarot — only two were actually Scots, but all were sentenced in Scotland in the years 1793 and 1794. A sixth man, George Mealmaker, who was sentenced a few years later, has good claims to be regarded as one of the group.

Their story can be understood only against the background of their time, the period of change and upheaval that came with the last years of the eighteenth century. In England and Scotland the Industrial Revolution was already under way, and the old order of society, based largely on agriculture and the land, was beginning to break up. Political change was in the air, too, and there was growing agitation for a more democratic system of government and for the reform of Parliament. Though the British parliamentary system was probably the most advanced in the world at that time, the mass of the people still had no vote, and, with a few exceptions, only men of landed property could sit in the House of Commons. "Pocket boroughs" or "rotten boroughs", with few inhabitants — Old Sarum was the most notorious, with only seven — had the right to return members to Parliament, while well-populated districts might have no representation at all. In practice, such a borough was usually controlled by the nobleman who owned most of the property within it, and who could give or sell the seat to any candidate he approved.

Such abuses had their roots far back in history, but they had been greatly aggravated by the Landed Property Qualification Act, which had resulted

I

from the struggle for power between Whigs and Tories in Queen Anne's reign. When, after years of Whig control, the Tories returned to power in 1710 they tried to consolidate their position by passing this Act. "The avowed purpose of the Qualification Bill," says Trevelyan, "was to prevent any Englishman who was not a squire from sitting in the Commons. Henceforth no one was allowed to sit who was not possessed of land to the annual value of £600 if a Knight of the Shire, and of £30 if a representative of a borough." They hoped by this to exclude many merchants and business men, who were more likely to be Whigs than were the conservative country gentlemen. It also meant that the boroughs became particularly valuable to ambitious politicians.

The Landed Property Qualification Act did not apply in Scotland, but since the Parliaments of Scotland and England had been united in 1707 any abuses in the system of election to the House of Commons affected Scotland, too. In any case the people of Scotland also suffered from the general restriction of the right to vote. So the demand for parliamentary reform that made itself increasingly heard as the eighteenth century drew towards its close found plenty of supporters in both countries.

Needless to say, the minority who held power and privilege were not going to give them up without a fight, and they found it easy enough to persuade themselves that the *status quo* was ordained by Providence and was in the best interests of the country. They had on their side the reluctance that many people always feel to changing old ways, and the alarm caused by such extreme views as those of Thomas Paine, who was not content to urge the reform of Parliament, but called for the overthrow of Church and Throne, and put his republican ideas into practice by helping the American colonists in their revolt against the Mother Country.

The outbreak of the French Revolution in 1789 deepened the gulf between conservatives and radicals. The former were confirmed in their suspicion that democracy meant bloodshed and anarchy, while the latter were inspired to reckless flights of oratory and enthusiasm. Societies with names like "Friends of the People" and "Friends of Liberty" sprang up all over the British Isles. On 16th October 1792 an association known as the "Friends of the Constitution and of the People" was formed in Glasgow, and one of the first names on its roll was that of Thomas Muir the younger, Advocate, of Huntershill, near Glasgow.

Many years later, in 1831, Peter Mackenzie wrote *The Life of Thomas Muir, Esquire, Advocate*, giving an account of the trials and tribulations of Muir, of whom he said: "A nobler man lives not this day within the city walls."

Thomas Muir was born in Glasgow on 24th August 1765, the only son of a respectable merchant. His father later bought Huntershill at Auchinairn, near Glasgow. Muir's mental growth was remarkable, and at the age of ten (or twelve according to some authorities) he was enrolled as a student in Glasgow University. As he was pious and industrious he studied divinity, and his elders were anxious for him to enter the Church.

Later his thoughts turned to law, and he studied to become a member of the Scottish Bar. He mastered foreign languages, collected rare books, and became proficient in useful knowledge, hoping to become a leader in his chosen profession. But he became embroiled in university politics, and it was alleged that he and his friends wrote offensive lampoons about unpopular professors. Incensed at these satires, the Faculty circulated a letter to all professors, urging them "not to admit Thomas Muir, and twelve other young gentlemen to their classes".

Muir was advised to apologize and to make peace with the professors as a means of restoring himself to favour. He refused, and, after graduating M.A. in 1782, left Glasgow for Edinburgh, where he studied law. In 1787 he was admitted a Member of the Faculty of Advocates.

Thomas Muir made many friends, because he spoke sincerely and eloquently on behalf of his clients, and his services as an advocate were much in demand. He was also ready to speak in public on his political views, which were fervently radical, especially when the French Revolution gave fresh fuel to his enthusiasm. When he joined the Friends of the Constitution and of the People in 1792, and became Vice-President, he was frequently called upon to address new branches on the aims and object of the parent association. These, as stated, should not have alarmed the authorities, since a condition of membership was that "it was incumbent on every person to subscribe a declaration, expressing his adherence to the Government of Great Britain, as established by King, Lords and Commons".

Says his biographer, Peter Mackenzie: "Muir always conjured his audience to adhere steadily to the principles of the Constitution: to be on guard against the villainous seduction of hired spies, who then unhappily began to brood on the land, and above all, he warned them against the dangerous consequences of tumult or insurrection, which would be fatal to the objects of their Association, and highly criminal."

Muir unfortunately did not heed his own advice. He became intensely partisan, and made many fiery speeches expressing sympathy with the French revolutionaries across the channel. This was asking for trouble, for by now the Prime Minister, William Pitt the Younger, was seriously alarmed lest the infection of the French Revolution should spread to the British Isles, and all over the country the authorities had informers at work, zealously noting down anything that might be interpreted as sedition. In Scotland this intelligence system was directed by the Lord Advocate, Robert Dundas, whose uncle, Henry Dundas, was Pitt's right-hand man and for many years wielded great power in Scottish affairs. At the time of the Scottish Martyr's trials Henry Dundas was Home Secretary.

The dossier of Muir's crimes gradually thickened as his organization printed and distributed propaganda pamphlets from Thomas Paine's *Rights of Man*. This work was written by Paine in answer to Edmund Burke's *Reflections on the Revolution in France*, which had powerfully influenced public opinion against the Revolution. In *The Rights of Man*, issued in parts between March 1791 and February 1792, Paine not only defended the French revolutionaries but implied that they had not gone far enough. He attacked monarchy and aristocracy, predicting their downfall in all the enlightened countries of Europe within seven years, and praised the American republic, which he had helped to establish.

Paine had gone to America in 1774, after he had lost his job as an excise-

3

man and had failed in business as a tobacco-miller, all his goods and chattels being sold for debt. Earlier in his career he had sailed on a privateer, finding his father's trade of stay-making, to which he had been apprenticed, too tame for him. His parents' Quaker religion also failed to appeal to his aggressive and turbulent character. In America he took an active part in the Revolution, and his pamphlet *Common Sense* had a tremendous effect there. George Washington credited it with having "worked a powerful change in the minds of many men", while Blanchard, Paine's biographer, says it caused the Declaration of Independence.

From 1787 Paine was in England and France, initially to perfect and market a pierless iron bridge, one of his many inventions, but mainly to act as a propagandist for republicanism in both countries. In August 1792 the National Assembly conferred French citizenship on him, and invited him to become a member of the French Convention, an invitation he decided to accept, since he was threatened with prosecution in England. He was warmly welcomed in France; meanwhile in England his trial for seditious libel went on and he was found guilty, though he was defended by the distinguished advocate Thomas Erskine. (Not understanding how a man could be tried in his absence, I asked my friend Mr Justice John Barry about it, and he explained that it could be done because Paine was charged with a misdemeanour, seditious libel; had he been charged with a felony his presence would have been required for a trial. In the written proceedings before the trial Paine pleaded not guilty, and at the trial did so through his counsel, Erskine.)

No wonder Tom Paine and all his works were anathema to the British Government. Worse still, the French leaders had shown by their treatment of Paine that they were not prepared to keep their revolution to themselves. On 19th November 1792, as Professor C. W. C. Oman records in the *Historians' History of the World*, the French Convention passed a decree offering assistance to "all subjects revolting against a tyrant". Two days later deputies from British associations came before the bar of the Convention in Paris, announcing their intention of establishing a similar Convention in their own country, and expressing their hopes that France would never lay down her arms as long as tyrants and slaves continued to exist.

Replied the President of the Convention: "Royalty in Europe is either destroyed or on the point of perishing in the ruins of feudalism. The declaration of the rights of man is a devouring fire which consumes all thrones" Such language was a direct incitement to the discontented British subjects to overthrow their own Constitution.

In December 1792 the Friends of the Constitution and of the People, with kindred societies, held a Convention in Edinburgh, attended by 160 delegates, among them Thomas Muir. Naturally the delegates liked the sound of their own voices and let off steam, and naturally, too, the Lord Advocate planted informers in their midst.

Muir read an Address from the Society of United Irishmen in Dublin to the Reformers in Scotland, which said, among other things: "We take the liberty of addressing you in the spirit of civic union, in the fellowship of a just and common cause. We rejoice that the spirit of freedom moves over the face of Scotland: that light seems to break from the chaos of her government;

and that a country so respectable in her attainments in science, in arts, and in arms; for men of literary eminence; now acts from a conviction of the union between virtue, letters and liberty; and now rises to distinction, not by a calm contented secret wish for a Reform in Parliament, but by openly, actively and urgently willing it, with the unity and energy of an imbodied nation."

Such sentiments seem harmless enough to a modern reader, but the mere name of the United Irishmen spelt rebellion to the Government, so their good wishes were enough to damn the Convention that received them, and to damn Thomas Muir for reading them.

In his *Lord Advocates of Scotland*, George W. T. Omond says: "The meetings of the reformers were private; but the Lord Advocate knew all that was going on. A spy had been hired to attend the meetings, under pretence of being a member. Who or what this spy was it is impossible to say. His letters are anonymous. He may have been a man named Watt, who was afterwards executed for treason, and whose defence was that he was acting for Government. Watt was well-informed of all that was going on, and sometimes sent a copy of the Minutes to the Lord Advocate."

Dundas now determined to make an example of a prominent reformer, says Omond, and Thomas Muir was the selected victim. On 2nd January 1793 he was arrested and taken before the Sheriff of Midlothian, charged with sedition, and lodged in the Tolbooth prison. Liberated on bail, he found to his sorrow that most of his friends had deserted him, for fear of being caught on similar charges.

Muir now made a fatal mistake. He decided to visit France, after arranging with his solicitor to advise him if and when criminal charges were issued against him. He reached Paris on the eve of the execution of Louis XVI, an act which he deplored, but was powerless to prevent. On 21st January 1793, beneath the sharp blade of the guillotine, the King of France was beheaded while the crowd shouted, "Long live the Nation!" "Long live the Revolution!" A few days later Pitt, horrified at the execution, bade the French ambassador leave England, and on 1st February the French Convention declared war. The war raged until 25th March 1802, when a peace treaty was signed at Amiens. Then it raged all over again until 1815 when Wellington defeated Napoleon at Waterloo.

While in Paris Muir received a letter from his solicitor, urging him to return to Edinburgh. He had been indicted to appear before the court on 11th February 1793 to answer a charge of sedition, but because of the war he was forbidden to leave France. Despite this, on 25th February 1793 a sentence of outlawry was declared by the Scottish Crown against Muir, followed by his being struck from the roll of the Faculty of Advocates.

In *The Life of Thomas Muir*, Peter Mackenzie states that the passport from the French Minister of Foreign Affairs describes Muir as "twenty-eight years of age, five feet nine inches high, hair and eyelashes of a chestnut colour, blue eyes, aquiline nose, small mouth, round chin, high forehead, long and full face".

In Paris, Muir met Barras, Condorcet, La Fayette, and many other distinguished people who showed him great kindness. A letter written some years later indicates that he also met Tom Paine. Eventually Muir was allowed to leave France. Later in 1793 he landed in Ireland, with a charge of outlawry hanging over his head, after which he crossed into Scotland.

He had been there an hour, says Mackenzie, when he "was pounced on by the minions of the law" and carried to the jail of Stranraer. Early in August 1793 he was taken to Edinburgh to stand trial.

The stage was now set for one of the most ruthless, biased, and venomous trials of the century.

CHAPTER TWO

ON 30th August 1793 Thomas Muir was brought to the bar of the High
Court of Justiciary, in Edinburgh, to answer charges of sedition.

Lord Cockburn writes of Muir's trial in his *Examination of the Trials for
Sedition in Scotland*: "This is one of the cases, the memory whereof never
perisheth. History cannot let its injustice alone."

In Cockburn's opinion, Muir was distinguished "by no superiority of
talent; he was, except in the imprudence of getting into the position of a
political prisoner in those days, a man of ordinary sense. His zeal for the
promotion of Liberty, but especially of parliamentary reform, was free of that
wildness of temperament which sometimes inflames reformers into absurdity
of project and dangerous ardour of disposition." Later in the same article,
Cockburn adds: "There were a few candid political opponents who were
startled by the poverty of the evidence of guilt; while all candid political
friends were loud in their protestations that there was no evidence whatever.
. . . It was the opinion of all who could be dispassionate then, and has come
to be the opinion of nearly everybody now, that Muir was really *Innocent*."

Muir was prosecuted by the Lord Advocate of Scotland himself. Dundas
was enraged at being harassed by advocates of parliamentary reform, and was
determined to smash the devotees of incipient revolution, French style.

Says Lord Cockburn: "The crime meant to be charged was sedition. But
instead of using the direct and simple term, the accusation is expanded and
multiplied into at least four separate charges." Here they are:

1. Whereas, etc., the wickedly and feloniously inciting, by means of seditious
speeches and harangues, a spirit of disloyalty and disaffection to the King and the
established government; more especially when such speeches and harangues are
addressed to meetings or convocations of persons brought together by no lawful
authority.

2. As also the wickedly and feloniously advising and exhorting persons to

7

purchase and peruse seditious and wicked publications and writings, calculated to produce a spirit of disloyalty to the King and government.

3. As also the wickedly and feloniously distributing seditious writing of the tendency aforesaid.

4. As also the wickedly and feloniously producing and reading aloud in a convocation of persons a seditious and inflammatory writing tending to produce in the minds of the people a spirit of insurrection, and the publicly recommending such seditious writing, are, *all and each, or one or other of them crimes.*

The charges were supported by a "statement of facts":

1. That the prisoner had attended meetings at Kirk-in-Tilloch and Milton, of a society for reform, in which he had delivered speeches, in which he seditiously endeavoured to represent the government as oppressive and tyrannical, and the legislative body of the State as venal and corrupt: especially by instituting a comparison between the pretended existing government of France and the constitution of Great Britain *with respect to the expenses* necessary for carrying on the functions of government, he endeavoured to vilify the monarchical part of the constitution, and to represent it as useless, cumbersome, and expensive.

2. That he had exhorted three people residing in Cadder, to buy and read Paine's *Rights of Man.*

3. That he had circulated the work of Thomas Paine, *A Declaration of Rights,* by the friends of reform in Paisley, *A Dialogue between the Governors and the Governed,* and *The Patriot,* and, in particular, that he did deliver and put into the hands of Henry Freeland, a copy of Paine's works.

4. That he had read an "Address from the Society of United Irishmen", to a meeting of the Convention of Delegates of the "Friends of the People", and had there expressed his approbation of its sentiments.

After discussing these sedition charges, Lord Cockburn states that one of the judges, Lord Henderland, said of the indictment, "It charges him particularly with attacking Kingly government, a pillar on which the Constitution hinges, and which, if undermined or pulled down, must give rise to the most serious consequences. Sorry shall I be, if of such a crime a man may be found guilty. But if the charges libelled on are found to be true, they must be found relevant to infer the pains of law; *and these pains include everything short of capital punishment."*

Another Judge, Lord Swinton, said "he had never heard such an indictment read, and he did not believe that in the memory of man there ever had been a libel of a more dangerous tendency read in that court. There was hardly a line of it which, *did not amount to high treason,* and which, if proven, *must infer the highest punishment the law can inflict."* (The term "libel" in Scots law is the equivalent of "indictment" in English law.)

Two more judges, Lord Dunsinnan and Abercromby, agreed with their colleagues, Henderland and Swinton, "as to the dangerous tendency of the crimes charged, and that if proven, the *highest* punishment should be inferred".

Lord Justice-Clerk Braxfield, chairman, then addressed the court: "The crime here charged is sedition, and that crime is aggravated according to its tendency; the tendency here is plainly to overturn our present happy Constitution — the happiest, the best, and the most noble constitution in the world,

8

and I do not believe it possible to make a better. And the books which this gentleman has circulated have a tendency to make the people believe that the government is *venal and corrupt, and thereby to incite rebellion*."

Robert MacQueen, Lord Braxfield, is stated in the *Dictionary of National Biography* to have been born in 1722 and to have died in 1799. After being educated at the grammar school of Lanark and at Edinburgh University, MacQueen was admitted as an advocate in 1744. He "quickly gained the reputation of being the best feudal lawyer in Scotland, and for many years possessed the largest practice at the bar." He assumed the title of Lord Braxfield on being appointed a Lord of Session on 13th December 1776, and on 1st March 1780 was appointed a Lord of Justiciary in the place of Alexander Boswell, Lord Auchinleck. On 15th January 1788 Braxfield was promoted to the post of Lord Justice-Clerk, and in this capacity he presided at the trials of Muir, Skirving, Margarot and others.

Lord Cockburn describes Braxfield as "a coarse and illiterate man, with a keen and vigorous understanding, a hard head both for drinking and thinking, and a tyrannical will. Strong built and dark, with rough eyebrows, powerful eyes, threatening lips, and a low growling voice, he was like a formidable blacksmith. His accent and his dialect were exaggerated Scotch, his language, like his thoughts, short, strong, and conclusive." Such was the judge whom Cockburn calls "the Jeffreys of Scotland". "He bullied the counsel, and his colleagues alike. Devoid of even a pretence of judicial decorum, he delighted while on the bench in the broadest jests and the most insulting taunts, 'over which he would chuckle the more from observing that correct people were shocked'."

It is worth noting that William Roughead, historian of many famous Scottish trials, gives a much more favourable portrait of Braxfield in his writings, and claims that Cockburn's account was a strongly biased one.

About a century after the trial of Muir, Robert Louis Stevenson wrote his last, unfinished novel, *Weir of Hermiston*, a story of the Scottish border, in which the chief character, according to the *Dictionary of National Biography*, was "founded on that of the famous judge Lord Braxfield".

Again we refer to Lord Cockburn for the trial of Muir, who had asked Erskine to be his counsel. Erskine agreed, but only on "the reasonable condition" that the conduct of the case should be left entirely to him. Unfortunately, "Muir had the folly to decline, partly from vanity, partly from despair". Said Erskine: "He declined my assistance. He pleaded his own cause — and you know the result."

The prisoner submitted a written defence, the substance of which he also stated verbally. He admitted that he had exerted every effort for parliamentary reform. "I am accused," said Muir, "of sedition. And yet I can prove by thousands of witnesses that I warned the people of the danger of that crime. I exhorted them to adopt none but measures which were constitutional and entreated them to connect liberty with knowledge, and both with morality. This is what I can prove. If there be crime, I am guilty."

Asked Lord Braxfield: "What exculpatory proof do you mean to adduce?"

Muir: "I have been accused of seditious harangues, and of circulating improper books, and that I intend to prove the reverse."

9

The Court desired to know, said Braxfield, "as it might save trouble, whether the prisoner admitted that he had recommended the particular books libelled".

Muir replied in the negative, but admitted that he had "advised reading books on all sides of the question". Braxfield then proceeded to pick the jury, and, says Cockburn, "The second person he called was Captain John Inglis — a gruff honest sailor. This person, though as violent a hater of everything that might be called popular liberty, had the candour to state 'that he was a servant of Government; that he understood Mr Muir was accused of a crime against Government; and that he did not consider as proper that Mr Muir should be tried by a jury composed of servants of Government: that his mind felt scrupulous — laboured under much anxiety, and he begged leave to decline being a juryman'."

Braxfield then informed Captain Inglis that "there was no impropriety in his being a juryman, and therefore he was *compelled* to serve". Comments Cockburn: "Is it not improper to compel a person to take his seat as a juror who honestly feels a bias against a prisoner?"

The fifteen jurors were all members of an "association of gentlemen" who had met in Parliament House, Edinburgh, on 7th December 1792, "to consider the present state of the country". Thomas Muir had also attended this meeting and signed his name as a member, but later his name was erased from the list without his consent. Now he was confronted by a jury composed of members of an association that had rejected him because "they did not think Mr Muir or his friends proper members". "So that the prisoner was put, by the presiding judge, voluntarily, into the hands of a jury of marked zealots — zealous, no doubt, for the best of all things, the Constitution, but zealous also against the prisoner as a supposed violator of it." The empanelling of this jury, Cockburn continues, was virtually the pronouncing of the verdict.

So there was little hope for Muir, though that part of the indictment charging him with having uttered seditious speeches was, in Cockburn's opinion, supported by no evidence whatever. Not merely the evidence for the defence, but much of that for the prosecution, showed that his addresses were all "strongly constitutional: urging reform, but deprecating revolution — recommending union and petitions, but dissuading from violence — praising France, chiefly on account of the cheapness of its government, and predicting the success of its arms, but uniformly preferring our own monarch for us". All that the Lord Advocate had to say to the jury on this branch of the case was that "asserting the superior economy of France, and *anticipating her military triumphs*, tended to make the prisoner's hearers like that country, and, so far, diminished their attachment to Britain, and thus provoked revolution".

The prisoner defended himself, says Cockburn, "with great spirit, and occasional eloquence". At one point he said, "I smile at the charge of sedition. I know for what I am brought to this bar. I will give you little trouble. I will prevent the lassitude of the judges: I will save you, the jury, from the wretched mockery of a trial — the sad necessity of condemning a man, when the cause of his condemnation must be concealed, and cannot be explained. What has been my crime? Not the lending to a relation of mine a copy of

Mr Paine's works; not the giving away a few copies of an innocent and constitutional publication; but for having dared to be, according to the measure of my feeble abilities, a strenuous and active advocate for an equal representation of the people, in the House of the people: for having dared to accomplish a measure, by legal means, which was to diminish the weight of their taxes, and to put an end to the profusion of their blood."

Mackenzie, in his biography of Muir, says that Muir "summarized article by article the accusation against him", and ended his plea: "Gentlemen of the Jury, I hasten to a conclusion. Much yet remains to say, but after the unremitted exertion of sixteen hours, I feel nearly exhausted. This is perhaps the last time that I shall address my country. I have explored the tenor of my past life. Nothing shall tear from me the record of my former days. The enemies of Reform have scrutinized, in a manner unexampled in Scotland, every action I have performed — every word I have uttered. Of crimes most foul and horrible I have been accused, of attempting to rear the standard of civil war, to plunge this land in blood, and to cover it with desolation.

"My crime is for having dared to be, according to the measure of my feeble abilities, a strenuous and active advocate for an equal Representation of the People in the House of the People. It is a good cause — it shall ultimately prevail — it shall finally triumph."

The prisoner paused for breath, and resumed his address: "Gentlemen of the Jury; the time will come when men must stand or fall by their actions — when all pageantry shall cease — when the hearts of all shall be laid open. If you regard your most important interests — if you wish that your conscience should whisper to you words of consolation, or speak to you in the terrible language of remorse, weigh well the verdict you are to pronounce. I am indifferent to my fate. I can look danger, and I can look death in the face, for I am shielded by the consciousness of my rectitude. I may be condemned to languish in the recesses of a dungeon. I may be doomed to ascend the scaffold. Nothing can deprive me of the recollection of the past. Nothing can destroy my peace of mind, arising from the remembrance of having discharged my duty."

According to Mackenzie, when Muir sat down there was a "unanimous burst of applause". He had spoken for nearly three hours, from about ten on Friday night to one on Saturday morning.

Muir's eloquence was of no avail, and he was found guilty. Cockburn's account continues: "Then came the great question whether the court could or would transport. But their Lordships soon settled this; because without a moment's pause, instantly after the verdict was given, they pronounced a sentence of transportation. He was not invited to say a word, by being directly informed that this was the sentence in contemplation. He was silent till it was too late to speak. Yet, exercising a discretion, the court sentenced a person in the rank of a gentleman, convicted of a first offence, and this offence Sedition, to transportation for fourteen years."

According to Cockburn, when the judges were discussing the sentence Lord Henderland informed his brethren that they had their choice of banishment, fine, whipping, imprisonment, and transportation. He considered that banishment would be improper, since it would only be sending to another country "a man dangerous to anywhere he might have the opportunity of exciting the same spirit of discontent, and sowing with a plentiful hand Sedition". Henderland was also opposed to a fine, because it "would only fall upon his parents, who had already suffered too much by the forfeiture of his bond", while whipping was too "disgraceful, the more especially to a man who had borne his character and rank in life". And imprisonment, the judge considered, "would be but a temporary punishment, when the criminal would again be let loose and again disturb the happiness of the people". He concluded, "There remains but one punishment in our law — transportation."

Lord Braxfield, after "expressing his concurrence with his brethren that transportation was the proper punishment for such a crime", mentioned that he was "troubled by a solitary doubt — he only hesitated whether it should be for life, or for the term of fourteen years".

So sentence was recorded: "We find the prisoner Guilty of the crimes libelled . . . we ordain and judge that the said Thomas Muir be transported beyond the seas . . . for the space of fourteen years . . . if after being transported he shall return to us, and be found at large, within Great Britain during the said fourteen years, without lawful cause, he shall suffer Death . . . and we ordain the said Thomas Muir to be carried back to the Tolbooth of Edinburgh, therein to be detained till he be delivered over to transportation.

Transportation was a dreaded punishment, as a story in the *Scots Magazine* for September 1789, headed "Transportation or Death", shows. It tells how, at the Old Bailey, a number of prisoners "who had received sentences of death, but whose executions had been delayed during the indisposition of the King, were asked whether they would accept his Majesty's mercy, on condition of their being transported to New South Wales during their natural lives". Eight of them "promptly refused to accept mercy on such terms, and preferred death. They were seriously exhorted by the Court, and told that if they refused the King's mercy they should be executed as soon as the Sheriff was available." Three hours later, as the Court was about to rise, the judges were told that five of the obstinate men had changed their minds "and entreated that they be permitted to accept the mercy of the Sovereign". The other three, still preferring death to transportation, were ordered to the condemned cells to await the Sheriff's pleasure. But the strain was too much, and two of the prisoners agreed to accept the Royal Mercy and a trip to Botany Bay. Two days later "the last of these deluded wretches was to have been executed outside Newgate. Every preparation was made; the sheriffs stayed the execution to the latest moment. Then the unfortunate man, finding himself on the brink of eternity, begged, and received, His Majesty's mercy on the terms first offered."

But Muir was not daunted. Mackenzie quotes him as saying, "I shall not animadvert upon the severity or the leniency of my sentence. Were I to be led this moment from the bar to the scaffold, I should feel the same calmness and serenity which I now do. My mind tells me that I have acted agreeably to my conscience and that I have engaged in a good, a just, and a glorious cause — a cause which, sooner or later, must and will prevail."

Ending his discourse on the tragedy of Muir, Lord Cockburn quotes a story told by Sir James Gibson-Craig, "who not only lived, but acted in these scenes during the trial of Muir. All were thunderstruck with the extreme severity of the sentence, and none more than the jury. They met after the Court rose, and expressed their opinion that the sentence was beyond all measures severe. They thought Muir's guilt had been so trivial that a few week's imprisonment would be a sufficient punishment. They resolved to prepare a petition for the court, but when they met, Mr Innes of Stow produced a letter he had received, threatening to assassinate him for his concurring in the verdict of guilty, on which the jury separated, considering it impossible for them to interfere."

One of the onlookers at this farcical travesty of justice was Samuel Romilly, a law reformer, born at Westminster in 1757. A descendant of a Huguenot refugee from France, Romilly became a clever linguist and translator. He studied law, and it is stated in the *Encyclopaedia Britannica* that "in the years that followed his call to the bar in 1783, he rose in his profession to become the outstanding chancery advocate in England. Romilly lived in Paris during the early years of the French Revolution, and ardently defended the rebels until their excesses and regicide sickened him. He returned to England a sadder and wiser man.

One of his special friends was Monsieur Dumont, a preacher from Geneva, who lived in Paris. Soon after Romilly returned to England he visited Edinburgh, and wrote to Dumont on 14th September 1793: "I am not surprised that you have been shocked at the account of Muir's trial. You would have been much more shocked if you had been present at it as I was. I remained there both days, and think I collected in the course of them, some interesting materials."

The above letter was printed in *Memoirs of the Life of Sir Samuel Romilly*, published in 1840. Jeremy Bentham, philosopher, jurist, and political reformer, also received a letter from Romilly written ten days after the trial of Muir. It appears in Romilly's *Memoirs,* and in the *Works of Jeremy Bentham.*

Wrote Samuel: "I am passing my time here very pleasantly; principally however, in a society which you would not at all relish — lawyers. Indeed, I doubt whether this would be a very safe country, at this moment, for you to be found in; for I heard the judges of the Justiciary Court, the other day, declare with great solemnity, upon the trial of Mr Muir, *that to say the courts of justice needed reform* was seditious, highly criminal, and betrayed a most hostile disposition towards the Constitution, of which the courts of justice form a most important part."

Later, in 1797, Romilly successfully defended John Binns, a delegate of the London Corresponding Society, on a prosecution for sedition. In 1806 he was sworn in as Solicitor-General and received a knighthood the same year. In 1808 he purchased for £3000 the representation of Wareham, Dorset, a rotten borough with 150 voters. Says the *Dictionary of National Biography*: "This compliance was a bad but then common practice Romilly justified to himself as, in view of the universal rottenness of the representative system, the best means of securing his own independence, for the sake of which he had twice declined the offer of a seat, once from Lord Lansdowne, and once from the Prince of Wales." In November 1818, after the death of his wife, Romilly shut himself in his house, and three days later cut his throat with a razor.

After his trial Thomas Muir was lodged in the Tolbooth of Edinburgh. On 10th November he wrote to his solicitor, Mr Moffatt: "I leave you and Mrs Moffat perhaps for ever, but your remembrance never shall be effaced from my mind. In public I can act the part of a man — I can meet everything with fortitude; but in private I must give way to feelings of nature. My dear and valued friend, in the remotest corner of the world your remembrance and that of Mrs Moffatt shall soothe me in my affliction, but my tears shall flow over the remembrance. I am really unwell. I cannot write much, nor have I time, but neither of you shall be wiped away from my heart."

Muir's heartbroken letter continues: "Let us all cultivate the paths of virtue. Let us all follow more closely than what we have hitherto done (misled by the pleasures, the follies, the occupation of this frivolous life) genuine Christianity, and with confidence we can indulge the transporting hope that we may again be united together, under the immediate presence of that Almighty Being in whom all truth, all justice, and all humanity concentrates. Let us look up to immortality, and although we may toss and tumble in the feverish night of Time, healing will come in the morning, and in the words of the inspired writer, the Sovereign Physician of Gilead shall heal our wounds."

After this exhortation to his friends, Thomas Muir concluded: "I am bidding you a long good-night. Never more shall we meet again in this sublunary sphere, but let it be our endeavours, by attending to our conduct here below, that we may meet in eternity above."

The above letter was printed in Volume II of the *Historical Records of New South Wales*, with a note that it was written on the eve of leaving the Tolbooth for the *Stanislaus* hulk, Woolwich.

Laments were loud throughout the British Isles at the harsh sentence imposed on Muir, and also on Palmer, whose trial began in September 1793. One of their sympathizers would almost certainly have been Robert Burns. On another occasion his expressions of sympathy with the reform movement nearly cost him his position as an exciseman. In Chambers's *Life and Works of Robert Burns* it is recorded that in a letter to Mr George Thomson, dated September 1793, Burns enclosed his famous ode beginning "Scots wha hae wi' Wallace bled", remarking that he had been roused into writing it by the "accidental recollection of that glorious struggle for liberty [the Battle of Bannockburn] associated with the glowing ideas of other struggles *not quite so ancient*".

This is quoted in the second volume of the *Historical Records of New South Wales* and the editor, F. M. Bladen, adds: "There can be little doubt that the result of the trials of Muir — on the 30th August — and Palmer — on the 12th September — was fresh in the mind of Burns when he composed the poem referred to; and it is more than probable that they were the 'struggles, *not quite so ancient*', to which he refers."

So it seems Burns was speaking for the reformers of his own time as well as for Bruce and his men before their famous victory of 1314 when he wrote:

> *Lay the proud usurpers low!*
> *Tyrants fall in every foe!*
> *Liberty's in every blow!*
> *Let us do, or die!*

CHAPTER THREE

THE HUNT was on. The trial and sentence of Thomas Muir was followed by more arrests on charges of sedition.

Public Enemy Number Two was the Reverend Thomas Fyshe Palmer, born in Bedfordshire in 1747, and descended from a respectable and well-to-do family. An article in the *Monthy Magazine* (vol. xxx, page 83) says that, according to his baptismal certificate, Palmer was baptized at Northhill, Bedfordshire, on 16th August 1747. He spent several years at Eton, and in 1765 was entered at Queen's College, Cambridge. In 1769 he took the degree of Bachelor of Arts, in 1772 that of Master of Arts, and in 1781 that of Bachelor of Divinity. For about a year he performed the duties of curate at Leatherhead in Surrey, but he had become dissatisfied with the doctrines of the Church of England, and in 1783 he severed his connection with it. He then went to Montrose in Scotland, to join a society of Unitarians who had opened a chapel there under the auspices of William Christie. Christie, described by the *Dictionary of National Biography* as "one of the earliest apostles of unitarianism in Scotland and America", was the son of a merchant and provost of Montrose. He was educated in the Presbyterian faith, but his theological studies convinced him that the Church of Scotland acknowledged "a false Popish deity", and he became a Unitarian.

According to the *Monthy Magazine*, Palmer remained in Montrose for twenty months, then moved to Dundee, where there was also a society of Unitarians. There he lived for several years, preaching frequently in towns and villages, and at Forfar, Edinburgh, he delivered "a series of discourses in vindication of Unitarian principles".

Because of his Biblical searchings he soon began writing theological tracts. His first was entitled *An Attempt to Refute a Sermon by H. D. Inglis, on the*

Godhead of Jesus Christ, and to Restore the long lost Truth of the First Commandment. The success of this tract encouraged Palmer to write *An Attempt to prove the Fallen Angels to have been only the Sons of Seth*. Other tracts were *An Attempt to explain Isaiah IX. 6* and *An Attempt to show that the Cock crowing which Peter heard was the sound of a Trumpet*. Such were the labours of the sincere Unitarian scholar during his decade at Dundee.

In his *Examination of the Trials for Sedition*, Lord Cockburn says of Palmer: "After obtaining a Fellowship in Queen's College, and a curacy in Surrey, some conscientious scruples about the Trinity made him forego very favourable prospects in the Church of England, and descend to the position of an Unitarian preacher, in which capacity he unfortunately set foot in Scotland. A scholar, a gentleman by family and manners, and of the purest moral character, he was highly esteemed by an extensive class of friends." But his zeal in the Unitarian cause also made him enemies, who, though unwilling to persecute him on religious grounds, were not displeased when his political activities gave them an opportunity to attack him.

As well as his Unitarian tracts, Palmer began publishing pamphlets in which he urged the reform of Parliament and universal suffrage. Then came the French Revolution in 1789, and the formation in England and Scotland of groups known as the "Friends of Liberty" and other names that had a sinister connotation in the ears of Prime Minister William Pitt and his colleagues. Very soon these liberty-loving groups were corresponding with the blood-crazed murderers of France, self-professed creators of a wonderful new world for downtrodden peasants.

On 12th September 1793 Palmer appeared before the Circuit Court of Justiciary at Perth, charged with seditious practices. The story is told in Howell's *State Trials*. The indictment stated that Thomas Fische (*sic*) Palmer was charged with "wickedly and feloniously writing or printing" a "seditious or inflammatory writing, calculated to produce a spirit of discontent in the minds of the people against the present happy constitution and government of this country, and to rouse them up to acts of outrage and violence, by insidiously calumniating and misrepresenting the measures of government".

The charge continued that "Thomas Fische Palmer is guilty actor or art and part and that during the month of July 1793, having been present at a meeting held at Dundee, which meeting denominated itself *A Society of the Friends of Liberty*, the said Thomas Fische Palmer did put into the hands of George Mealmaker, weaver in Dundee, a manuscript or writing, of a wicked or seditious import, in the form of an address to their Friends and Fellow Citizens; and feloniously written or composed by the said Thomas Fische Palmer."

The offending pamphlet was actually written by Mealmaker, not Palmer. Here are some extracts from it:

"Friends and fellow citizens; That portion of liberty you once enjoyed is fast setting, we fear, in the darkness of despotism and tyranny! Too soon, perhaps, you who were the world's envy, as possessed of some small portion of liberty, will be sunk in the depth of slavery and misery, if you prevent it not by your well-timed efforts. . . .

"Is not every day adding a new link to our chains? Is not the executive

Thomas Fyshe Palmer
Scottish National Portrait Gallery

Palmer in prison
Mitchell Library

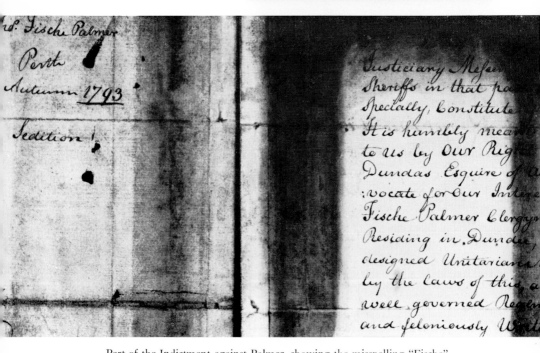

Part of the Indictment against Palmer, showing the misspelling "Fische"

branch seizing new and unwarrantable powers? Has not the House of Commons (your ownly security from the evils of tyranny and aristocracy) joined the coalition against you? Is the election of its members either fair, free or frequent? Is not its independence gone, while it is made up of pensions and placemen? . . .

"We have done our duty, and are determined to keep our posts, ever ready to assert our just rights and privileges as men, the chief of which we account the right of universal suffrage, in the choice of those who serve in the House of Commons. . . .

"You are plunged into a war, by a wicked ministry and a compliant parliament, who seem careless and unconcerned for your interest, the end and design of which is almost too horrid to relate, the destruction of a people, merely because they will be free. By it your commerce is sore cramped and almost ruined. Thousands and ten thousands of your fellow citizens, from being in a state of prosperity, are reduced to a state of poverty and misery. A list of bankruptcies, unequalled in former time, forms a part in the retinue of this quixotic expedition, the blood of your brethren is pouring out, and all this to form chains for a free people, and eventually to rivet them forever on yourselves. . . ."

In the indictment the Crown accused Palmer of delivering to "William Skirving of Strathruddie, 100 copies of the said seditious writing, and which were distributed by him to various booksellers". The reading of the charges was followed by a list of witnesses against Palmer, including Edward Leslie and Robert Miller, booksellers of Dundee, who bought copies of the address from William Skirving. Forty-five jurymen were then called, and fifteen were chosen.

Lord Eskgrove then asked Palmer if he were guilty of the crimes laid against him in the indictment.

Mr Palmer: "I am not the person named in the indictment."

Lord Eskgrove: "And that you plead?"

Mr Palmer: "Yes, my lord."

Mr Haggart, counsel for Palmer, then explained that the indictment charged "Thomas *Fische* Palmer", whereas the prisoner was "Thomas *Fyshe* Palmer". A family named Fische Palmer lived in Sussex, "but from that family the prisoner has not the honour to descend".

Haggart backed up his objection by quoting similar errors in courts of law, from 1619 to 1791, when a man named Low was charged as Law. The learned lords gave their opinions that the cases quoted did not affect the case in point. Lord Eskgrove then commented that if the defence insisted that the indictment be properly served it would only delay the trial another fifteen days, till a new indictment could be served, and the prisoner would be in jail that much longer, "so that it is a mere matter of moonshine, which can serve the prisoner no good purpose".

Once again Palmer was asked by Lord Eskgrove how he pleaded, and he replied, "I am not guilty, my lord."

Haggart's next move was to attempt to show that the pamphlet was not seditious. "I admit that the publication in question contains some strictures on the House of Commons, and implies censure on the conduct of the executive government," he said, "but who can maintain that this is not warranted by the liberty of the press, and by the first principles of our government?" He proceeded to give examples of similar language, which had apparently not been regarded as seditious by the authorities, since no prosecution had followed. Hoping no doubt that the name of Edmund Burke would carry weight, since his *Reflections on the Revolution in France* had won the approval of the Tories, he quoted a speech Burke had made in the House of Commons when advocating a Reform Bill. In this Burke had said that "Kings are naturally lovers of low company", which, when quoted, prompted an interruption by Lord Eskgrove, "Then low company should like Kings."

Haggart, still quoting Burke, continued: " 'Kings are so elevated above the rest of mankind, that they must look upon all their subjects as on a level; they are rather apt to hate than to love their nobility, on account of the occasional resistance to their will, which will be made by their virtue, their petulance, or their pride. It must indeed be admittted that many of the nobility are as perfectly willing to act the part of flatterers, tale bearers, parasites, pimps and buffoons, as any of the lowest and vilest of mankind can possible be. But they are not properly qualified for this object of their ambition. The want of a regular education, and early habits, with some lurking remains of their dignity, will never permit them to become a match for an Italian eunuch, a mountebank, a fiddler, a player, or any regular practitioner of that tribe. The Roman emperors threw themselves into such hands, and the mischief increased, till the decline, and ruin of the empire.' "

Palmer's counsel asked the Court, "What is this but saying, 'Kings in general are fond of low company'? But was this language of Mr Burke thought seditious? No, it was meant to enforce a great plan of reform. The plan was approved, and was carried; and no prosecution was thought of against Mr Burke."

After taking a deep breath, Mr Haggart launched into another quoted speech, this one made in the House of Commons on 31st May 1793 by a member, Mr Wharton, who said, "All that was valuable to the people of this country, all the provisions which were stipulated to secure the peace and prosperity; the individual liberty and the general property of the people of this land, had all been since the revolution taken away. All."

The criticisms made in the offending pamphlet of the House of Commons and the system of election to it were compared by Haggart to a petition from the Friends of the People in London to the House of Commons in May of that year. Part of this read: "Your petitioners inform your honourable House, and they are ready to prove it at your bar, that they have the most reasonable grounds to suspect that no less than one hundred and fifty of your honourable members owe their elections entirely to the intereference of peers; and your petitioners are prepared to show, by legal evidence, that forty peers, in defiance of your resolutions, have possessed themselves of so many burgage tenures, and obtained such an absolute and uncontrolled command in very small boroughs in the Kingdom, as to be enabled, by their positive authority, to return eighty-one of your honourable members."

After quoting this, Mr Haggart said, "My lords, whether they can prove the fact or not, here is the language, and that language is not looked upon as libellous or seditious. Can it be said, that eighty members introduced by peers, is not a high aristocratical influence? I pray God, that petitions and all legal means may be used, that such language as this may be used again and again till this pestilence in the constitution is rooted out."

Page after page of Howell's *State Trials* is filled with Haggart's earnest plea on behalf of his client. He quoted Milton's *Areopagitica* and also Hume's *Essay on the Liberty of the Press*, both of which Erskine had cited in his defence of Paine.

Mr Maconochie, the prosecutor, then took over, and one by one dismissed Haggart's arguments. He denied that the legislature was corrupt; he denied the claim for universal suffrage; and insisted that a coalition between Parliament and King was necessary. If it were not for societies calling themselves "Friends of the People", he said, there would be no war with France, since the French would "never have been so mad as to attack the British nation".

Eventually witnesses were called, Henry Davidson, a Crown witness, being the first. Next witness was George Mealmaker, a weaver of Dundee, who admitted that he was the author of a handbill (produced in court), that he was a member of the Friends of Liberty Society, being once a treasurer and once a president. He "could not remember" when questions were asked him. George was a very unsatisfactory witness. This was understandable, because he was later prosecuted for his part in the Dundee meeting.

Eleven witnesses were called on behalf of Palmer, including "James Ellis, Junior, cotton-spinner from Glasgow, at present residing in the house of Thomas Fyshe Palmer". Ellis stated that he lived in Mr Palmer's house in that part of the town of Dundee "known by the name of Methodist Close".

One day in June, Ellis said, he was stopped by a lad, George Mealmaker, a Dundee weaver. The two youths then attended a meeting at which there was an address to "our fellow citizens". Ellis said he saw the manuscript of this, and it was in the handwriting of George Mealmaker.

After questioning by Mr Haggart, Ellis said, "Mr Palmer and I were going up to Mr Palmer's house. Several people stopped us in the Close, and George Mealmaker said to Mr Palmer, 'I belong to the Society of the Friends of Liberty, that meet in the Berean Meeting House.' They told Mr Palmer that they intended to publish an address to their fellow citizens, and that they would be glad of Mr Palmer's assistance in it."

Palmer asked the Friends of Liberty how many belonged to it, and was told "that thirty people usually meet there, composed chiefly of tradesmen and labourers".

"Then," said Palmer, "you are so few in number, I think it a great folly in you to think of publishing anything. It would answer very little purpose and would only bring an expense upon people that are little able to bear it."

Mealmaker replied, "We are not like the other society, for we have money by us, and we will publish it." Palmer said "it was folly to publish anything at present".

Eventually Mealmaker and his cronies prepared an address, which Palmer read. Said Ellis, "I saw Mr Palmer deliver back this address to Mealmaker, saying, 'As I am not a member, I have not taken the liberty to alter a single word but one.'"

More witnesses were called on behalf of Palmer, followed by Crown witnesses, after which Lord Abercromby addressed the jury. "Gentlemen, Mr Palmer has been indicted for the publication of a writing alleged to be seditious. It certainly shows abundance of that party zeal, of which there have been so many examples. But though the language is not to be commended for its moderation, it is another question whether such terms are seditious, and punishable as a state crime. The language of the party is intemperate, abusive, too often slanderous, without candour, charity or decency, disgusting to all lovers of quiet and moderation."

The judge who liked "quiet and moderation" now stigmatized Mr Palmer in blistering words as the villain of the piece. He attacked Thomas Paine and his extravagent doctrine on *The Rights of Man*, he criticized the defence counsel for advocating the liberty of the press; and said that, though an end might be lawful, it would not justify unlawful means.

After this outburst, the judge stated that, in his opinion, Palmer was not the author of the handbill that caused all the trouble. "Mealmaker composed and wrote it, and the fact is proved as well by his own testimony, as by other evidence." Palmer's publication of it was guilt enough, and the time at which it was done aggravated the offence. "It was published in July last, after the French Revolution had taken place; after the progress of that revolution had agitated the public mind; after unheard-of crimes, unexampled in the history of nations had been committed, and all the horrors of that revolution had taken place; after the writings of Paine had been disseminated with unremitting assiduity; after they had poisoned the minds of the lower order of people; and after an alarm had been spread in this country. That was the season chosen for the publication of this writing. You will consider these circumstances still farther to evince the evil tendency of this paper."

At two o'clock on 13th September 1793 the jury found "the address mentioned in the libel to be a seditious writing, tending to inflame the minds of the people"; they found Thomas Fyshe Palmer "art and part guilty of writing the said address" — in other words, of being an accessory to its writing — "and that he is guilty of causing the said address to be printed, and that he is guilty of distributing, and causing to be distributed, the said inflammatory writing".

Lord Eskgrove thanked the jury, and Lord Abercromby passed his comments, namely that a clergyman's job was "to instruct citizens in their duty to God and man, and not become excited to crimes of the most dangerous nature".

After this Palmer asked permission to speak a few words, which was granted. "My lords," he said, "I can appeal, with conscious sincerity, to the great Searcher of hearts, for the good intentions and unrightness of my conduct. My life has been employed in the dissemination of what I conceived to be religious and moral truths. My friends know with what ardour I have done this, at the sacrifice of all my worldly interests. But during the late great political discussions, it was naturally impossible, in a man of my sanguine disposition to remain an unconcerned bystander."

After Palmer ended his appeal by declaring his faith "in that great Being whom I serve", he added, "Perhaps, my lords, I am out of time in mentioning that three witnesses were not called, who would have sworn that on the 6th July last George Mealmaker declared he wrote every word of this address, independent of any one else."

Palmer now named the three witnesses, but the judges ignored his statement, and the clerk read their sentence — transportation for seven years.

The downfall of the Reverend Thomas Fyshe Palmer and Thomas Muir can be attributed to their burning zeal to free their country from the shackles of the Tories and Whigs who controlled the House of Commons with their system of "pocket boroughs", thus depriving the masses of a right to vote. They believed that their purpose of parliamentary reform could be achieved by verbal exhortation. They were right, but they were men before their time. Nearly forty years later they were vindicated.

The prejudiced trial and imprisonment on the hulks of Muir and Palmer raised the hackles of William Godwin, a dour fighter for political justice, who indignantly wrote to the Editor of the London *Morning Chronicle*, as follows: "Sir, the situation in which Messieurs Muir and Palmer are at this moment placed is sufficiently known within a certain circle, but is by no means adverted to by the public at large. . . . All the consolations of civilized society are pertinaciously refused to them. Property, whether originally their own or the gift of their friends, is to be rendered useless. Supplies of clothing have been graciously received on board the vessels, but stores of every kind and *books* have constantly been denied admission. The principle which has been laid down again and again by the officers of Government is — *they are felons like the rest*."

Godwin then sailed into the Government. "This, sir," he growled, "is a species of punishment scarcely precedented in the annals of mankind. Tiberius, and his modern antitype, Joseph the Second, are mere novices in the art of cruelty compared with our blessed administration. Joseph took judges from the bench, men accustomed to reflection, to deference and elegant gratification, and made them scavengers in the streets of Vienna. Mr Pitt probably took the hint from this example. But he has refined upon his model, inasmuch as he has sent the victims of his atrocious despotism out of the country. If I must suffer under the barbarian hand of power, at least let me suffer in the face of day. Let me have this satisfaction, that my countrymen may observe my disgrace. Let them learn a great lesson from my suffering. It is for them to decide whether it shall be a lesson of aversion to my guilt, or abhorrence against my punisher. On that condition, I will stand on their pillories, and sweep their streets with satisfaction and content. But to shut me up in dungeons and darkness, or to transport me to the other side of the globe, that they may wreak their vengeance on me unobserved, is base, coward-like, and infamous."

Godwin was now warming to his theme as he wrote: "Perhaps, Mr Editor, I may be told that, in holding up these proceedings to the indignation of my countrymen, I am guilty of sedition . . . Mr Dundas told Mr Sheridan, when that gentleman applied to him officially upon this subject a few months ago, that *he saw no great hardship in a man's being sent to Botany Bay*. . . . I can readily believe that to a man so obdurate in feeling and unhumanised in manners as Mr Dundas, a privation of the sources of intellectual pleasure may appear no hardship. . . . We declaim against the French, and we imitate them in their most horrible atrocities."

But Godwin's voice was a voice crying in the wilderness, and his scathing indictments of Pitt and Dundas were ignored.

News of Palmer was given in an item in the Belfast *Northern Star* of 2nd December 1793: "Mr Palmer was taken out of Perth Jail by a party of dragoons, about midnight, and conveyed in a post-chaise to Kinghorn, and from thence on board Captain Ogilvie's yacht, lying in Leith Roads. We hear that the Sheriff-Depute of Perthshire ordered Mr Palmer to be hand-cuffed, but the officer of dragoons who commanded the escort would not allow such ungentlemanly conduct. On Friday evening, sailed from Leith Roads the *Royal George*, yacht, Captain Ogilvie, with Thomas Muir and Thomas Fyshe Palmer on board, whose trials have furnished to the world matter of such extraordinary discussion."

The *Annual Register* of London, 1st December 1793, stated: "Mr Thomas Muir and the Reverend T. F. Palmer arrived in the river [Thames] from Leith. Orders were sent down for delivering them to Duncan Campbell, the contractor for the hulks at Woolwich, the former on the *Prudentia*, and the latter in the *Stanislaus*. They were in irons, among the convicts, and were ordered to assist them in common labour on the banks of the river. Mr Muir is associated with 300 convicts, among whom he and Mr Palmer slept after their arrival. Mr Muir is rather depressed in spirits, but Mr Palmer appears to sustain his misfortune with greater fortitude."

Part of a letter written on 10th January 1794 by the Reverend Theophilus Lindsey is quoted from the *Memoirs of Lindsey* in Volume II of the *Historical Records of New South Wales*. "Since I last wrote, opinions have varied about the destiny of Mr Palmer and Mr Muir, as the Scottish Judges have, upon revisal, adhered to the sentence pronounced upon them. Mr Palmer's health and spirits are most cheerful; Mr Muir far from well in health since the cold weather set in; both of them supported by their integrity and future hopes. Some friends who visited the hulks on Wednesday had a commission from some others to offer a purse to Mr Palmer and Mr Muir. The former declined taking anything, but Mr Muir thankfully accepted it. Mr Palmer afterwards altered his mind."

In another letter Mr Lindsey informed his friend "that the amount of the contribution was between five and six hundred pounds, and that it was vested in the hands of a committee of seven for the benefit of Messrs Palmer, Muir, Skirving, and even Margarot, who as a joint sufferer was not to be overlooked, though his general character was not so high as the others". We shall follow the stories of Skirving and Margarot in later chapters.

Theophilus Lindsey, like Palmer, had left the Church of England and become a Unitarian minister. The *Dictionary of National Biography* tells us that he opened a chapel in Essex Street, London for public worship in April 1772. In 1812 his friend Dr Thomas Belsham, also a Unitarian minister, wrote *The Memoirs of the Reverend T. Lindsey*, in which he describes Lindsey's friendship with the Reverend Thomas Fyshe Palmer, and in which the letters quoted above appear. Of Palmer, Belsham writes, "This gentleman, in consequence of perusing the writings of Dr Priestley and Mr Lindsey, became a decided Unitarian, and being a man of ardent active spirit, he devoted himself to the propagation of those principles which to him appeared scriptural and evangelical." In telling the story of Palmer's downfall he says that "the extreme inhumanity" of the sentences passed upon the reformers "excited general indignation and horror: and that not only in England but in foreign countries".

On 9th January 1794 Lady Carysfort, sister of Lord Greville, the Foreign Secretary, wrote to the Home Office, saying that she was enclosing a letter from Dr Palmer, of Peterborough, brother to the Reverend T. F. Palmer, in which he asked that "a lad by the name of James Ellis" might have permission to go with him as a free settler. This was the lad who lived in Palmer's house in Dundee and who gave evidence at his trial. Permission was granted, and Ellis travelled to Port Jackson with his master.

The *Morning Post* of 13th January 1794 stated that the King in Council had signed an order for the transportation of Muir and Palmer to Botany Bay. The vessel in which they were to have been transported was "so much decayed that she is obliged to be condemned. Mr Muir is so extremely ill that the physician who attends him has not the least hope of his recovery. In such a situation no unfortunate man can present stronger claims to the Royal clemency."

The condemned transport was the *Canada*. She was replaced by the *Surprize*.

In the *Historical Records of New South Wales*, Volume II, is an unsigned letter attributed to the Home Office, Whitehall, dated 14th February 1794, and addressed to Lieutenant-Governor Francis Grose at Sydney. (In the *Historical Records of Australia* this letter is attributed to Under-Secretary King.) "You will observe," says the writer, "from copies of certificates of the sentences of Muir, Palmer, Margarot, and Skirving, who are amongst the convicts on board the *Surprize*, that they were convicted of the crime of sedition, considered as a public offence. I have no doubt but that their present situation, the sufficiency of their own understandings, and the nature and constitution of the settlement they are going to, will prove motives (if any be necessary) sufficiently strong to preserve them from any attempt hostile to the peace and good order of your Government. At the same time, you will, of course, keep a watchful eye over their conduct, and for their sakes, as well as for the sake of the settlement, give them clearly to understand what must be the consequence of any such attempts on their parts.

"Although directions have been given that the persons above mentioned should not be suffered to carry out with them any publication of a seditious or dangerous tendency, yet I take the opportunity of submitting to you whether it will not be highly necessary with this view that their effects should be carefully examined previously to their landing at Port Jackson."

The letter ended with the information that a young man of the name of Ellis had been permitted by Secretary Dundas to accompany Palmer in the *Surprize*, but on his arrival he was to be considered as a free settler.

On 24th March 1794 the *Oracle and Public Advertiser* stated: "It is remarkable of these two gentlemen [Muir and Palmer] that, minutely as they accord in political opinion, their religious tenets are as far asunder as possible. Mr Palmer is a strenuous Unitarian, and has for many years been the pastor of an Unitarian congregation. Mr Muir, on the contrary, who, notwithstanding his profession of the law and habits of life, is an accomplished theologue, is a warm advocate for the doctrines of the Trinity."

CHAPTER FOUR

THE AFTERMATH of the trials of Muir and Palmer has been told by George Omond in *The Lord Advocates of Scotland*. In December 1793 Mr Secretary Dundas wrote to Lord Braxfield, stating that representations had been made to the Government against the legality of the sentences on Muir and Palmer, and requesting the opinion of the judges. Lord Braxfield, in transmitting the verdict of the court, which was that the sentences were legal, added a private note "urging that the Royal Mercy should not be extended to the condemned men".

Omond continues: "The Lord Advocate could depend on receiving ample assistance from the judges, who, though not corrupt, had already shown themselves to be prejudiced and unscrupulous. It was rumoured that the powers of the Lord Advocate were to be increased. Hitherto the Act of 1701, the Habeas Corpus Act of Scotland, had been a safeguard against undue delay in bringing prisoners to trial, and other modes of oppression; but it was now reported that the Act of 1701 was to be suspended in Scotland, also the Habeas Corpus Act in England."

It was said that if this were done, Lord Advocate Dundas would possess all the powers that "Bloody Mackenzie" had exercised a century before. This gentleman, otherwise known as Sir George Mackenzie of Rosehaugh, was King's Advocate from 1677 to 1686, and again in 1688, earning his nickname by his ruthless prosecution of the Covenanters after the battle of Bothwell Bridge in June 1679. "No King's Advocate," he declared, "has ever screwed the prerogative higher than I have. I deserve to have my statue placed riding behind Charles II in the parliament close." The *Dictionary of National Biography* comments: "Mackenzie's career as public prosecutor can only be defended if in law, as in love and war, 'all things are fair'."

Lord Advocate Dundas hankered to possess similar powers, and his opportunity came in 1793, when a Convention of Reformers met again in Edinburgh during October, November, and December. On 5th December the leaders of the Convention — William Skirving, Maurice Margarot, and John Gerrald — were arrested, Margarot and Gerrald at a meeting of the Convention, and Skirving, who was not present, later in the day.

Skirving, you will remember, had been mentioned at Palmer's trial as having received and distributed copies of the "seditious writing". He was the son of a prosperous farmer and was educated at Edinburgh University for the Church — according to Cockburn the "Secession Church" — but became a tutor in the family of Sir Alexander Dick of Prestonville. Later he began farming in Kinross-shire, and wrote articles on agriculture. He was once a candidate for the Chair of Agriculture in the University of Edinburgh.

On 6th and 7th January 1794 William Skirving of Strathruddie, lately tenant of Damhead, described as Secretary to the British Convention, was tried before the High Court of Justiciary for sedition, "a crime of a heinous nature, and severely punishable". On the Bench sat Lord Braxfield, chairman of the panel of judges who had tried and sentenced Thomas Muir to fourteen years' banishment at Botany Bay on 30th August 1793. Assisting him were Lord Swinton, Lord Eskgrove, Lord Dunsinnan, and Lord Abercromby.

Cockburn, in his *Examination of the Trials for Sedition in Scotland* reviews in detail the story of William Skirving, whom he describes as "a person of good character". He lists "the facts set forth in the sedition charge" as follows:

1. That the prisoner Skirving had circulated the Dundee paper for his connection with which Palmer had already been condemned.
2. That he had been an active member of the Society called the Friends of the People, and had, as its Secretary, circulated a seditious handbill.
3. That he had been equally involved with that Society after it had assumed the new name and character of the convention of delegates of the people associated to obtain universal suffrage and annual parliaments.
4. That in both associations Skirving had made seditious speeches and motions.
5. That after the convention had been dispersed by the civil magistrate, he, who had previously resisted, endeavoured to reassemble it.

Continues Lord Cockburn: "The indictment sets forth that the members of Skirving's association did in the months of October, November, and December 1793, at Edinburgh, in imitation of the proceedings of the French Convention, call each other by the name of *citizen*, divide themselves into sections, appoint committees of various kinds, such as of *organization*, of *instruction*, of *finance*, and of *secrecy*, inscribe their minutes with the first year of the British Convention."

At Skirving's trial, Solicitor-General Blair alleged that because Skirving and his fellow members had copied the French revolutionaries and regicides in this way, it was their intention to copy them still further by murdering the King and taking over the country.

Forty-six "divers persons" were listed as witnesses against Skirving, including six handwriting experts. After the charges against him were read, he was asked by Lord Braxfield, "What do you say to this, Mr Skirving? Are you guilty or not?"

"I am conscious of no guilt, my lord."

"Have you any counsel for you?"

"No, my lord, I have the misfortune to have no counsel whatever."

Lord Eskgrove: "Mr Skirving very well knows that if he had wished for counsel, and had applied to the court, he might have had counsel."

Mr Skirving: "Such is the apprehension of your prejudice against the Friends of the People, that it has gone forth that an agent before the court said, it was almost giving up his business to be seen doing anything for the Friends of the People; and therefore, I thought I would go to the court, and do as well as I could without counsel. It is very unfortunate that I have had so little time to prepare for my defence. However, conscious of innocence, I must trust myself in the hands of the court, and make the best defence I can."

Lord Eskgrove: "We know very well that both the agents and the court have so much compassion that they never refuse to assist any panel." ("Panel" in Scots law means "prisoner" or "the accused".)

Lord Justice Braxfield: "The meanest subject that comes to this court may have counsel if he applies for it. Do you wish to have counsel now?"

Mr Skirving: "I should be very glad, but it would now be taking any gentleman unawares."

Solicitor-General Blair then harangued the judges and jury on the "heinous" offence committed by the prisoner in the dock. On and on he went; one would think that he was paid by the word, as he hammered home the charges, repeating the seditious crimes of Skirving with slight variations.

That afternoon, when the court recessed, Skirving said, "My lord, may I not be admitted to bail?"

"No," said Lord Braxfield. "It is contrary to the rule of the court."

Some of the statements made by delegates to the Convention were quoted for the information of the Court, such as the words: "The landholder is called upon to coalesce with the Friends of the People, lest his property be soon left untenanted; the merchants, lest the commerce of the country be annihilated; the manufacturer, whose laudable industry has been arrested in its progress; the unemployed citizen, the great mass of labouring and now starving poor, and finally the rabble are called upon by the remembrance of their patriotic ancestors, who shed their blood in the cause of freedom, and to whose memories even the enemies of that cause are compelled to pay an involuntary tribute of applause."

The prosecutor conceded that the landowner, the merchant, and the manufacturer, all having property, might lawfully be courted, and that the unemployed citizen had hopes which might be appealed to without crime, "but it was held that the *rabble* could only be invited for their physical strength, which disclosed a design to use force if necessary".

"Calling upon the rabble!" exclaimed Lord Swinton, one of the judges. "How are the rabble to do it? Can they do it any other way than by outrage and violence?"

Comments Lord Cockburn: "Since Lord Swinton was not shocked at the starving poor being invited it is not easy to understand his horror of the rabble." Another statement by the Solicitor-General in support of his charge against Skirving was that "the very name British Convention carries Sedition along with it". The word "delegate" was treated as equally criminal. Cockburn points out that "These are two ancient and innocent terms in the law of Scotland indicating nothing either unusual or alarming. Not only had a Convention of Delegates, composed of men of high station and acknowledged loyalty, sat undisturbed and unsuspected in Edinburgh shortly before this period, for the promotion of burgh reform; but our royal burghs were directed by statute to elect their representatives in the House of Commons by means of delegates; and for above three centuries these burghs had annually assembled at Edinburgh in their municipal parliament as a *convention*, in which, except as a delegate, no member could be received." In any case, the idea that an imitation of the terms and forms used in the French Convention necessarily or even probably implied an intention to imitate French king-killing and massacre was absurd.

Lord Cockburn says that the fifteen jurymen were chosen on the principle "that those only could be trusted who, as the Lord Advocate stated, were prejudiced in favour of the British Constitution". So the dice was loaded against Skirving. "Lord Braxfield's charge to the jury was worthy of himself," says Cockburn. "He sets out in the case against Skirving by instructing the jury what sedition is, and his definition, "I take the crime of sedition to be the violating the peace and order of society": and it is intended with different degrees of aggravation; according to what is the object of it; when sedition has a tendency to overturn the constitution of this country it borders upon high treason; and if it goes that length it loses the name of sedition, and is buried under the greater crime of high treason; and a very little more than is contained in this indictment would have made it the crime of high treason."

Lord Braxfield, after inflaming the minds of the jurors by twisting the charge of sedition towards high treason, added that the Convention was held during the time when "this nation is engaged in a bloody war with France, consisting of millions of the most profligate monsters that ever disgraced humanity. Justice will never enter into their ideas, but they swallow all before them. And I say gentlemen, that the greatest union in this nation is necessary, to support us under this war. If you are of the opinion that these meetings are of a seditious nature, and of a seditious testimony when the question comes home to the panel at the bar, you must find him guilty."

Lord Braxfield, with none to say him nay, then exceeded the bounds of all legality when he referred to Palmer's conviction as morally, if not legally conclusive against Skirving. "Gentlemen," said Braxfield, "Fyshe Palmer's publication, of all that I ever read, is of the most seditious tendency, and a more wicked publication it was not possible for human invention to devise; and accordingly Palmer was very justly indicted for that composition, and he was found guilty at the last circuit at Perth by a most respectable jury; in consequence of which he is condemned to banishment by transportation." Because Skirving had little knowledge of the law, and acted as his own counsel, Braxfield got away with it.

After lunch on the second day of the trial the jury returned to their seats and were asked by Lord Braxfield for their verdict.

Alexander McKenzie, chancellor (that is, foreman) of the jury, replied, "We are all in one voice, finding William Skirving guilty of the crimes libelled."

"Gentlemen, you have returned a very proper verdict," said his Lordship, "and I am sure you are entitled to the thanks of your country for the attention you have paid to this trial."

Lord Eskgrove approved of the verdict, saying, "Your lordship did pronounce a sentence of banishment by transportation against Muir; and I cannot, from the tenor of this indictment, find that the crime of which this man is convicted is one whit less."

Lord Swinton concurred. "I conceive nothing less than that which was inflicted upon Mr Muir. I do not know but the crime deserves more; but we cannot do less than punish the same crime by inflicting the same punishment." He added, "In this case the Convention wished for universal suffrage and annual parliaments. One of these is a most ridiculous and absurd doctrine — universal suffrage. Nothing can be so absurd. Annual parliaments, or a shorter duration of parliaments, may be a matter of argument."

Lord Dunsinnan considered the punishment suggested "as moderate and proper, and I most heartily concur with your Lordships".

Lord Abercromby admitted that these societies contained many good men, who were led astray and deluded by their leaders. "I am disposed to believe that there are many well-disposed persons in every part of the Kingdom who joined these Societies without any wicked purpose, believing that their sole object was to render our Constitution, excellent as it is, still more perfect, without entertaining the most distant idea of overturning that constitution."

Lord Braxfield then said, "I have always considered sedition as the most dangerous crime that can be committed. I think we cannot discharge our duty to the country unless we inflict a severe punishment. Mr Muir was transported for fourteen years; and the old hesitation in that case was whether it should be limited to fourteen years or not."

He then pronounced the sentence, "that the said William Skirving be transported beyond seas . . . for the space of fourteen years from this date", and if he should be found at large within any part of Great Britain during that time he should suffer death.

Skirving replied to his judges with dignity. "Conscious of innocence, my lords, and that I am not guilty of the crimes laid to my charge, this sentence can only affect me as the sentence of man. It is long since I laid aside the fear of man as my rule, I shall never walk by it. And, my lords, I could not be ignorant of the sentence, because I knew it long before this. I had a letter from London this very morning, informing me that such a sentence was to take place. . . . I know that what has been done these two days will be rejudged. That is my comfort, and all my hope."

Never were words spoken more truly. Acts of Reform during the next hundred and fifty years established universal suffrage and removed many abuses, and William Skirving, tenant farmer of Strathruddie, and erstwhile secretary of the British Convention, was vindicated.

Says the *London Morning Post* of 17th January 1794: "Mr Skirving, who was lately sentenced to fourteen years' transportation in Scotland, leaves a wife and eight helpless children behind him."

CHAPTER FIVE

Maurice Margarot, Wine Merchant — Michael Roe Tells his Story — Margarot's Sympathies with French Revolution — Friend of Thomas Hardy — London Corresponding Society — Rotten Boroughs — Hardy and Margarot Congratulate French Revolutionaries — Margarot Pamphleteer — Margarot and Gerrald Delegates to Edinburgh Convention — Universal Suffrage Demanded — Margarot Arrested — Margarot's Trial, January 1794 — Crowds Follow Him to Court — Lord Provost Disperses Cavalcade — Margarot Attacks Braxfield — Astounds Judges — Guilty — Sentenced to Transportation — Cockburn's Comments — Margarot Joins Muir, Palmer, and Skirving in "Surprize" Transport — Mrs Margarot Allowed to Join Him — Margarot a Trouble-maker.

PUBLIC Enemy Number Four in the list of Scottish Martyrs was Maurice Margarot, who had come from London to Edinburgh to attend the British Convention, and who was arrested there, as we have seen, on 5th December 1793. For a record of his early life, I am indebted to Michael Roe, in an article published by the Institute of Historical Research in May 1958. Says Mr Roe: "As his name suggests, Margarot, born in 1745, was not of English stock. His father was a wine and general merchant, operating in Portugal and France, although nominally resident in London where his home had been a rendezvous for the radical faction in the days of Wilkes and Liberty."

My research pal, Jeffrey Gibian, after a busy time scanning the pages of directories, writes from London: "The 1765 London Directory lists for the first time, 'Maurice Margarot, Wine Merchant, Castle Street near the Mews'. I followed it through the Kent's Directories for the years until 1781, when it no longer appeared."

After a classical education at the University of Geneva, Margarot was living in France when the Bastille was stormed by the revolutionaries on 14th July 1789. We next find him in England as a member of the London Corresponding Society, founded by Thomas Hardy, a bootmaker, who had come to London from his native Stirlingshire in 1774. A thoughtful and intelligent man, Hardy took an interest in politics and particularly in parliamentary reform. He planned the London Corresponding Society "as a means of informing the people of the violence that had been committed on their most sacred rights, and of uniting them in an endeavour to recover their rights". In his *Memoirs* Hardy describes how the Society was launched by himself and eight of his friends at the Sign of the Bell, in Exeter Street, the Strand, early in January 1792. When they had finished their bread and cheese and porter for supper and their pipes afterwards, "the business of Parliamentary Reform was brought forward". Hardy now proposed rules which were approved by those present, who agreed to pay one penny each weekly to promote the objects of the Society. A week later nine persons joined, followed in the third week "by twenty-four new members, which made the treasury rich to the important amount of four shillings and one penny".

Hardy's chief argument to attract subscribers was that "a majority of the people are not represented in Parliament; that the majority of the House of Commons are chosen by a number of voters, not exceeding twelve thousand; and that many large and populous towns have not a single vote for a representative, such as Birmingham, 40,000 inhabitants, Manchester 30,000, Leeds 20,000, besides Sheffield, Bradford, etc., etc." Meanwhile the rotten borough of Old Sarum, with a population of seven, had the right to send two members of Parliament to Westminster. No wonder that Hardy and his pals were hostile.

I do not know whether Margarot was a foundation member of Hardy's London Corresponding Society, but he was soon prominent in its activities. Says Michael Roe: "On 2nd April 1792, the London Corresponding Society issued its first address, signed by Thomas Hardy but written by Margarot and expressing several of the themes to which he clung until death. Liberty was declared man's birthright; his supreme duty, abhorrent though tumults and violence might be, the preservation of that liberty. The present was a time of crisis and degeneration, in consequence of a partial, unequal and therefore inadeqate Representation, together with the corrupt methods in which Representitives are elected; oppressive taxes, unjust laws, restrictions of liberty and wasting of the public money, have ensued."

On 27th September 1792 Thomas Hardy and Maurice Margarot carried a congratulatory address from the London Corresponding Society to the National Convention of France, forecasting that the triple alliance of the people of America, France, and Britain, would "give freedom to Europe and peace to the world".

Before the end of 1792 "Margarot had written two further pamphlets, the first maintaining that although men should be rewarded in proportion to their talents, equality before the law should be absolute; the second, couched as a letter to the Home Secretary, Dundas, demanded the speedy introduction of parliamentary reform".

Throughout 1793 Margarot busied himself with the affairs of the Corresponding Society, and in November he and Joseph Gerrald arrived in Edinburgh as delegates to the British Convention of the Friends of the People. They were the dominant figures in debates, says Michael Roe, and "doubtless took an important part in composing the Address which the Convention published on 19th November". The Norman Conquest, asserted this document, had first planted the "tree of feudality" in England and, despite Magna Carta and the expulsion of the Stuarts, its bitter fruits remained. The throne was now endangered, not by the Convention, but by evil Ministers who encouraged the King to emulate James II. If the teachings of the Prince of Peace were heeded in this crisis, the national debt would be alleviated, and commerce and manufactures would flourish. The aim of the Convention, however, was the restoration of annual parliaments and universal suffrage.

As the sessions of the Convention went on, the authorities, as we have seen, decided on drastic action, and early in December, Margarot, Gerrald, and Skirving were arrested. Michael Roe points out that since Muir and Palmer had been charged with sedition for propagating similar views a few months earlier, and had been sentenced to transportation, there could have been little doubt that similar punishment would be inflicted on this occasion.

On 13th January 1794 "Maurice Margarot, Merchant in Marybon, London, lately residing at the Black Bull Inn Edinburgh", was indicted for sedition, the said Mr Margarot "having been named a delegate by an association of Seditious people calling themselves the Corresponding Society of London".

Margarot later published the story of his trial, which runs into 186 pages of close-set type, full of the author's egotistical opinions. All accounts agree that Margarot had a field day with their lordships on the Bench, and swapped insult for insult in a way that must have driven them crazy. Knowing he was set for fourteen years' banishment to Botany Bay, he must have decided to give his judicial audience a display of histrionics, harmful to his cause but delightful to the gallery.

Even before he came into the Court he was the centre of dramatic scenes, described by Lord Cockburn, who was fifteen years old at the time and living in Edinburgh, his father being Sheriff of Midlothian. On the day of Skirving's trial, he says, "I was sitting in school in the High Street, when I saw a crowd coming out of the Parliament Close, following a little, black, middle-aged man, who was put in a coach, from which the people proceeded to take off the horses." This was Margarot, who had been listening to Skirving's trial. When he came out the populace thought he had been discharged, so they drew his coach "in triumph to his lodgings in the Black Bull, at the head of Leith Walk". Released from school, young Cockburn and his friends joined the procession. "I ran alongside the carriage, and when I could get near enough, thought it excellent entertainment to give an occasional haul; for which I later got as severe a rebuke from the Lord Advocate as if I had committed some base immorality."

A few days later, Margarot came from the Black Bull for his own trial, attended by a procession of the populace and his Convention friends, with banners and what was called a "tree of liberty". This tree was in the shape of the letter M, twenty feet high and ten wide. "The honour of bearing it up by carrying the two upright poles was assigned to two eminent conventionalists, and the little culprit walked beneath the circular placard in the centre, which proclaimed liberty and equality, etc. The popular idol in this scene was a little, dark creature, dressed in black, with silk stockings and white metal buttons, something like one's idea of a puny Frenchman, a most impudent and provoking body." Young Cockburn watched this scene from the old Post Office near the North Bridge. The Post Office and the adjoining houses had been secretly filled with constables, and sailors from a frigate, all armed with sticks and batons.

The "tree of liberty" arrived at the north end of the bridge, and as it did "Provost Elder and the magistrates appeared, all robed, at the south end. The day was good. There was still not one person on the bridge between the two parties. But the rear of each was crammed with people who filled up every

CITIZEN SKIRVING
Secretary to the Britifh Convention ———
A Tried Patriot and an Honeft Man. ——

William Skirving
Frontispiece of The Trial of William Skirving

of Great Britain ffrance and Ireland
Defender of the faith To
                        Macers of Our Court
of Justiciary Messengers at arms our Sherif
in that part Conjunctly and severally
specially constitute Greeting Whereas
It is humbly Meant and Complained to
us by Our Right Trusty Robert
Dundas Esquire of Arniston Our Ad:
vocate for Our Interest Upon William
Skirving Tenant or lately Tenant in
Damhead now designing himself of

inch as those in front moved on. The magistrates were in a line across the street, with the Provost in the centre, the city officers behind this line, and probably a hundred loyal gentlemen in the rear of the officers. The two parties advanced steadily towards each other in silence, till they met just about the Post Office." It was a tense and exciting moment for the young schoolboy.

"The Provost stepped a pace forward, so that he almost touched the front line of the rebels, when, advancing his cane, he commanded them to retire. Without waiting one instant to see whether they meant to retire or not, the houses vomited forth their blugeoned contents; and in two minutes the tree of liberty was demolished and thrown over the bridge, the street covered with the knocked down, the accused dragged to the bar, and the insurrection was over."

The *Scottish Register* of 15th January 1794, reporting the case, said that on the morning of Margarot's trial he was accompanied to the court by "a concourse of people holding a canopy over his head, inscribed with the words, *Reason, Liberty, Equality*. The Lord Provost, attended by peace officers, and supported by a press-gang, dispersed the cavalcade, demolished the canopy, took the bearers into custody, and attended Mr Margarot to the bar of the court of Justiciary, where he was put on trial." Lord Braxfield angrily commented on "the disturbance to the Court of Criminal Justice, by the mob which assembled this morning to conduct this man to his place of trial with triumph, with shouts, clamour, noise and violence; clearly directed to intimidate court and jury and prosecutor in the discharge of their duties".

Margarot opened the Session with the question, "Clerk of the Court, where is the Lord Justice General for Scotland, I don't see him in his place?"

Not receiving a satisfactory answer to his question, Margarot went on: "I hold that this Court is not competent to try me. My lords, I am cited before the Lord Justice General of Scotland, the Lord Justice-Clerk, and Lords Commissioners of Justiciary. We know that this is the highest court in Scotland. We know that there is no higher office in Scotland than that of Lord Justice General, and we know that if it was an unnecessary post, it would not have £2000 a year salary, annexed to it. . . . The centre-stone, the principal officer of the court, and the man who represents the King is not present. The indictment is loose, and renders it null and void. I have done my duty, and I demand to be discharged from your bar."

Their lordships were not impressed, but Margarot continued to harangue them, demanding, insisting, pleading, and bouncing them to produce the Lord Justice General. Before the eloquent prisoner paused for breath he had spoken over a thousand words to the five astounded judges hearing the case, until he was interrupted by Lord Braxfield. "What do your lordships say to this objection?"

Their lordships unanimously repelled the objection and told Margarot to stand up and hear the libel (or indictment) read against him.

"What do you say to this?" asked Lord Braxfield. "Are you guilty of the charges contained in it, or not guilty?"

Mr Margarot: "My lord, guilt does not stand in your bar at present."

Lord Braxfield: "Are you guilty or not guilty? You must answer the question."

Mr Margarot: "I am not guilty." He then added that there were flaws in the indictment. He demanded to be shown the Act of Parliament which said sedition was "a crime of a heinous nature". He asked for a definition of high treason, and quoted Erskine's definition of sedition. Margarot claimed that he was unaware until he visited Scotland that there was a Grand Inquisitor, and stated that the meetings of the Friends of the People attended by him were perfectly normal and free from sedition. Then he started on the British Constitution, and how it was slanted against them by the Grand Inquisitor.

"My lords, our transactions have been legal. The illegal actions have been entirely on the part of our prosecution. We have experienced the fate of general warrants: we have experienced the fate of a State Inquisition. Good God! Has not a man living under the British Constitution a right to examine the Constitution? I am told that it is the finest institution in the world; and yet I feel my pocket emptied daily with taxes; I feel my liberties taken away one after another; and yet I must not meet with my neighbours to the number of twelve, to discuss those injuries I daily feel, and to enquire after the means of obtaining redress, but immediately comes a Crown lawyer, claps the word *Sedition* on it, and I am punished."

Whenever the prisoner paused for breath, one of the judges had his say, but never got far before Margarot again took the stage.

Suddenly Margarot produced his trump card. "Now, my lord, comes a very delicate matter. I mean to call upon my Lord Braxfield, and I hope that the questions and the answers will be given in the most solemn manner. I have received a piece of information which I shall lay before the Court. First, my lord, are you upon oath?"

Braxfield: "State your questions and if they are proper questions, I will answer them."

Margarot: "Did you dine at Mr Rochhead's at Inverleith last week?"

Braxfield: "And what have you to do with that, sir?"

Margarot: "Did any conversation take place with regard to the trial?"

Braxfield: "Go on, sir."

Margarot: "Did you use these words: 'What should you think of giving him a hundred lashes, together with Botany Bay', or words to that effect?"

Braxfield: "Go on. Put your questions if you have any more."

Margarot: "Did a lady say to you that the mob would not allow you to whip him?"

Braxfield: "Go on."

Margarot: "And, my lord, did you not say that the mob would be the better for losing a little blood? These are the questions that I wish to put to you. Deny them, or acknowledge them."

Braxfield to his co-judge: "Do you think I should answer questions of that sort, my Lord Henderland?" Lord Henderland loyally stuck to his chief, and replied, "No my lord; they do not relate to this trial." Lord Eskgrove also backed up his chief by saying, "What may have been said in a private company cannot in any way affect this case." Lords Dunsinnan and Swinton also concurred with their fellow judges "that not one of these questions is proper, not one of them is competent; and ought not to be allowed in the court". And so Margarot's trump card was out-trumped.

"If Justice Braxfield had spoken as was imputed to him, it was plainly improper in him to try a case he had so prejudged," says Cockburn. "It was generally understood that the Justice had uttered the sentiments imprinted to him, and that a lady had incautiously repeated them. Mr Rochead, at whose house the words were said to have been spoken, kept a luxurious bachelor's table, and had a dinner party every Sunday at Inverleith."

Among the guests were Lord Cockburn's father, also Lord Advocate Dundas, Lord Braxfield, and a few ladies. These friends enjoyed Braxfield's remark "as not a bad sentiment for the times, and laughed at Margarot's impudence and defeat". So Braxfield cleverly got out of the noose by refusing to answer the question. If he had been innocent he could have denied the allegation, instead of leaving the other judges on the Bench to make the decision and defeat justice.

Eventually, when Margarot talked himself dry, sixteen witnesses entered the box one at a time, and parroted their tale of seditious utterances at the meeting on 5th December.

After two days the obedient jury found the prisoner guilty, and Lord Justice-Clerk Braxfield pronounced his sentence of transportation beyond the seas for fourteen years, and ordained that he should be "carried back to the Tolbooth of Edinburgh therein to be detained till he is delivered over for being so transported".

Replied Mr Margarot, for once almost dumb, "My lords, I thank you."

Our learned friend Lord Cockburn, in his analysis of the case of Maurice Margarot, comments that Margarot, though said to have been rather a clever man, "made a long and injudicious harangue in his own defence. No enemy, anxious to deprive him both of hope and acquittal, and of sympathy in conviction, could have made a worse defence. He does not appear to have had the remotest conception where the strength, and still less the weakness, of his case lay; nor did he state or reason it, even according to his own view, with any force, sense, or plausibility. Throughout he was defying without formidableness, and insolent without effect."

Cockburn continues: "But there was nothing to justify the rude and cruel criticism of Lord Braxfield, who the very instant that Margarot was done, and before he himself began his summing up, interposed this observation: 'You have gone on for four hours, and I would not allow you to be interrupted. If you had not been a stranger I would not have heard one third of what you have said in four hours, which was all sedition from beginning to end.'"

Comments Lord Cockburn: "Even if this statement had been true, which it was not, and even although it had not implied an admission of his Lordship's incorrectness, in quietly listening to the commission of a crime in his own court, it was a coarse advantage of a judge to take of any prisoner in making what he thought his defence. But it was a hint to the jury."

Cockburn considers that the proceedings of the Supreme Criminal Court in these sedition trials give "by far the most frightful, and the justest idea of the spirit of those times". "They were political prosecutions, during a period of great political excitement; and therefore, however faction might have raged, everything done by the Court ought to have been done calmly, impartially, and decorously. The general prevalence of public intemperance was the very

35

circumstance that ought to have impressed more deeply upon judges the duty of steady candour, and of that judicial humanity which instinctively makes every right-minded occupier of the judgment seat interpose between a prisoner and prejudice."

In Cockburn's opinion, the judges not only showed bias against the prisoners, but were absolutely straining for convictions. "With all their pre-possessions the judges were not cruel, nor even consciously unfair. But being terrified, and trying those who were causing their alarm, they could scarcely be expected to enter the temple of justice in a state of composure. If ever there was an occasion when justice might have shone, simply by being just, this was one." Then, Cockburn goes on, the judges further showed their bias in fixing upon the sentence, which according to their discretion, could be anything from one hour's imprisonment to transportation for life. "Assuming transportation to be lawful, it was conceded not to be necessary, and it was not then, nor at any time, used in England as a punishment for sedition. At that period it implied a frightful voyage of many months, great hardship in the new colony, an almost complete extinction of all communication with home, and such difficulty in returning, that a man transported was considered as a man never to be seen again." Yet transportation was the punishment chosen.

So it was off to the Tolbooth for Margarot, where on 24th January 1794 he wrote to Thomas Hardy in London: "Dear Hardy, I thank you, my valuable friend, for the kind concern you show; but I wish the London Corresponding Society may not forget me. If you publish my trial it might be necessary to place a print of my handsome figure in front, if so, Mrs Margarot can furnish you with a miniature, whence an engraving can be taken; if that is done, pray let the engraver put into my hand the paper, containing the questions to Lord Justice Braxfield, and let the last of them be legible, viz.: *Did you not say that the mob would be the better for losing a little blood?*"

Margarot went on to tell Hardy, "We have had an padlock put upon our door, and the captain of the Tolbooth is not entrusted with the keys at night, but delivers them to the magistrates." After commenting on the action of the Duke of Portland, and his brother, Lord Edward Bentinck, "for the abuse of parliamentary seat-jobbing, which should be made more public", Margarot wrote, "Armed associations are, I perceive, now set on foot by the rich where-fore should not the poor do the same? Are you to wait patiently until 20,000 Hessians and Hanoverians come to cut your throats? And will you stretch forth your necks, like lambs, to the butcher's knife, and like lambs content yourself with bleating? Pray let me hear from you soon; remember me to Muir and Palmer, and all suffering brethren." At that time, Muir and Palmer were imprisoned on a hulk in the Thames awaiting transfer to a transport bound for Botany Bay.

Margarot's letter, seized by Bow Street runners, was produced at the trial of Thomas Hardy, whose story will be told in a later chapter. It was printed in Howell's *State Trials*.

From Newgate Prison on 18th February 1794 a Mr John Kirby, presumably the Governor, wrote to Patrick Campbell, master of the *Surprize*: ". . . the bearer, Mary Margarot, is the wife of Maurice Margarot, a most valuable good woman, yet she is desirous of accompanying him to Botany Bay. If she could be indulged, I am convinced her conduct will gain her regard and respect."

On 1st April Mr A. S. Hammond of the Navy Office wrote to Under-secretary Nepean that the contractors had been instructed that a separate place for Muir, Palmer, Margarot, and Skirving, had been provided, and also that £30 had been allowed for Mrs Margarot's diet on the voyage.

On 27th March Margarot had written from the *Surprize* at Spithead to the Right Honourable Henry Dundas, the Home Secretary, a letter breathing rebellion and defiance, and demanding that explicit instructions be issued to Captain Campbell and others with reference to the treatment of Mrs Margarot and himself on the transport, and also upon his arrival at the place of banishment.

"Sir, I have a demand to make turning entirely upon what I apprehend is a constitutional point, and as such requires explanation. I wish to know, Sir, the extent of my sentence, and of the power which exercises it. Arrived at Botany Bay, am I to be a slave, the transferable property of the King of Great Britain, and be forced to labour under the goad of a task-master? Is that to be the lot of an Englishman, or, am I on landing there to be restored to liberty? And if so, will that liberty authorize me to remove my self from New South Wales to any other part of the world not belonging to Great Britain, or must I remain there? You will easily discover the importance of these questions, and, as a gentleman, I presume you will answer them yourself."

Maurice Margarot ends his letter to Dundas on a satirical note. Says Maurice: "I cannot close without returning you my unfeigned thanks for all the severities I have experienced by your express order. Bolts, padlocks, handcuffs, confinement in damp pestilential places along with common felons, stinted ship allowances of provisions, all these, Sir, tho' highly prejudicial to my three fellow sufferers, and likely to prove fatal to two of them, have had a different effect on me. They have convinced me that, however, you may think proper to punish my body, my mind preserves its independence, and remains invariably attracted to the cause of the people and thorough Parliamentary reform, which you but accelerate by repeated severities."

I cannot find any reply to this letter; probably Dundas did no deign to make one.   •

Mr Margarot was also proving a thorn in the side of his fellow-passengers. A letter from the *Surprize* at Spithead, dated 21st April, from three officers going to Australia, was sent to Under-Secretary King with reference to Mrs Margarot sharing a cabin with servants of government. "This we could not reasonably object to, as she is a free woman. . . . But Mr Margarot is also accommodated in the same cabin; this is extremely irksome to us, and we have disputed much that a person suffering a sentence of the laws of the country should be in the same place with the officers of Government. You know, sir, having the liberty of coming into the cabin will create intimacy, and intimacy begets words. Their sentiments are specially adverse to ours. As a loyal subject, but particularly having the honour of bearing my sovereign's commission, I consider it as my duty to suppress. On the other hand, it shall be my chief study to tend my feeble assistance to make, not only the situation of them, but every person on board, as comfortable as possible. If Mr Margarot is accommodated so by your orders, far be it from us to dispute it."

James Thomson, ship's surgeon, one of the signatories to this letter, had previously travelled to Sydney as surgeon on the *Atlantic* in 1791. He was now returning to Sydney as Assistant Colonial Surgeon.

Harmony was restored, at least for a time, when Mrs Margarot was allowed to share a cabin with the children of Mr John Boston, a free settler, of whom we shall hear more later.

CHAPTER SIX

THE FIFTH of the Scottish Martyrs to be tried was Joseph Gerrald, born on 9th February 1763 at St Christopher in the West Indies, where his father, who was of Irish descent, had settled as a planter. So says the *Dictionary of National Biography*, which also tells us that he was brought to England as a child and placed in the care of Doctor Samuel Parr at Stanmore school. "Parr conceived the highest opinion of his abilities, but was nevertheless obliged to expel him for 'extreme indiscretion'."

Samuel Parr is treated at length in the same Dictionary, in which he is described as a "pedagogue". Born in 1746 or 1747 at Harrow-on-the-Hill, he was precocious, and declared that he could remember being suckled by his mother. He learnt Latin grammar when four years old, and "played at teaching sermons". Samuel went to Harrow School and later taught there for a time, one of his pupils being Richard Brinsley Sheridan. In 1771 he started a rival school at Stanmore. There, though he "laid great stress upon Greek", he allowed the boys to substitute English poetry for classical verses, at the risk of a flogging if the English were bad. "He not only admired cricket, and smoked his pipe among the spectators, but encouraged pugilism, and arranged that fights should take place at a place which he could see from his study window." At the end of 1776 he closed his school at Stanmore and continued his teaching career at other schools, so, though no date is given for Gerrald's attendance there, it must have been between 1771 and 1776.

The Reverend William Field, in *Memoirs of the Life, Writings and Opinions of the Reverend Samuel Parr, LL.D.*, refers to Parr's painful agitation at "the cruel fate of one of his earlier pupils, the richly-gifted, the greatly imprudent, but dreadfully injured, Joseph Gerrald; to whom he was attached with a fondness truly paternal; and by whom he was beloved, with all the sincerity and warmth of filial affection". Field says that Gerrald possessed an estate of £3000 a year in the West Indies, "but a large portion of it was consumed during long litigation". He describes Gerrald as possessing high talents, attainments and rectitude, a keen sense of honour, firmness never to be shaken, and "courage never to be daunted, in what he conceived to be a good cause. Unhappily in a course of dissipation, he wasted his fortune, and injured his health; and yet, in the midst of all, he never renounced his virtuous principles, and never wholly neglected his intellectual improvement."

Back to the *Dictionary of National Biography*, which states that Gerrald, having returned to the West Indies, "married — according to one account rashly — a lady of St Christopher, who soon afterwards died leaving him with two children. Reduced to comparative poverty, he went to America, where for four years he practised at the bar in Pennsylvania. In 1788 he came to England to prosecute a lawsuit in connection with his property. . . . He renewed his acquaintance with Dr Parr in a grateful letter."

From this time Gerrald became active in the agitation for parliamentary reform. He enrolled himself, says Field, "among the bold and ardent patriots, who, about the time of the French Revolution, stood forward in the great cause of political renovation, with more zeal, it must be owned, than discretion; with the greatest purity of intention, no doubt, but with too much theoretical extravagance, and too little practical wisdom". In 1793 Gerrald published a pamphlet entitled *A Convention the Only Means of Saving Us from Ruin*. In this he stated that a Convention should be elected to represent the people of Great Britain, and also urged universal suffrage in the election of delegates.

Came the great day when a British Convention of "Friends of the People assembled in Edinburgh to discuss ways and means of saving us from ruin". Gerrald and Margarot, as told earlier, attended as delegates from the London Corresponding Society, and on 5th December 1793 their arrest brought the Convention to a sudden end.

Before leaving the Convention hall, Joseph Gerrald read this prayer: "O Thou Governor of the Universe! We rejoice that, at all times and in all circumstances, we have liberty to approach Thy throne; and that we are assured that no sacrifice is more acceptable to Thee, than that which is made for the relief of the oppressed. In this moment of trial and persecution, we pray that Thou would be our defender, our counsellor, and our guide. O be Thou a pillar of fire to us, as Thou wast to our fathers of old, to enlighten and to direct us; and to our enemies a pillar of cloud, of darkness, and confusion."

Gerrald was released on bail, and returned to London, where he heard of the trial and conviction of Skirving and Margarot. According to Field, he was "seriously advised and earnestly entreated" by his friends and his "revered tutor", Dr Parr, to "save himself from a relentless persecution, by flight; and they generously offered to indemnify his bail against all pecuniary fortfeiture. But every such proposal, he resolutely rejected, conceiving it to be a violation of honour."

Among the papers of Dr Parr printed in Field's *Memoirs* was a memorandum of Gerrald's decision to die if necessary in a good cause.

"He heard my proposal attentively," wrote Parr, "but with no emotion of joy. After calmly discussing the propriety of the proposal, he refused to accede to it, saying: 'My honor is pledged; and no opportunity for flight shall induce me to violate that pledge. I gave it to men whom I esteem and respect, and pity; to men who, by avowing similar principles, have been brought into similar peril; to men who were confirmed in those principles and led into that peril by the influence of my arguments, my persuasions and my example.'"

At this crisis in the life of Joseph Gerrald, who was deliberately putting his head in the noose, after seeing the fate of Muir, Palmer, Margarot, and Skirving, he was visited by William Godwin, who in February 1793 had written an *Enquiry Concerning Political Justice*, which rocked the occupants of the ancient halls of Westminster, who had consistently denied proposals for universal suffrage. His letter to the *Morning Chronicle* in defence of Muir and Palmer has already been quoted. C. Kegan Paul, in *William Godwin: His Friends and Contemporaries*, quotes a letter from Godwin to Gerrald, dated 23rd January 1794. Wrote Godwin: "I cannot recollect the situation in which you are in a few days to be placed without emotions of respect, and I had almost said of envy. . . . Your trial, if you so please, may be a day such as England, and I believe the world, never saw. It may be the means of converting thousands, and, progressively, millions, to the cause of reason and public justice. You have a great stake, you place your fortune, your youth, your liberty, and your talents on a single throw. If you must suffer, do not, I conjure you, suffer without making use of this opportunity of telling a tale upon which the happiness of nations depends. Spare none of the resources of your powerful mind."

William Godwin continued his exhortation to Gerrald with further advice. "Never forget," he wrote, "that juries are men, and that men are made of penetrable stuff; probe all the recesses of their souls. Do not spend your strength in vain defiance and empty vaunting. Let every syllable you utter be fraught with persuasion. What an event would it be for England and mankind if you would gain an acquittal!"

Asked Godwin, "Is not such an event worth striving for? It is in man, I am sure it is, to effect that event. Gerrald, you are that man. Fertile in genius, strong in moral feeling, prepared with every accomplishment that literature and reflection can give."

He warned Gerrald to study the placemen of the jury. "'I know,' I would say to this jury, "that you are packed, you are picked and culled from all the land by the persons who have at present the direction of public affairs, as men upon whom they can depend; but I do not fear the event; I do not believe you will be slaves. . . . I have been told that there are men upon whom truth, truthfully and adequately stated, will make no impression. It is a vile and groundless calumny upon the character of the human mind. This is my theory, and I now come before *you* for the practice.'"

Lots more of this sound advice, but not sound enough. The jury were men who depended upon Dundas and his hirelings for their livelihood. It was a case of "find Gerrald guilty — or else".

Back to Godwin: "You stand on as clear ground as man can stand on. You are brought there for meeting in convention to deliberate on grievances. . . . Depend upon it, that if you can establish to their full conviction the one great point — the lawfulness of your meeting — you will obtain a verdict. That point is fully contained in the Bill of Rights, is the fundamental article of that constitution which Englishmen have been taught to admire."

William Godwin's final plea: "Above all, let me entreat you to abstain from harsh epithets and bitter invective. Show that you are not terrible but kind, and anxious for the good of all. Truth will lose nothing by this. Truth can never gain by passion, violence, and resentment. It is by calm and recollected boldness that we can shake the pillars of the vault of heaven. How great will you appear if you show that all the injustice with which you are treated cannot move you: that you are too great to be wounded by their arrows; that you still hold the steadfast course that becomes the friend of man, and that while you expose their rottenness you harbour no revenge. . . . Farewell; my whole soul goes with you. You represent us all."

On 3rd March 1794 Joseph Gerrald was brought to trial in Edinburgh on a charge of sedition. The full story of his four days in the dock has been told in Howell's *State Trials*, covering 151 pages and consisting mainly of dry-as-dust discussions between the prisoner and the five learned gentlemen on the bench, who had already decided to banish him to Botany Bay. The trial was just a formality.

Lord Cockburn, in his account of the case, writes: "None of these previous cases (Muir, Palmer, Skirving, Margarot) has sunk so deeply into the heart of posterity, as Gerrald's, not so much from his superior innocence, as from his character and heroism. He was an Englishman, a gentleman, and a scholar; a man of talent, eloquence, and fidelity to his principles and associates; the rashness of whose enthusiasm in the promotion of what appeared to him to be the cause of liberty, though not untinctured by ambition or vanity, was the natural result of the political fire which at that time kindled far less inflammable breasts. The purity of his intentions was above all suspicion."

Gerrald's conduct throughout his trial contrasted strikingly with that of his judges. "The feebleness of his health, which obviously left him no chance of surviving his anticipated sentence, gave his case additional interest. He appeared at the bar with unpowdered hair, hanging loosely behind, his neck nearly bare, with a large collar, doubled over; so that he was not unlike one of Vandyck's portraits."

This was the French costume of the day, and one of the symbols of his party. His adopting it on this occasion gave great offence, "and no doubt he appeared in it, from a desire to show his opponents that he did not shrink from displaying the outward badge of his principles".

When proceedings began on 3rd March 1794 Gerrald asked for counsel, saying that as he was totally ignorant of the laws of the country he had applied to "several gentlemen of the profession" to take his case, but they had all refused. The judges agreed to grant his request, and the case was postponed for seven days while Gerrald discussed his defence with the men appointed.

The trial opened on 10th March 1794, with Gerrald objecting to Lord Braxfield's trying him, on the grounds that Braxfield had prejudged his case when he remarked at a dinner "that the members of the British Convention deserved transportation for fourteen years, and even public whipping". Readers will recall that Maurice Margarot had made a similar objection, but his protests were ruthlessly ignored.

After Gerrald made this statement Lord Braxfield left the chair while the remaining judges deliberated this point. They then attacked the prisoner for his insolence in daring to traduce Lord Braxfield. "His objection is a very high insult upon the dignity of this Court!" Lord Swinton exclaimed. "He now stands at the bar, charged with a crime little less than treason. The insolence of his objection is swallowed up in the atrocity of his crime."

Comments Lord Cockburn: "Yet the trial had not begun. And what a symptom is it of a Court, when the judges treat a declinature of one of their number, on a ground of supposed legal or of supposed personal impropriety, as an insult!"

Lord Abercromby then took up the cudgels on behalf of his departed chief and said, "There is no such thing as a common law disqualification of a judge." After stating that he had no intention of intimidating Gerrald, Abercromby added, "I have no hesitation in saying that if the prisoner should be convicted of the crime charged against him I shall say that even fourteen years' transportation is too slight a punishment for an offence of such magnitude."

Hell hath no fury like a judge scorned. So the noble Lords, Henderland, Eskgrove, Dunsinnan, Swinton, and Abercromby, after vilifying the prisoner, repelled the declinature, and Lord Braxfield was recalled from outer darkness to resume his place as chairman of the bench.

The indictment was read, and Gerrald rose to address the Court. He did this at length, quoting numerous authorities, and then said, "Gentlemen, my feelings, my exertions, and my state of health have exhausted me."

Lord Henderland: "You may sit down, Mr Gerrald, and take a little breath."

Mr Gerrald: "I thank your lordship."

Having rested a few minutes, Gerrald began quoting legal decisions since Magna Carta and answering the charges against him, while the judges wagged their heads, without any intention of reversing their verdict.

Lord Cockburn quotes a remark from Lord Henderland to the jury, "Gentlemen, as to the activity of the prisoner at the bar, you have his speeches", and comments that it had not at that time been proved that Gerrald had ever made a speech.

Lord Eskgrove was another judge who transgressed the laws of justice, when he said of Gerrald and his companions: "They were endeavouring to obtain universal suffrage and annual parliaments. As to universal suffrage, I never heard that it had obtained in the British Constitution, and therefore, though it may be lawful to obtain a change, yet if it is a change of that sort, it goes to show that it was not their intention to improve the Constitution, but to subvert and overthrow it." Yet this change, Cockburn points out, had been advocated with impunity by many eminent men before that time, "and it is now one of the ordinary subjects of unchecked public discussion, which shows how careful a judge should be not to assume his political principles to be eternal truths, or to hold everything to be clearly wicked which alarms him".

Solicitor-General Blair opened the case for the prosecution with the remark that "he expressed his strongest possible concurrence with the Court in the opinion that seeking universal suffrage is not only dangerous, and inconsistent with the nature of the government, but seditious. It is a subversion of that form of government under which we live, and this form of government having been fixed at the Revolution, such a change can never be advocated without carrying with it its own evidence of seditious intention." Blair finally instructed the jury "that the point they had to try was whether, on a review of the whole facts, the prisoner's intentions were pure, or were seditious, wicked and criminal".

Says Lord Cockburn: "From the first, the prisoner was a doomed man. Independently of panic and general prejudice, the jury were directed, by authorities to which, when conveying doctrines so acceptable, they were very willing to yield sometimes, that the mere advocacy of the reform which the Convention avowed its anxiety to promote, was in itself criminal; and at other times, that this advocacy was at least so conclusive as evidence of seditious intention that no rational juror could doubt it. And from the moment Gerrald admitted it, he stood virtually condemned. He proclaimed his principles to the last, and was sacrificed with the chaplets he was proudest of on his brow."

Cockburn then discusses Gerrald's address to the Court, "which amidst great merits, had numerous defects. Chiefly anxious about his universal suffrage and annual parliaments, he labours this hopeless topic, while he is far too short and casual on what ought to have been his great theme, the right, under the Constitution, of every one to recommend what the majority may think unconstitutional and dangerous reforms."

One part of Gerrald's address that touched Lord Cockburn was this: "If, at any early period of my life, it had been announced to me that the task of defending the rights and privileges of nine millions of people would have devolved upon me, a simple individual, I should certainly, from my youth up, have devoted my whole time, that I might be enabled to execute so sacred and important a trust. Unfortunately my health has been much impaired by continual sickness."

Then came this peroration: "What ever may become of me, my principles will last for ever. Whether I shall be permitted to glide gently down the current of life, in the bosom of my native country, among those kindred spirits whose approbation constitutes the greatest comfort of my living; whether I be doomed to drag out the remainder of my existence amidst thieves and murderers, a wandering exile on the bleak and melancholy shores of New Holland, my mind, equal to either fortune, is prepared to meet the destiny that awaits it."

Joseph Gerrald then made a Latin quotation, but, not being a Latinist, I called upon my friend Cardinal Gilroy for help. His Eminence replied that the lines were taken from Horace's Satires, Book 2, Satire 1. Continued Cardinal Gilroy: "An expert to whom I handed your letter has furnished the attached information, which, I trust, suits your purposes."

From this I learnt that the passage from which Gerrald quoted reads:

> . . . *seu me tranquilla senectus*
> *exspectat seu mors atris circumvolat alis,*
> *dives, inops, Romae, seu fors ita iusserit exsul,*
> *quisquis erit vitae scribam color.*

Translation of the above: ". . . whether a peaceful old age awaits me, or Death envelops me with its gloomy wings; whether rich or poor; whether at Rome or, should Fortune so ordain, as an exile, whatever may be the complexion of my life, I will write."

After this Latin resignation to his fate, Gerrald resumed his plea in English. "To be torn a bleeding member from that country which we love is indeed painful in the extreme. But all things cease to be painful when we are supported by the consciousness that we have done our duty to our fellow-creatures. . . . Gentlemen, my case is in your hands. You are Britons. You are freemen. You have heard the charge. You have heard the evidence. And you know the punishment that follows upon conviction."

Says Lord Cockburn: "Some who were present and still remember the scene, say that during the delivery of his address he had occasionally to struggle with a deep-seated cough." But the judges remained unmoved. Cockburn records an episode which, he says, discloses the temper with which Gerrald's defence was received on the bench. "Gerrald was commenting on the change in human institutions, and the consequent duty of toleration in new doctrines. He quoted the example of Christianity, which was originally attempted to be crushed, partly on account of its novelty, an example which has been cited a thousand times by divines and pious philosophers, as a case which ought to make all ages cautious in condemning moral changes merely on account of their being innovations." Gerrald's words were: "After all, the most useful discoveries in philosophy, the most important changes in the moral history of man, have been innovations. The Revolution was an innovation: Christianity itself was an innovation."

Interruption from Lord Braxfield: "All that you have been saying is sedition! And now, my lords, he is attacking Christianity!"

Lord Henderland: "I cannot sit here as a judge without saying that it is a most indecent defence."

Mr Gerrald: "I conceive myself as vindicating the rights of Britons at large; and I solemnly disclaim all intentions of attacking Christianity."

Commented Lord Cockburn: "No religiousness on the part of their Lordships could account for this shocking perversion of what the prisoner had said. But none of the judges was religious. Braxfield's very name made the pious shudder. And the very moment before he interrupted Gerrald he chuckled over a profane jest of his own, on our Saviour's success as an innovator, a jest too indecent to be recorded, but which transpired next day, because his brethren on the bench thought it too good to be kept to themselves, and which has never been forgotten."

The *Dictionary of National Biography* quotes Braxfield's indecent jest. "When Gerrald ventured to say that Christianity was an innovation, and that all great men had been reformers, *even our Saviour himself*, Braxfield chuckled in an undertone: 'Muckle he made of that, he was hanget'. On another occasion he is said to have told an eloquent culprit at the bar: 'Ye're a verra clever chiel, man, but ye wad be none the waur o' a hanging.'"

The trial of Joseph Gerrald lasted four days, during which thousands of words were spoken for and against the prisoner. Braxfield, addressing the jury, said, "I look upon Gerrald as a very dangerous member of society, for

I dare say, he has eloquence enough to persuade the people to rise in arms."

Mr Gerrald: "Oh my lord! My lord, this is a very improper way of addressing a jury. It is descending to personal abuse. God forbid that my eloquence should ever be made use of for such a purpose."

Braxfield: "I don't say that you did so, but that you had abilities to do it."

Lord Braxfield concluded his words to the jury: "Gentlemen, if you are satisfied that this meeting is seditious, I don't see how it is possible to avoid the consequence of finding this prisoner guilty art and part of the crime charged; but, gentlemen, it is not my verdict to be returned. You will return such a verdict as your consciences will direct."

The jury retired at eleven o'clock and returned twenty minutes later, "and they all in one voice found Joseph Gerrald guilty of the crimes libelled".

Lord Braxfield thanked them. Turning to the prisoner, he said, "Mr Gerrald, now is your time to speak, if you have anything to say."

"My lords," replied Gerrald, "I have an objection to state at this verdict." He then pointed out that the written evidence of the case consisted of several hundred pages, which could not have been read in less than six or seven hours. The jury had returned after twenty minutes; therefore they "neither did, nor could they, consider the great body of written evidence placed before them".

The prisoner discoursed lengthily on this point until Braxfield interjected: "Mr Gerrald, have you anything to say, now is the time?"

Gerrald: "My lord, I have very little to say. I am a little hurt, as I am surprised at the verdict, inasmuch as I find that the Public Prescutor in the House of Commons anticipated the fate which I was to meet. But, my lord, I trust that a moral and enlightened world, collectively, will do justice to the purity of the motives which have actuated my conduct; and I glory in being the advocate of a cause, with which is complicated truth, justice, and freedom, which I know must and will ultimately triumph."

Lord Braxfield next turned to his brethren on the bench and asked for their opinions upon the punishment to be inflicted. They were unanimous that although transportation was a very severe punishment, the prisoner deserved it. After which Lord Justice-Clerk Braxfield pronounced the sentence, which was transportation for fourteen years.

Howell's *State Trials* gives the information that the jury was "composed exclusively of members of an association calling itself the 'Friends of the Constitution'". This was a very different body from the "Friends of the Constitution and of the People" to which Muir belonged, having been formed "for the express purpose of suppressing the movement for parliamentary reform", and having "denounced the 'Friends of the People' for attempting to kindle the torch of civil war, and to lay the country in blood and destruction". Many of the jury were also placemen in the service of the Crown.

Nearly a century later, in 1891, Lord Rosebery wrote a biography of Pitt the Younger, the man who, as Prime Minister, was responsible for the prosecution of the Scottish Martyrs in 1793. Says Lord Rosebery: "These trials sank deep into the minds of the Scottish people. Half a century afterwards, a memorial was erected to the victims on one of the loftiest sites in Edinburgh; while Fox expressed in an ejaculation what it still thought of those who sentenced them: 'God help the people who have such judges!' "

CHAPTER SEVEN

Now THAT the Scottish Martyrs were rounded up and awaiting banishment to Botany Bay, Prime Minister Pitt and his henchmen began preparations to finish off Thomas Hardy, founder of the London Corresponding Society. Hardy was arrested on 12th May 1794 on a charge of high treason, and after being examined several times before the Privy Council he was committed to the Tower of London to await trial, together with eleven of his associates.

In his biography of William Godwin, C. Kegan Paul quotes notes written by Mary Shelley, Godwin's daughter. Said Mary of her father's reaction when he heard that the grand jury had found a true bill against the twelve men, "He well understood, that had these trials been followed by a verdict of *guilty*, he would have subsequently shared their fate as their friend and intimate associate."

Godwin understood the motives of the authorities in accusing people of high treason, when the real charge was sedition, and when Chief Justice Eyre made the charge and explained the law of treason according to the Statute 25, Edward III, Godwin seethed with indignation, and fiercely wrote a counter-charge. "He looked on this crisis as one of awful moment to all Englishmen. The law of high treason, accurately defined by the statute, and ably commented on by the best lawyers, was to be stretched and bent for the destruction of these men. They had met in conventions for the sake of furthering a plan to obtain annual parliaments. This was their apparent crime; it remained to discover the guilt of high treason beyond so innocuous an outside."

Godwin wrote page after page exposing the King's Ministers and Chief Justice Eyre, fully aware that if his appeal failed he was destined for the same fate as his friends. "The effect of this appeal," said Mary Shelley, "when it became widely spread through the paper, was memorable. Hitherto men had

47

heard that the King's Ministers had discovered a treasonable conspiracy, and had arrested the traitors. They believed this. No project was believed too wild or wicked for those who had imbibed the infections of the French Revolution, nor could any believe that the highest and most solemn council of the State could have proceeded against twelve subjects of the realm but on clear grounds. The charge of the Chief Justice did not dissipate the illusion."

But Godwin's fluent pen and sound argument reached the citizens of London before the trial, and many of those who had believed that the accused were certainly guilty of treason "began to perceive that a design to reform Parliament was not treasonable, and that however wrong-headed, and even reprehensible it might be to associate for such a purpose, this was no cause why men, otherwise innocent, should themselves and their families be subjected to the frightful pains and penalties of treason".

The story of Hardy's trial is told in Howell's *State Trials*, and the events leading up to it in the *Memoirs of Thomas Hardy*, published in 1832. On the title page of the latter work the author states that herein is the story of his endeavours to promote parliamentary reform, until his arrest on a false charge of high treason on 12th May 1794.

A preface to the *Memoirs*, dated 16th October 1832 and written by Hardy's friend D. McPherson, says, "The duty now devolves on me, of informing the reader, that Mr Hardy, having lived to see the final sheet of his memoirs from the press, breathed his last about eight o'clock on the morning of the 11th instant."

This means that Thomas Hardy died thirty-eight years after his battle with bureaucracy to diffuse political knowledge among the people of Great Britain and Ireland through the London Corresponding Society, the members of which "devoted themselves to the cause of justice and humanity". This also means that Hardy lived long enough to see the principles for which he had battled triumph, because on 7th June 1832 the Reform Bill received the royal assent. This was the beginning of a process of parliamentary reform that continued until universal suffrage became part of the British way of life.

In his *Memoirs* Hardy chose to write "in the third, rather than in the first person, to obviate the necessity of calling the great *I* so repeatedly to my assistance". He states that he was born on 3rd March 1752 in the parish of Larbert, Stirlingshire, about one mile from the forest of Torwood, famous in Scottish history as the place where, in the hollow trunk of a large oak-tree, many of the exploits of the great patriot, Sir William Wallace, were planned. Hardy no doubt had a fellow-feeling for Wallace, like him a fighter for freedom and like him imprisoned in the Tower of London. But Hardy was more fortunate than Wallace, who was executed in 1305 as a traitor, though he owed no allegiance to the English King.

Walter Hardy, Thomas's father, was a sailor. He died at sea in 1760, leaving a wife with little means of support. Her father, Thomas Walker, a shoemaker, took young Tom under his care, and put him to school to learn writing, reading, and arithmetic, at the cost of a penny a week. Leaving school, Thomas was taught shoemaking, after which he worked as a builder's assistant, but an accident in which a scaffolding collapsed, killing one man and injuring another, caused him to return to shoemaking. In April 1774 he took passage

MAURICE MARGAROT.

Questions put to the Lord Justice Clerke.

Marg: *Did you use these words — What sho.d you think of giving
him 100 lashes together with Botany Bay — or words to that purpose.*

L.d J.Clk: *Go on — put your quest.s if you have any more.*

Marg: *Did any person — Did a Lady say to you that the Mob
would not allow you to whip him, & my Lord did you
not say that the Mob would be the better for letting a
little* BLOOD.

Published as the Act directs Feb. 17. 1794 by H.D. Symonds N.o 20 Paternoster Row

Maurice Margarot
From the account of his trial, with "Questions Put to the Lord Justice Clerke"

Henry Cockburn

on a ship to London, arriving there "with no more than eighteen pence in his pocket".

While working at his trade in London Hardy, "being of a contemplative and serious turn of mind, met many of the middle and lower classes of Dissenters". In 1781 he married "the daughter of Mr Priest, a carpenter"; she bore him children, but they all died young. In 1791 he took a house in Piccadilly, where "he began to feel the pressure of taxes, and it required no great penetration, to be able to trace it to the corrupt practices of men falsely calling themselves the represenatives of the people, but who were in fact, selected by a few individuals, who preferred their own aggrandisement to the interest of the community". He asked himself: "Was the cause of the people hopeless? Must they and their posterity forever groan under this intolerable load? Could not the nation, by a proper use of its moral powers, set itself free?"

As we have already seen, Hardy's answer to these questions was to form the London Corresponding Society in January 1792. The story of its activities has been told in the chapters dealing with the trials of its two eminent members, Margarot and Gerrald. In his *Memoirs* Hardy writes of the Society's first address in adding, "This was written by Mr Margarot." But Hardy signed it, and was legally responsible for what Margarot had written.

Here are a few of the resolutions that accompanied this address:

"*Resolved*: that every individual has a right to share in the government of that Society of which he is a member, unless incapacitated.

"*Resolved*: That it is no less the *right* than the *duty* of every citizen, to keep a watchful eye on the government; that the laws, by being multiplied, do not degenerate into oppression; and that those who are entrusted with the Government, do not substitute Private Interest, for Public Advantage.

"*Resolved*: That in consequence of a partial, unequal, and therefore inadequate Representation, together with the *corrupt* method in which Representatives are elected; oppressive taxes, unjust laws, restrictions of liberty, and *wasting of the public money*, have ensued.

"*Resolved*: That the only remedy to those evils is a fair, equal, and impartial Representation of the people in Parliament.

"*Resolved*: That this Society do express their *abhorrence* of tumult and violence; and that, as they aim at Reform, not anarchy; reason, firmness, and unanimity are the only arms they will employ, or persuade their fellow-citizens to exert, against *Abuse of Power*."

Copies of these resolutions were sent to the Societies for Constitutional Information established in London, Sheffield, and Manchester; they were later published in the newspapers, and distributed by the London Corresponding Society in the form of handbills. "Thousands of them were circulated in London, and throughout the country."

Then in September 1792 came the "Congratulatory Address to the National Convention of France" by Hardy and Margarot, on behalf of the London Corresponding Society, full of high-flown rhetoric which must have had an ominous sound to the ears of Authority — for example, "What is freedom? What are our rights? Frenchmen, you are already free, and Britons are preparing to become so."

Before the end of the year the London Corresponding Society had correspondence with every society in Great Britain, "which had been instituted for the purpose of obtaining, by constitutional means a Reform in the Commons House of Parliament". About this time — Hardy does not give the date — Margarot and Hardy signed an *Address to the Nation*, written by Mr Felix Vaughan, Barrister-at-Law, and a member of the London Corresponding Society. This was written in reply to attacks made on the London Corresponding Society by "an Association for protecting property against republicans and levellers", which Hardy said was formed by the Government to disseminate propaganda against the London Corresponding Society.

Nearly one year passed, during which "Societies for Reform" spread throughout England and Scotland, the movement culminating in the Convention in Edinburgh that ended with the arrest of Margarot, Gerrald, and Skirving. Now it was the turn of Thomas Hardy: "On a memorable morning in May 1794, I heard a thundering knock on the door of my home, No. 9 Piccadilly."

The door-knockers included several Bow Street runners. They held Hardy, ratted his pockets, seized his papers, and when asked by the prisoner why he was thus treated, showed him a paper, which was a warrant for this arrest on a charge of high treason. As we have seen, Hardy was examined by the Privy Council, and was later committed to the Tower by a warrant dated May 1794 and signed by twelve Privy Councillors, including William Pitt, the Prime Minister.

The same William Pitt, nearly a decade earlier, had on 18th April 1785 introduced a bill in the House of Commons in which he proposed to suppress thirty-six pocket boroughs, and transfer their representation to various towns and counties. The suppression of such boroughs was one of the main objectives of Hardy and his friends, so Pitt should have been in the dock with them.

The Governor of the Tower was instructed that Hardy was not to be allowed communication with other traitors in the Tower. "Nor is pen, ink, paper, books or newspapers to be permitted to him."

Hardy records that a week before his committal to the Tower "the Bill for suspending the Habeas Corpus passed the Lords."

Says the *Encyclopaedia Britannica*: "In times of public danger it has occasionally been thought necessary to suspend the Habeas Corpus Act. This was done in 1794 (by an act annually renewed until 1801) and again in 1817, as to persons arrested and detained by his Majesty for conspiring against his person and government." By this Act freedom of speech was effectually banned for many a year.

After Hardy had been in the Tower for some days, "the faithful partner of his bosom, who was in an advanced state of pregnancy, obtained permission to pay him a mournful visit, and was allowed to see him twice a week in the presence of a jailer". On 11th June London was illuminated to commemorate Lord Howe's victory over the French Fleet. On that night, a mob of ruffians assembled before Hardy's house, No. 9 Piccadilly, and "assailed the windows with stones and brick-bats. They then attempted to break down the shop door, and swore, with the most horrid oaths, that they would either burn or pull down the house. Weak and enfeebled from her situation, Mrs Hardy shouted to her neighbours, who advised her to escape through a small back window. This she attempted, but being very large around the waist, she stuck fast, and it was only by main force that she could be dragged through, much injured by the bruises she had received." Mrs Hardy visited her husband once again in the Tower. It was her farewell, "for they were doomed never again to see each other in this vale of tears". Soon afterwards, on 27th August, she was taken in labour and delivered of a dead child, and herself died.

Mrs Hardy left an unfinished letter to her husband, which she had begun on the day of her death, saying, "I hope the Spirit of God is both with you and me, and I pray that He may give us grace to look up to Christ. There all the good is that we can either hope or wish for, if we have but faith and patience, although we are but poor sinful mortals. My dear, you have it not in —"

So Thomas Hardy mourned in the Tower for his beloved wife, while awaiting trial for high treason. The trial began at the Old Bailey Sessions on 28th October 1794. A grand jury had returned a true bill against Thomas Hardy, John Horne Tooke, and ten others. On the bench "were Lord Chief Justice Eyre; Lord Chief Baron Macdonald; Mr Baron Hotham; Mr Justice Buller; Mr Justice Grose; and others his Majesty's justices, etc."

Prosecuting the twelve prisoners were the Attorney-General, Sir John Scott, the Solicitor-General, Sir John Milford, and six other legal luminaries. Hardy was the first to be tried. Assisting Thomas Hardy was the Honourable Thomas Erskine, who had defended Paine, and Mr Gibb, later to become Lord Chief Justice of the Court of Common Pleas.

After the jury were sworn in, the Attorney-General asked them to give serious attention to "this great and weighty cause, namely High Treason, with which the prisoner is charged". He quoted Lord Hale: "The crime of High Treason is the greatest crime against faith, duty and human society, and brings with it the most fatal dangers to the government, peace, and happiness of a Kingdom or State, and therefore is branded with the highest ignominy and subjected to the greatest penalties that the law can inflict."

The case droned on, as the clever lawyers subtly interpreted the words of Margarot and Hardy in their *Address to the Nation* as "compassing the death of the King". This, they inferred, revealed a conspiracy to use universal suffrage as a ruse to set up a new legislature and to form a convention to assume control of civil and political authority, and "rip up monarchy by the roots". The papers of the London Corresponding Society, which had been seized by the Bow Street Runners, were produced and quoted in court, also a letter in which the Society returned thanks to Mr Thomas Paine, who appears to have been a visitor-member, for the publication of his "Second Part of the *Rights of Man*, combining Principle and Practice".

Hour by hour the Attorney-General dredged the correspondence of the London Corresponding Society with similar societies in England and Scotland, imputing sinister significance to innocent facts. When he was exhausted his corps of informers gave evidence against Hardy, quoting from his letters to other societies, and their replies. This was Erskine's chance to examine the witnesses, and he sailed into them hour by hour, and day by day.

Among the papers seized from the files of Thomas Hardy and the London

Corresponding Society was a printed pamphlet entitled *Proceedings of the Public Meeting held at Sheffield, in the open air, on the 7th April, 1794.* There was also *An Address to the British Nation, being an Exposition of the Motives which have determined the People of Sheffield to Petition the House of Commons no more on the subject of Parliamentary Reform.*

This meeting at Sheffield of the Friends of Justice, Liberty, and Humanity was held at three o'clock in the afternoon on the Castle Hill, Sheffield, "to consider upon the propriety of addressing the King, in behalf of the persecuted patriots, citizens Muir, Palmer, Skirving, Margarot and Gerrald; also of again petitioning the House of Commons for a reform in the representation of the people, and to determine upon the propriety of petitioning the King for the abolition of negro slavery".

The pamphlet stated that despite heavy rains having fallen, "from ten to twelve thousand people were assembled". The petition to the King stated that if the five Scottish Martyrs "had been really guilty of crimes, then punishment should doubtless have been proportionate to their offences". After entreating His Majesty to consider the case of these unfortunate prisoners, the pamphlet continued with a plea to him not to let it be recorded in history that he or any of his judges transported men for fourteen years because they dared to speak the same words that had helped to advance His Majesty's Prime Minister to his high situation. "Let it not be said that men of education, of refined sentiments, of the most virtuous and benevolent characters, were severed from their dearest connections, and plunged into dungeons with thieves and prostitutes; let it not be said, that fathers were torn from their wives and children, and sons from their aged parents, because they had the virtue openly to condemn the corruptions of government; let it not be said, that it was as great a crime to speak the TRUTH as to be guilty of felony. But rather, O King, let it be recorded that George III had the wisdom, the humanity, and the justice, to step in betwixt these severe and cruel sentences and their execution."

Henry Yorke, as chairman, had then addressed the meeting, and observed that the cause for which the Scottish Martyrs were now suffering had been advocated in the year 1783 by Mr Pitt, the Duke of Richmond, and other men.

The other pamphlet, *An Address to the British Nation*, was then read to the court. Very lengthy, it ended with a demand for "equality of rights with which is included equality of representation, without which terror is law, and the obligations of justice are weakened; because unsanctioned by the sacred voice of the people", and called on the "People of Scotland" to take their part. "The banks of the Forth, the Fields of Bannockburn and Culloden, and that tribunal of Edinburgh, which has disgraced your capital, shall yet bear testimony to the cause for which Fletcher wrote, and Wallace bled."

Another address produced in court was signed by John Lovett and Thomas Hardy on 14th April 1794, to their friend Joseph Gerrald, still imprisoned in Scotland since his trial on 3rd March 1794. "We behold in you, our beloved friend and fellow-citizen, a martyr to the Glorious Cause of Equal Representation, and we cannot permit you to leave this degraded country without expressing the infinite obligations the people at large, and we in particular, owe to you for your very spirited exertions in that cause upon every occasion;

but upon none more conspicuously, than during the sitting of the Convention at Edinburgh, and the consequent *proceedings* (we will not call it trial) at the bar of the Court of Justiciary." Deploring that the laws of the country had fled, the address ended: "We again pledge ourselves to you and our country, never to cease demanding our rights from those who have usurped them, until, having obtained an Equal Representation of the People, we shall be enabled to hail you once more with triumph to your native country. We wish you Health and Happiness; and be assured we never, never shall forget your name, your Virtues, nor your Great Example."

At long last Erskine was allowed to address the jury. After enumerating a score of cases to show that the charge of high treason should not have been brought, Erskine informed the jury that "irreverent expressions against judges are not acts of High Treason. I am no advocate for disrespect to judges, and think that it is dangerous to the public order; but putting aside the insult to the judges now in authority; the reprobation of Jeffreys is no libel, but an awful and useful memento to wicked men."

Erskine then told the story of how "Lord Chief Justice Jeffreys denied the privilege of English law to an innocent man" when he sentenced Sir Thomas Armstrong to death in 1684. Armstrong's daughter prayed that God Almighty's judgments might light upon the judge, and, said Erskine, they did, for death "speedily followed this transaction". Erskine was taking a long chance on the jury's historical ignorance, since Jeffreys in fact lived for another five years after Armstrong's execution.

Not satisfied with scaring the soul-case out of the jurors with the name of "Bloody" Judge Jeffreys, Erskine now called upon the Duke of Richmond to give evidence. After His Grace was sworn, Erskine produced a letter written by Richmond on 15th August 1783 to Lieutenant-Colonel Sharman, Chairman to the Committee of Correspondence, assembled at Lisburn, Ireland. The letter stated: "I have been honoured with a letter from Belfast, dated 19th July, by the delegates of forty-five Volunteer Corps, for taking steps to forward their intentions on the subject of a more equal representation of the people in Parliament." Too long to reproduce here, this famous epistle pointed out the corrupt state of boroughs in Ireland, and the opinion of the people, "That the Constitution can be restored to its ancient purity and vigor by no other means than parliamentary reform".

Charles Lennox, third Duke of Richmond and Lennox, was born in London in February 1735. The *Dictionary of National Biography* tells us that he was "educated at Westminster School, where Cowper remembered seeing him set fire to Vinny Bourne's greasy locks and box his ears to put it out again". After graduating at Leyden University, Lennox joined the army and distinguished himself at the Battle of Minden. He succeeded his father as Duke in 1750, and in 1756 took his seat in the House of Lords. He quarrelled with King George III, denounced the policy of the Crown with references to the American colonies, and in 1775 "declared that the resistance of the colonists was neither treason or rebellion, but is perfectly justifiable in every possible political and moral sense". Four years later, in May 1779, he "supported a motion for the removal of the causes of Irish discontent by a redress of grievances; and in reference to a union between England and Ireland declared that he was for a union, not a union of legislatures, but a union of hearts, hands, of affections and interests".

Continues the *Dictionary of National Biography*: "On 2nd June 1780 Richmond attempted to bring forth his Reform Bill. The three main features of the proposal were annual parliaments, manhood suffrage, and electoral districts. It was rejected without a division, and practically without discussion." In May 1782 the Duke urged the appointment of a committee for parliamentary reform — again without success. Then in 1783 he wrote his famous letter on reform to Lieutenant-Colonel Sharman, which eleven years later was read at the trial of Thomas Hardy. This letter was reprinted, and "became the very scripture" of all the societies promoting universal suffrage. The Duke also gave evidence at the trial of John Horne Tooke, and his testimony was of great value in the defence of both men.

The next witness for Hardy was also a distinguished man — Richard Brinsley Sheridan, best known to our century as the author of *The School for Scandal*. Born in Dublin in 1751, Sheridan was educated at Harrow; as a young man he fought duels over Elizabeth Linley, who later became his wife, and he studied law. The *Encyclopaedia Britannica* states that when he entered Parliament in 1780 for Stafford "he is said to have paid the burgesses five guineas each for the honour of representing them. His first speech in Parliament was to defend himself against the charge of bribery, and was well received." Sheridan was in and out of the Ministry for many years; he became penniless over the failure of the Drury Lane theatre; he lost thousands in gambling, and when he died on 7th July 1816 he was buried with great pomp in Westminster Abbey.

Asked whether he knew Thomas Hardy, the prisoner, Sheridan said he had met him once, in March 1793. "I had given notice in the House of Commons," said Sheridan, "that I intended to bring forward a motion, to propose a committee to inquire into the seditious plots, and the proceedings of the Societies which were supposed to be promoting sedition or treason."

Mr Erskine: "At that time was the convention which had been assembled in Scotland sitting, or had it been dispersed?"

Sheridan: "I do not recollect. Having this notice in the House of Commons, I thought it my duty to inquire into the existence of these societies, and their conduct, being a great believer in the supposed plots. I sent for Mr Hardy. He came, and I took the precaution to have two gentlemen present. I then showed Mr Hardy a publication which had been delivered at the House of Commons, and the House of Lords, reporting the proceedings and the addresses of these societies. Mr Hardy went over that book with me, and complained that it calumniated the Society he belonged to."

Lord Chief Justice Eyre: "It is not regular to go into a general narration, Mr Sheridan. The point you are called upon to prove is that Mr Hardy offered to assist you in disclosing everything he knew, and to assist you in bringing forward the inquiry."

Sheridan: "I certainly will confine myself to that. Mr Hardy observed that the information was accurate; that the places mentioned of their places of meetings were correct, but that the object of the Society was much mis-stated.

They had nothing in view but a parliamentary reform according to the plan of the Duke of Richmond."

Mr Erskine: "What did Hardy declare the object of the Society to be?"

Sheridan: "Obtaining, by peaceful means, a parliamentary reform upon the Duke of Richmond's plan."

Erskine: "Will you state what assistance Hardy offered you?"

Sheridan: "He went through the lists, and upon my asking him whether these societies having been dispersed they continued at public houses, he declared they did not. . . . I asked Hardy if they still continued to meet, and he said yes. He had no objection to give me the list of the houses where they met, and that I might read it, if I pleased in the House of Commons."

Erskine: "Did Hardy know that you intended making a motion in the House of Commons on this subject?"

Sheridan: "I told him that distinctly; I took down a great many of the houses where he said they met. I had the paper in my hand the next day when I moved in the House for a Committee to inquire into the conduct of these societies."

Erskine: "Did Hardy offer you further help?"

Sheridan: "He offered me every assistance. He offered me a sight of the correspondence, copies of all his letters, if I chose, and expressed a wish that my motion might be successful."

Sheridan, cross-examined by the Attorney-General, "steadfastly adhered to his statement that Hardy was anxious to have an investigation into his affairs, and had nothing to conceal".

Mr Attorney-General: "Are you a member of the Constitutional Society?"

Sheridan: "I do not know whether I am or not. I was an original member with the Duke of Richmond. I do not know whether I have withdrawn my name, but I have not attended since the year 1783."

After the ninth day, Lord Chief Justice Eyre summed up the 100,000 words of evidence given by witnesses and informers, and charged the jury to consider their verdict.

One of the jury: "My Lord, we wish to have a copy of the indictment to take with us."

Lord Eyre: "I suppose there will be no objection to your taking out the indictment. Gentlemen, I must apprise you, that after you have withdrawn there can be no refreshment. Do you wish to take any moderate refreshment before you withdraw?"

One of the jury: "My Lord, we thank you, we shall not have occasion for any."

The jury withdrew at thirty minutes after noon, returning at thirty-five minutes after three o'clock. Thomas Hardy was then sent to the bar.

Clerk of the Arraigns: "Thomas Hardy, hold up your hand. Gentlemen of the jury, look upon the prisoner. How say you, is Thomas Hardy guilty of the high treason whereof he stands indicted, or not guilty?"

Foreman: "Not guilty."

Clerk of Arraigns: "Did he fly for it?"

Foreman: "Not that we know of."

Prisoner: "My fellow countrymen, I return you my thanks."

55

The prisoner was discharged.

Lord Chief Justice Eyre: "Gentlemen of the jury, I ought to take the first opportunity after this laborious attendance, very sincerely to thank you for the readiness with which you have sacrificed so much of your personal convenience, and with which you have undergone the fatigue of this trial."

Footnote to the above in Howell's *State Trials*: "The jury slept at the Hummums every night from the 29th October, attended by the proper officers of the court, sworn in the usual form."

Comments Thomas Hardy: "The trial lasted nine days, after the fullest investigation that ever took place in this or any other country, after which Hardy was pronounced *Not Guilty*, by the unanimous voice of as respectable a jury as ever was empanelled. A jury which with unremitting patience, underwent a fatigue and confinement unparallelled in the annals of our courts of justice. A jury, on whose awful voice depended the liberty of eleven million citizens. A jury, whose integrity established on a firm basis the first and most important pillar of the English Constitution — The Trial by Jury — which had been on the decline, and much tampered with, and thereby, entitled themselves to the grateful applause of the present and future generations."

When the words "Not guilty" were pronounced by the foreman of the jury, Hardy tells us, "the Sessions House, where the court sat, was rent with the shouts of applause. A vast multitude caught the joyful sound, and like an electric shock, the glad tidings spread through London, and were conveyed quicker than the regular post could travel, to the most distant parts of England, where all ranks anxiously awaited the result of the trial."

While the crowds were hooraying with joy on a bleak and rainy afternoon, Hardy slipped out through the debtor's door of the Old Bailey where a coach awaited to take him to the house of his brother-in-law in the Strand, "for he had no house of his own, nor family to welcome him". But he had not gone far before he was recognized, and the crowd stopped his coach, turned out the horses, and drew it along Fleet Street, the Strand, Pall Mall, and St James Street. At No. 9 Piccadilly, his former home, now ruined by the mob, they stopped for a few minutes in solemn silence. Thence they proceeded to Haymarket, and back again to Lancaster Court, where he alighted and addressed the people from the window in a short speech, "after which they gave three cheers, and quietly dispersed".

The discharge of Hardy was followed by the six-day trial of Mr Horne Tooke, then by those of the Reverend Jeremiah Joyce and of John Thelwall. Says Hardy: "The prosecutors, finding they could not obtain a conviction, declined proceeding with the trials of the other defendants." How different from the infamous trials in Perth and Edinburgh, where a picked jury of Government placemen, and judges who knew no mercy, condemned five men to a living death at Botany Bay!

Of Hardy's fellow-sufferers, John Horne Tooke was possibly the most prominent, an early and active member of the London Corresponding Society, "a steady and intrepid champion of freedom and an unflinching supporter of parliamentary reform". The Reverend Jeremiah Joyce, also a member of the Society, was a friend of Palmer's and, like him, a Unitarian minister. He was tutor to the sons of the Earl of Stanhope, Pitt's brother-in-law, and it is said that one reason for his arrest was that Pitt wanted to irritate Stanhope. Thelwall, the last of the group to be tried, was a typical do-anything-oncer—lawyer's clerk, editor, poet, and enthusiastic political reformer. At the beginning of his trial he handed a note to his counsel, Erskine, saying he wished to plead his own cause. Said Erskine, "If you do, you will be hanged!" Replied Thelwall, "Then I'll be hanged if I do." After his release, he published *Poems Written in Close Confinement in the Tower and Newgate*. He later became a teacher of oratory, specializing in the cure of stammering.

In spite of the favourable outcome of these trials, the days of the London Corresponding Society were numbered. The suspension of the Habeas Corpus Act had given the Prime Minister power to imprison without trial, making political agitation too dangerous for the time being, and Thomas Hardy returned to his bootmaking business. In November every year a party was given for him by his friends and admirers to celebrate his release from Newgate.

As stated earlier, Hardy died on 11th October 1832, the year that Parliament passed the first Reform Bill, thus beginning the process of reformation which had been the aim of the London Corresponding Society and which, forty years earlier, its members had agreed to support with a levy of one penny a week.

CHAPTER EIGHT

Hardy Visits the Martyrs at Portsmouth — A Cast of Thomas Muir's Face — Tributes to the Martyrs — Letters from Palmer — Skirving Writes of the "Stone Cut Out Without Hands" — Letter from Muir — The Martyrs Championed in Parliament — Stanhope Seeks an Inquiry into Muir's Case — Sheridan's Petition for Palmer — Adam's Speech — Dundas Defends the Judges — Fox Attacks Braxfield and Swinton — Mentions Rowan's Letter — Ellis on the "Surprize" — John Boston and Family — Departure for Botany Bay.

BEFORE Hardy was arrested, he had paid a visit to the Scottish Martyrs on board the *Surprize* at Portsmouth. Many years later he told of this in a letter dated 3rd March 1821, to his friend Mr Witherspoon of Cheapside, in which he enclosed an engraving of a bust of Thomas Muir: "When the *Surprize* transport was lying off Portsmouth at Motherbank, in which those persecuted patriots, Muir, Palmer, Margarot, and Skirving were sent to Botany Bay, I was on board of her, and saw Mr Banks, an eminent statuary, take a cast from Mr Muir's face, from which he made a bust, and from which the enclosed engraving is taken. It is a good likeness."

Well, there they were in March 1794, the chosen four at Portsmouth on the convict transport *Surprize*. The fifth man, Joseph Gerrald, was in the Tolbooth at Edinburgh awaiting his fate. George Mealmaker was still free in Dundee, waiting for something to happen. After the four prisoners went aboard the *Surprize* they received an "address from the Society for Constitutional Information, London", dated 28th March 1794, which began: "Friends and Fellow Citizens, Although we have been silent, yet we have by no means been the unconcerned spectators of your conduct and sufferings." The members of the Society expressed "honest indignation at the steps taken by their enemies who are the enemies of Public Liberty, the men who are conspiring against the happiness of mankind. . . . The history of liberty, for whose sake you are doomed to a long and unmerited exile, will afford, in the present instance, that consolation that former martyrs to the same cause have experienced; the consolation, that you *will not*, you *cannot*, suffer in vain. Men may perish, but truth will prevail; neither persecution, nor banishment, nor death itself, can finally injure the progress of those principles which involve the general happiness of man." The Society assured the four martyrs that "the memory of your virtues shall never be effaced from our breasts; the cause for which you have struggled, is a glorious cause; the world that has witnessed your exertions shall witness ours also".

A reply from the *Surprize*, dated 16th April 1794, was sent by the Reverend

58

Thomas Fyshe Palmer to his "Fellow Citizens" of the London Constitutional Society, saying: "I have long since looked upon your Society with admiration and esteem, considering it as the source and school of most of the political information, which by the blessing of God, has overspread England. That my conduct is approved by such a Society, is my pride and joy."

After some comments on "the history of liberty", Palmer discussed his trial in Perth on 12th September 1793. "My jury," wrote Palmer, "was three times packed by the servants of the Crown before it sat on me. In the first instance by the Sheriff's deputy, placemen appointed by the Crown; in the second by the Crown agent, lord advocate, etc., at Edinburgh, and in the third, by the justiciary lords who tried the cause. These last, arbitrarily appoint the fifteen persons who are to sit upon the accused."

Palmer then remarks on the lack of fair play by the justiciary: "The strongest objections are mere air as the lords alone are the judges of the validity of them. A majority of the fifteen jurymen condemns." This meant that if the prosecutors could find "eight servile tools in fifteen", the liberties and lives of all Scotland were at their mercy. "Trial is condemnation. The sentence is appointed before-hand by the Minister, and mine was known a full week in Edinburgh before it was uttered." Thus Palmer claimed he had suffered an "infamous robbery of the first right of Englishmen, a trial by jury fairly chosen".

In the Shepherd Papers, in the library of Manchester College, Oxford, are a number of original letters written by Palmer and Gerrald. Copies of these letters are now in the Mitchell Library, Sydney. A letter from Palmer on board the *Surprize*, dated 23rd April 1794, to an unknown friend, shows his gratitude for favours rendered. "It is not kind you will say to leave one of my best friends and benefactors the last to be written to. As proof of my esteem I answer that the last line I write in this hemisphere is to you. But in truth it is but for a few days only past that I have been capable of thought. My prison so damp and unwholesome with twenty-four people talking, swearing and blocking the light of our little hatchway, God knows is little calculated to adjust it. I am afraid you will think me still not recovered. I am not yet murdered, and I hope by the blessing of God to save my persecutors from this guilt."

Palmer then thanked his friends for a gift of the *Cambridge Intelligencer*, a paper he held "in the highest esteem". After stating that he expected the *Surprize* to drop down to St Helen's the next day, the letter concluded, "Farewell, dear Sir, my next will be more interesting, and I hope more entertaining. I am with a grateful heart that rejoices to see such sympathy towards virtuous suffering whoever be the object."

On 17th April 1794 William Skirving wrote from the *Surprize* to the London Constitutional Society thanking them for "their consoling address, which has excited me, as also the hearts of each of my fellow martyrs for the important cause of Universal Suffrage, and annual parliaments, the most lively sensations of gratitude and esteem". Skirving applauded the Society for their strong stand, and he was also impressed with their statement that "We do not, we cannot suffer for such a cause in vain", and that "the importance of the cause of freedom is too great to the world to expect it to be accomplished without opposition". He fervently hoped "that the day is not very distant, when you will again receive us on British shores, the welcome children of a free and happy people". His letter ends: "Our enemies are the enemies of public liberty; the men who conspired against the happiness of mankind. But though the mighty are combined, though they should so far prevail, as to scatter utterly in their vain apprehension the friends of truth, that truth, the principles of which are already established, is the *stone cut out without hands, and shall become a great mountain, and fill the whole earth*, for He who first commanded the ligh to shine out of darkness, is its almighty Patron."

Not being versed in matters Biblical, I wrote to my friend Reverend Father Francis J. Gorman, S.J., Director of the Jesuit College of Saint Ignatius, Riverview, Sydney, asking about Skirving's quotation.

Wrote Father Gorman: "William Skirving was quoting the Old Testament, Book of Daniel, Chapter 2. The general theme of the book is the uniqueness of the God of the Israelites. Daniel, in the early chapters, relates his experiences in the Court of the King of Babylon, where he served as a slave. In this chapter, Daniel interprets a dream of King Nabuchodnoser, which the court magicians were unable to interpret."

This was the dream of Nabuchodnoser (or Nebuchadnezzar): "He saw a colossal and bright statue; its appearance was frightening. The head was of gold, the breast and arms of silver, the legs of iron, the hips of bronze, the feet partly of iron and partly of clay. While he stood wondering at the statue, a stone was cut from the mountain, without any human agency, and fell on the feet of the statue, smashing it to pieces. Nothing was left of it. The fragments were carried away by the wind and *the stone became a great mountain filling the earth.*"

Further comments on the King's dream from Father Gorman: "The dream symbolized the overthrow of all earthly Kingdoms and the setting up of the universal reign of God's Kingdom on earth, after the coming of the Messiah. The materials, gold, silver, iron, clay, represent different earthly kingdoms to be overthrown and superseded by another Kingdom set up by God, different from all others, and indestrucible and eternal, spiritual and universal. It is widely argued what historical Kingdoms are symbolized by the four metals and there is no agreement on their identity. Their function seems to be merely to indicate that one Kingdom will succeed another until finally the Messianic Kingdom spreads over the earth and all opposition to it will be overcome ... when Christ and His teachings rule all men's hearts."

The letters of Palmer and Skirving to the London Constitutional Society were followed by a letter from Thomas Muir, on the *Surprize* transport, dated 24th April 1794.

Wrote Muir: "That the spirit of Freedom is not extinguished, but still retains its former energy, in defiance of the artifices and the violence of despotism, is an object of high consolation to my mind. Engaged in the sacred cause of Man, individual man is an atom of little value; and in speaking of himself, when he recollects and contemplates the principles of his conduct, should disdain to use the term suffering. Without a vain affection for myself, I disdain the assumption of extraordinary merit. The man who has acted in obedience to the law of his conscience, has simply discharged his duty; and the contrary supposition would involve him in guilt."

After commending the Society for their aims and objects, Muir concluded: "Your exertions in attempting to procure a fair representation of the people in parliament are meritorious. . . . in proportion to the number, and to the rapidity of those tremendous scenes which in succession pass the eye, *All All* of them deriving their existence from this violation of our constitutional rights, let your ardour in procuring a rectification of what is wrong be increased, confident you will obtain the blessing of that Being, whose great design is the happiness of his creation."

While Muir and his mates were languishing in jail, their plight was often mentioned in Parliament. Lord Cockburn tells us that on 31st January 1794 the Earl of Stanhope moved, in the House of Lords, for an address to the King, "beseeching that the sentence against Thomas Muir be not carried into effect until the House shall have had time to inquire into his case. His Lordship had, apparently, been very ill-instructed, for he took up objections that were quite untenable."

Not to be deterred by this failure, Sheridan on 24th February 1794 presented a petition to the House of Commons, "in favour of Palmer who was then on the transport which was to convey him to New South Wales. The petition described his sentence as *illegal, unjust, oppressive,* and *unconstitutional,* and prayed for such relief as the House should think proper."

Arguments raged over the legality of the sentence, and "Mr Whitbread, Senior, fell into the strange blunder of claiming mercy for the prisoner (Palmer) on the ground that he was insane". Mr Sheridan then explained that "the lunatic was the prisoner's brother".

On 10th March 1794 the subject was again brought up in the House of Commons by Mr Adams, a lawyer, "a thorough Scotchman by birth, tastes and interests. He had prepared himself thoroughly on the facts and the law of the case, and made the most admirable speech. It was full, luminous, sound, strong, without one offensive word; and besides glancing at the improprieties of the trial, laid open the illegality and the cruelty of the sentence, the exposure of which was his particular object."

Dundas then defended the verdict of the Scottish judges, saying that it was sound law, and was attacked by Sheridan and Charles William Fox. Fox said: "If the day should ever arrive, if the tyrannical laws of Scotland should ever be introduced, in opposition to the humane laws of England, it would then be high time for my honorable friends and myself to settle our affairs, and retire to some happier clime, where we might at least enjoy those rights which God has given to man, and which his nature tells him he has a right to demand."

After pausing to get his second wind, the celebrated orator resumed: "Indeed, sir, so striking and disgustful are the whole features of this trial, that when I first heard of them, I could not prevail upon myself to believe that such proceedings had actually taken place. The charge itself, and the manner in which that charge was exhibited, made my blood run cold."

Mr Fox now asserted that Muir and Palmer had done "no more than what had been by Mr Pitt and the Duke of Richmond. Then there is one strange assertion made by one of the Lords of Justiciary. He says that no man has a right in the Constitution, unless he possesses a landed property. How absurd, how nonsensical, how ridiculous!"

Mr Fox was referring to Lord Justice-Clerk Braxfield, who had observed in his charge to the jury: "Mr Muir might have known that no attention could be paid to such a rabble. What right had they to representation? He could have told them that the parliament would never listen to their petitions. How could they think of it? A government in every country should be just like a corporation; and in this country, it is made up of the landed interest, which alone has the right to be represented; as for the rabble, who have nothing but personal property, what hold has the nation of them? What security for the payment of their taxes? They may pack up their property, and leave the country in the twinkling of an eye, but landed property cannot be removed."

After this outburst Fox attacked Lord Swinton, who, he said had been undecided whether to send Muir to the gallows, or to the wild beasts, or to Botany Bay for fourteen years, and had informed the defendant that the Court happily selected the mildest punishment — though Fox himself had his doubts about that.

"He had always entertained the highest veneration for the character of a judge, and his indignation was roused to find that the learned Lord Swinton instead of discharging his duty with the gravity becoming the bench, had acted with ignorance, levity, and hypocrisy."

Fox then referred to the publishers of Paine's book, who were convicted and sentenced to pay a fine of £100, and also to Archibald Hamilton Rowan, who was convicted of writing the Address from the United Irishmen to the Convention of reform societies in Scotland. Rowan, the author of the letter, was sentenced to two years' imprisonment, said Fox, whereas Muir, who only read the letter at the Convention, was sentenced to fourteen years' transportation.

But the Tory Party remained unmoved by the speeches of Fox and the Whig party, and as they were in the majority, the cases of the Scottish Martyrs were hopeless.

Besides the four Scottish Martyrs and the other convicts, the soldiers, and the government officials on the *Surprize*, there were several free settlers — James Ellis, the Scottish lad, servant to Palmer, John Boston, his wife and three children, and Matthew Pearce and his wife, who was pregnant. Mrs Margarot, as we have seen, shared a cabin with Boston's children.

John Boston's letter applying for permission to settle in New South Wales is printed in the second volume of the *Historical Records of New South Wales*. He had written on 5th December 1793 to Under-secretary King: "I take the liberty to entrude your attenion to my pretensions having the honour to solicit you to send me out as a settler to New South Wales. I was brought up as a surgeon and apothecary, but have never since followed that profession. I have since made my particular study of those parts of chemistry that are more particularly usefull in trade and business. Have, therefore, a knowledge of brewing, distilling, sugar-making, vinegar-making, soap-making, etc. I have been in business as distiller, but was unsuccessful, I likewise have a theoretical and some practical knowledge of agriculture. I flatter myself, sir, should you think fit to examine my pretensions, you would find me possess that general knowledge which I consider would be usefull in an infant colony like New South Wales. I take the liberty to mention that I am a married man, and have three children; that my views are not ambitious; and should I in this application be so fortunate as to succeed, I will make it my pleasure to exert myself in every respect for the advantage of the Colony."

The application was approved, and in a letter from Whitehall dated 15th February 1794 the Right Honourable Henry Dundas informed the Lieutenant-Governor of New South Wales, Major Francis Grose, that the *Surprize* carried "two settlers who have been well recommended, with their respective families. . . . One of them, Mr Boston, will I hope prove particularly useful to the settlement by curing fish and making salt." If Dundas had known more about Boston's politics he would have been less enthusiastic.

One 2nd May 1794 the *Surprize* suddenly up-anchored and was gone from Portsmouth, headed for Botany Bay. A warship convoyed her for the first part of her voyage of thirteen thousand miles.

CHAPTER NINE

*"Surprize" at Rio de Janeiro — Convict's Flux — Diabolical Mutiny
Plot — Palmer and Muir Charged with Conspiracy — Ringleaders in
Irons — Maurice Margarot — John Grant, Informer — Soldiers Propose
Murdering Officers — First Officer Macpherson under Arrest —
Draper's Evidence — John Boston Accused of Sedition — Muir Drunk
and Disorderly — "Narrative of the Sufferings of T. F. Palmer and W.
Skirving" — Palmer's Version of the Mutiny — Grant's Forgery —
Spies on Martyrs — Lying Story of Joseph Draper — Palmer Pays for
Ellis's Cabin Passage — Margarot as Campbell's Confidant — Camp-
bell's Quarrels with Macpherson — H.M.S. "Suffolk" Called In —
Accusations — Floggings — Men in Irons — Palmer's Sufferings —
"Infernal Brothel".*

FIRST news of the transport was in a letter from Rio de Janeiro, dated 2nd
August, to the Commissioners of the Navy, signed by Patrick Campbell,
master, saying the *Surprize* had arrived there on 2nd July. After describing the
difficulty in obtaining fresh water, owing to the town's pipes being broken,
Captain Campbell remarked, "Several of the convicts having symptoms of
a flux just after our arrival, we though it prudent not to go to sea with them
in that state. But owing to the very great care and skill of Mr Thompson the
surgeon, there is not now a sick person in the ship."

Then came startling news. Says Captain Campbell: "There has been a most
diabolical scheme laid, and very near attempted to be put into execution, and
Messrs Palmer and Skirving apparently the advisors and ringleaders of it.
I keep them separate from other persons, and have got most of the ringleaders
in irons until we get to New South Wales, where the business will be
investigated, and copies of the whole transmitted to your Honourable Board.
I have done everything in my power to be cautious in so critical a situation,
nor am I in the least anxious; but all the people under my care have been
treated in a manner that will keep me and the civil officers appointed by
Government from reproach, altho' I am aware that every effort will be used
by the friends of Palmer and Skirving to slander those whose throats they
would have cut. I must, in justice to Mr Muir, say that he does not appear
to have had any hand in the plot."

Captain Campbell then eulogized Maurice Margarot, who "has throughout the whole of this business, and ever since he came on board, behaved in
a manner honorable to himself, and not only pleasing but serviceable to us".

Campbell stated that he had been warned of his danger by "John Grant,
a convict, but who had behaved with the greatest degree of propriety and
good order" and who "gave me information that he had heard the deserters, in

OMNE SOLUM FORTI PATRIA.

I.KAY 1794

JOSEPH GERRALD

A Delegate to the British Convention.

Joseph Gerrald

Samuel Parr

William Godwin

the Irish language, which he understood from its analogy to the Gaelic language, concerting measures to seize the ship by attacking the cabin and murdering myself". These "deserters" were soldiers who had deserted and been captured, and had been given the choice of being shot or joining the New South Wales Corps.

Grant told the Captain that all the soldiers would join the mutineers, and Campbell accordingly put in irons six of the deserters whom Grant pointed out as the ringleaders. Campbell's account continues: "I had observed Mr Macpherson, My Chief Officer, for some time guilty of great irregularities and ill-treating the women convicts; in a continual state of intoxication, and also absenting himself from my table without any visible cause . . . I thought the present a proper opportunity to give him friendly advice. I therefore called him into my cabin, and was advising him, not as a commander, but as a friend, for his ungentlemanly and un-officer-like behaviour, and begged him to remember his station in the ship at this critical time amongst a lot of assassins, and reminded him of his family at home who depends on him, but he flew in my face, and abused me by telling me he was as good a man as myself, and challenged me to fight him, adding that the present was the proper time for it, and on coming up on deck in the presence of the ship's company, he repeated his abusive language and challenge. I therefore put him under arrest."

Campbell set down other evidence that had persuaded him mutiny was brewing. One sinister incident on 30th May was described as follows: "A cask of porter being broached, it was put under the care of a sentinel, with orders not to allow any to be drawn from it but by the steward. In the afternoon, on inspecting the cask, it was found quite empty, whereupon James McLean and Joseph Brotherwood, the former one of the deserters, who had been doing duty, were put in irons." While this was being done McLean told the sergeant "that the soldiers were fools to allow themselves to be used so; that they were able, and ought to right themselves".

Campbell also stated that on 1st June John Starling, a convict, gave him information "concurring in omnibus with Mr John Grant that he heard them say that they had a person in the ship to head them." After stating that Messrs Muir and Margarot on this and every occasion had offered their willingness to protect the ship, Campbell proceeded to Monday, 2nd June, when he went on board the Commodore's ship and told him all that had happened. In consequence Macpherson was taken ashore under arrest.

On that same day Joseph Draper, a soldier, said that in April, while the transport was lying at Spithead, Skirving and Palmer asked him if he knew if the convicts would be on their side "to attack the sentinel and kill or heave him overboard, then rush on the quarter-deck and secure the captain, officers, the arms and ammunition, and then those who did not side with the party were to be shot or hove overboard; that William Carswell, a convict, William Neale, James McLean, Thomas Barton and himself were to be the chief actors; that Mr Palmer told him he had a man to direct the ship, and that he could get numbers of sailors to join them for money, as he had plenty". On and on went Joseph Draper's story of the alleged plot, of money he had been paid, and of spirits generously supplied to him. Draper, who was unable to read and write, signed his statement with an X. Says F. M. Bladen, historian and barrister, who edited the second volume of the *Historical Records of New South Wales*: "This soldier, in consequence of an attempt to raise an insurrection in Quebec, had been condemned to be shot, but was pardoned on condition of serving in the New South Wales Corps."

More evidence in similar strain from James Gilthorpe, a convict, William Neale, William Evans, James Somerville, a convict, and finally John Grant, who appears to have been founder and fomenter of the alleged conspiracy.

Continues Captain Campbell: "John Grant, who keeps accurate memorandum of what daily occurs, declares that on the 14th April, when lying at Spithead, Mr Boston went to Portsmouth, and on his return came to supper with Messrs Palmer, Skirving, etc., as also did Mr Macpherson, the chief mate." After supper, "politics were introduced and in mentioning the King, Mr Boston drank 'Damnation to the King, his family, and all crown'd heads; that they were absolute tyrants, and ought to be extirpated from the face of the earth.'"

More treasonable words to the same effect, then Mr Boston added, "That until we followed the example of France we must consider ourselves in a state of slavery . . . the present war was a King's war, and must be terminated by the intervention of the people, and he did not doubt that he would soon see all Europe engaged in a civil war."

After this outburst, according to Grant, Boston said "that in the town of Birmingham he would undertake to raise thirty thousand people under arms in less than fourteen days, and that he knew it was their intention to raise commotions, and used every persuasion with Mr Ellis to induce him to go there to purchase buttons and manufactures for barter at New South Wales".

Grant's statement to Captain Campbell concludes: "That when Mr Boston was with Palmer, Skirving, etc., more disloyal toasts were drunk than on any other occasion; that since the confinement of Mr Palmer, Boston told Grant that he was to carry on a distillery at New South Wales; that Palmer was to advance the money, and receive half the profits . . . that he, Palmer and Ellis were to live all together during the time of Mr Palmer's sentence, and thereafter to go to America. That it was agreed upon 'twixt Skirving, Palmer, and Macpherson that the latter would come in to their mess and leave the Captain's table." Finally John Grant averred that "he had often heard Boston avow himself a Jacobin".

Captain Campbell also wrote to the owners of the *Surprize* in London, repeating the story of the alleged conspiracy and the events outlined in these pages. He again referred in complimentary terms to Margarot, who had behaved "with every degree of propriety", and to Grant, and said that Muir did not appear to have had anything to do with the conspiracy. "As to anything else respecting him, Palmer, or Skirving, let the testimony of evidence which you will receive speak for itself."

Though Muir escaped suspicion as far as the conspiracy was concerned, he did not manage to keep out of trouble altogether. With Campbell's letter to the Commissioners of the Navy was a letter signed by William Baker, a Civil Superintendent bound for Botany Bay. Baker backed the charges of Captain Campbell that Palmer and Skirving had formed a conspiracy to take the ship, and added that on Monday, 28th July 1794, the ship "laying at Rio de Janeiro", Thomas Muir was in conversation with William Skirving, "who, in consequence of being concerned in a conspiracy to murder the captain and take the ship, is under confinement and in the care of a sentinel". Muir conversed with Skirving contrary to directions forbidding it. "When I told him in the mildest manner that in so doing he acted wrong . . . he answered he had only been borrowing a book." Baker afterward walked around the quarter-deck, while Muir "stood by the roundhouse door, uttering a number of disrespectful words". At first Baker took no notice, seeing he was drunk, which happens as often as he can get liquor". Muir then said, "They had sent a set of rascals and scoundrels on board". With that, Baker "struck him in a slight manner, when he fell down".

Baker's statement was verified by Samuel Reddish, Sergeant in the New South Wales Corps, who concluded, "Mr Muir desired Mr Baker to give up talking, as he was 'infinitely beneath his notice', and thereupon Mr Baker struck him. . . . this happened before eight of the clock in the morning and that Muir was intoxicated."

Palmer and Skirving told a different story of the alleged mutiny, and their version was published in *A Narrative of the Sufferings of T. F. Palmer and W. Skirving during a Voyage to Botany Bay, 1794*. This narrative was sent to England soon after the *Surprize* reached New South Wales and was published there. It runs to twenty-two pages of small print, from which I shall extract the main points, to offset the tales told by Captain Campbell and his cohort of convict yarn-spinners.

Palmer states that on 11th February 1794 he was taken from the *Stanislaus* hulk, and put aboard the *Surprize* transport, where he found Muir, Skirving, and Margarot, "all of them from Newgate in handcuffs". With Palmer was a convict named John Grant. Grant's father, a Highland farmer, had sent him from the plough to be an attorney in London. "By the interest of Mr Dundas, as he relates, he was appointed sheriff depute of Invernesshire. It was in this situation that he committed a forgery of about £20, the penalty of which crime is death in Scotland, but through legal chicanery, and the mercy of the Scotch judges, he was saved from the gallows."

Palmer then states that while on the revenue cutter that brought himself and Muir from Leith Roads to London, Grant, hoping for a free pardon circulated a rumour that Palmer and Muir were going to murder the captain and run away with the ship to France. Fortunately Captain Ogilvie, who knew Palmer and Muir, ignored the story.

Palmer goes on: "Mr Muir, Mr Skirving and myself had no doubts in our minds of Grant being a spy upon our conduct, in the *Surprize*, as well as in the cutter. He was put into the same room, and he slept in the same bed as me, yet as he was destitute we suffered him to mess at our cost. He had, however, nearly defeated our kindness by his own folly, for he was charged by three witnesses of stealing from Mr Muir two guineas and five shillings, and of breaking open one of my boxes."

Eighteen soldiers shared their sleeping quarters; of these sixteen were deserters. "Six of them were ironed, hands and feet; among them was Joseph Draper, once condemned to be shot for an attempt to assassinate Prince

Edward. He afterwards became my accuser." Draper had been a tailor, and when his irons were taken off he worked at his trade. "I always paid him ready money," says Palmer, "till the time of leaving Portsmouth Harbour, when he wished that the few shillings I owed him might remain in my hands. During our stay in Portsmouth I contracted a dangerous illness arising from the severity of my confinement. The place was continually wet and cold in the day time; and in the night it was hot almost to suffocation by twenty-four persons being put in a small space under close wooden hatchways unperforated with a single hole. My life was despaired of by the medical men on board."

Draper now asked Palmer and Skirving to advance him money to buy articles of trade in Portsmouth, but, wrote Palmer, "I positively refused. I had discovered too many shabby things about him, and held him in abhorrence. The young friend (Ellis) who voluntarily accompanied me into exile, had not the same sentiments. He advanced Draper eighteen shilling of my money, without my knowledge, and contrary to my orders. Poor Mr Skirving, from the benevolence of his temper, advanced him forty shillings, which Draper engaged to work out. Little did Skirving suppose that this would be construed as a bribe for the purpose of murdering Campbell and the principal officers."

John Grant now began his Machiavellian tactics by "whispering to Mr Ellis that there was a design among the soldiers to mutiny, and to sail the ship into some part of France. Ellis well knew the man, and suspecting his treacherous designs ordered him to hold his tongue."

Unpleasant though living conditions might be for the Scottish Martyrs, they were far better off at first than most of the other convicts, having paid £40 each for a "cabin passage". "My friend Mr Ellis," writes Palmer, "who, by leave of the Ministry, went out as a free settler, finding when he came on board that all the free settlers had a cabin passage paid for by government, made application for one but was refused. I stayed to the last hoping that government would pay it but they refused." Eventually Palmer paid Campbell £36 15s. for a cabin passage for Ellis.

There were now two messes for cabin passengers, Palmer continues, and the Captain wished to unite them, to save expense. Accordingly he invited Palmer, Skirving, and Margarot to dine in the great cabin. Muir dined alone. Palmer readily agreed, and the arrangement continued for ten days, when "without deigning to make any apology" Campbell ordered him from the table at dinner, and bade him go down to the steerage and mess with Skirving and Mr and Mrs Margarot. "I felt the ignominy of this treatment ; my dislike to the steerage led me to form a mess with my friends Mr and Mrs Boston and Mr Ellis in Mr Boston's cabin."

Several days elapsed, until on 31st May, "Captain Campbell pretended to have discovered a bloody plot among the soldiers, to excite a mutiny, and to murder himself and the officers, and afterwards carry the ship to France. He ordered the mate to call all hands on deck, and commanded six of the soldiers, viz. Draper, Evans, Neale, Barton, Griffiths, and McLean, to be put into double irons. One of them asked the reason and Campbell told him that if any one of them dared to speak, he would blow out his brains."

Now the plot thickens. "Mr Margarot had from the beginning been paying his court to Campbell, and from the time of this pretended discovery of the mutiny, unblushingly appeared as his councillor, friend and confidant. Whenever he spoke it was in a confidential whisper. At all times and in all hours they were in deep consultation. Some days previously Margarot was instructed with the important secret of the mutiny, and even furnished with arms to assist in quelling it; and was observed to say to Campbell, with a significant wink, *keep your eye on the old gentleman,* meaning me."

Then came a violent row between Captain Campbell and Macpherson the mate. Words ensued, "Macpherson was divested of authority, and a file of soldiers marched him down as a prisoner in his cabin". Worse still, "Mrs Margarot had the cruelty to say 'that she did not doubt but that Macpherson was at the head of the mutiny plot'."

Palmer and a few of his friends were of the opinion that the "mutiny" was a diabolical fiction. They were concerned for Macpherson, and "at the desire of Doctor Thompson, Mr Boston and some others", Palmer drew up a petition in his favour.

The petition, addressed to Captain Campbell and signed by sailors, settlers and passengers on the *Surprize*, briefly stated that the signatories were worried at the unhappy differences that had taken place between Mr Macpherson and the Captain. They pointed out that they had no security for Captain Campbell's health, and "should he be deranged from any of the many calamities which we are liable to, there is none on board who is acquainted with the passage and has the nautical skill of Mr Macpherson".

Campbell ignored the petition, and next morning when the *Surprize* came up with H.M.S. *Suffolk*, whose captain was Commodore of the convoy, "Campbell by trumpet repeated the story of the alleged mutiny in which the principal officers were concerned." Campbell then went on board the *Suffolk* and convinced the Commodore, Captain Rainier, that Macpherson was dangerous. In the course of the day, Macpherson was sent on board the *Suffolk*, and Campbell "assured us on his return, that he was condemned to be ironed hands and feet, to be fastened to an iron bar on the poop, to be exposed there day and night in all weathers, and to be fed with only bread and water".

Campbell now distributed arms to the sailors and settlers, armed watches were appointed, and the Captain himself was "cased with pistols and daggers". He also mounted two blunderbusses in the roundhouse, bolted the door, and put on a great act; "his performance would have done credit to any stage".

After this act, Campbell told Skirving about the mutiny, and that gentleman honestly replied that he did not believe a word of it. "He made the same reply when it was mentioned a second time, and added that if ever it had any foundation, he was certain that neither himself, Palmer, Muir or Margarot had the least interest in it." Campbell apparently agreed with Skirving's statement, then a few minutes later told Muir that Skirving and Palmer were the ringleaders of the plot. A day later he told Boston that he knew at Spithead that Palmer was in the plot.

Next morning Palmer received word from Campbell to attend him upon the quarter-deck. "I went up totally ignorant of what was doing in the ship. To my astonishment I found the deck full of people." Among them were Dr Thompson, Grant the forger, Draper the deserter and attempted murderer, a lieutenant from the *Suffolk*, Mr Page, and Captain Campbell "accoutred like a perfect Robinson Crusoe. He had a belt of pistols around his body, pistols in his breast, in his waistcoat and breeches pockets, a sword and a dagger." Close to the quarter-deck were five of the imprisoned soldiers, and two convicts, Carswell and Gilthorpe, all in double-irons. Draper was at large on the deck. The military were all in arms behind the prisoners, and the whole ship's company beyond them. Skirving was then called, and Campbell stated that Draper had accused Skirving and Palmer "of attempting to excite a dangerous mutiny, of intending to murder himself and the principal officers, and to run away with the ship". After this the Captain "gave us another touch of the histrionic art, as he walked up and down the deck in affected sorrow, and declared that nothing ever gave him so much concern in his life. *Nothing* by God!"

Draper then read his accusation in the presence of Skirving and Palmer, declaring that they gave him "money, tea, sugar, rum, and clothes, besides promising him much more for the purpose of murdering our principal officers, and that they had men ready to run away with the ship to France".

As Palmer mentioned earlier, James Ellis had given Draper money in Portsmouth to buy supplies. Now his kind action was being twisted into bribery. Listening to all this rigmarole was Lieutenant Page from the *Suffolk*, who had been sent on board the *Surprize* to hear the allegations. Next witness was John Grant, the Scottish forger, who testified that he had heard the deserters plotting.

Campbell then had a conference with Lieutenant Page and the principal officers, after which the seven accused soldiers "were stood in a row, and every second man ordered to be flogged immediately, and the rest on the next day. The sentence was put instantly and severely into execution. They were again promised their liberty and intercession with the Governor of New South Wales if they would confess. At the same time Campbell assured them that this was but a beginning of their punishment if they did not confess, which should be inflicted weekly until such time as they were hanged from the yard-arm."

But the accused men denied knowledge of any plot, "except James Gilthorpe, the convict cook. He could not bear his punishment. He pretended to have something to reveal, and was taken to the roundhouse where his declaration was taken down and his irons knocked off. The next day Carswell was severely flogged, but this was the last of the punishment."

The remaining prisoners were then "loaded with extra leg-irons to the weight of sixty pounds. At night they were carried on the poop. A heavy chain was run through their hand and leg-irons, and the chain was fastened to Campbell's bed below. They were unable to lay down on their bed, or to be in any other posture than doubled with their chins and knees both together. Their food was only a biscuit and a half per day, one quart of water, and three ounces of salt meat for each man."

In this manner the prisoners were exposed to the burning heat of the tropics by day, and the dews by night, their backs bleeding from floggings. Campbell told them that if they stirred or made a noise he would fire at them through the ceiling of the roundhouse, and he gave "strict orders to the sentinel that if they rattled but a link of their chain, or even groaned, he would run them through".

Palmer and Skirving were ordered into custody. Lieutenant Page represented a temporary confinement as necessary to our honour," says Palmer. "We demanded a speedy and rigorous trial. I told him I despised his mercy, and demanded justice." Page and Campbell then promised justice, "though it would seem that it was then determined to keep us prisoners to the end of our voyage, a period of nearly five months".

Palmer and Skirving were now put in a small cabin six foot square. "The bed was only two foot wide, in which it was meant that we two bulky men should sleep together. I sent word to Captain Campbell that it was too narrow, and he facetiously replied that I should soon sleep in a narrower, meaning my coffin. We were denied the privilege of the worst of felons, to breathe an hour in the day the fresh air upon deck. I was forbidden all books, papers, pen and ink. My money, trunks, and clothes were taken from me, and I was refused clean linen and my own stores."

Palmer continues. "Our cabin was in the midst of that infernal brothel of which I had so often expressed my dislike. The language of Newgate was virtue and decency compared with what I was doomed to hear. My neighbours were divided from me by only a wooden partition, the women were perpetually engaged in clamours, brawls and fighting."

The *Surprize* carried sixty women convicts, who were engaged in the ancient game with the sailors of swapping favours for favours. And so, while the buxom wenches from Wapping on Thames industriously worked their passage to Port Jackson, the devout Unitarian minister feverishly wrestled with the narrative of his sufferings en route to Sydney Town, "denied even the privilege of washing".

CHAPTER TEN

THE *Surprize* arrived at Port Jackson on 25th October 1794 about eight in the evening. That night, Palmer tells us, Captain Campbell went to the Governor's house "with a monstrous bag of papers, containing the original charges, and copies of the evidence he had been able to procure against us. As I guessed, the first impression from Campbell's great art and plausibility, was very formidable. The Governor had formed the worst opinions of us. Some officers coming on board, I gave them letters I had for them. The Governor received some, likewise, especially one from Mr Alderman Macauley which was of great service to me."

"The Governor" referred to was Lieutenant-Governor Major Francis Grose, of the New South Wales Corps, who had been in charge of the Colony since the departure of Governor Phillip.

Here are a few facts about Grose collected from the *Australian Encyclopaedia*: Francis Grose was born in Surrey, England, in 1754, and entered the army in 1775, serving in the American War of Independence, during which he was twice wounded, and was present at the Battle of Bunkers Hill. In June 1789 he was ordered to raise and take command of a corps for service in New South Wales; this became known as the New South Wales Corps. On 14th February 1792 Grose arrived in Sydney with the appointment of Lieutenant-Governor of the Colony. In December of the same year Phillip sailed for England and Grose took command. His residence was built on a site that is now the corner of George and Grosvenor streets, where the office of the Union Steamship Company of New Zealand stands.

Among the officers who welcomed the *Surprize* was Captain David Collins, Judge-Advocate of the Colony. Collins, an officer of the Royal Marines, had also fought in the American War of Independence, and had arrived in New

South Wales with the First Fleet. Though he had no legal training he held the office of Judge-Advocate until 1796, when he returned to England. Later he became Lieutenant-Governor of Van Diemen's Land. His book, *An Account of the English Colony in New South Wales*, is one of the most valuable histories of early settlement in Australia. In it he recorded the arrival of the *Surprize*, "having on board sixty female and twenty-three male convicts, some stores, and three settlers. Among the prisoners were Messrs Muir, Palmer, Skirving and Margarot, four gentlemen lately convicted in Scotland for the crime of Sedition."

Continued Collins: "A guard of an ensign and twenty-one privates of the New South Wales Corps were on board. Six of these people were deserters from other regiments brought from the Savoy prison; one of them, Joseph Draper, we understood had been tried for mutiny (of an aggravated kind) at Quebec. This mode of recruiting must have proved as disgusting to the officers as it was detrimental to the interests of the settlement. If the corps was raised for the purpose of protecting the civil establishment, and of bringing a counterpoise to the vices and crimes which might naturally be expected to exist among the convicts, it ought to have been carefully formed from the best characters; instead of which we now found a mutineer (a wretch who could deliberate with others, and consent himself to be the chosen instrument of the destruction of his Sovereign's son) sent among us, to remain for life, perhaps, as a check upon sedition, now added to the catalogue of our other imported vices. The *Suprize* anchoring in the cove after dark, she saluted at sunrise the following morning with fifteen guns."

Palmer and Skirving were also busy that morning, taking steps to defend themselves against Campbell's charges. They sent a petition to the Governor, which is reprinted in the second volume of the *Historical Records of New South Wales*. In it the petitioners, "Thomas Fyshe Palmer, clerk, late of Queen's College, Cambridge, and William Skirving of Strathruddie, gent.", tell the story of their voyage on the *Surprize*, and of how they were accused of leading "a conspiracy of convicts and soldiers to carry the ship into some part of France or America. . . . They heard this accusation with astonishment, indignation, and horror. Obnoxious to the Ministry of Britain for their political sentiments, and for their public conduct, they undoubtedly are, but in the course of their trials the morality of their characters was acknowledged by their official prosecutor."

After denying all complicity in the conspiracy, they state that "they propose to institute a criminal charge against Captain Campbell", and ask that "every circumstance relating to their conduct should be minutely and severely investigated".

Lieutenant-Governor Grose replied on the same day: "The recommendations you have brought to several gentlemen of the colony will ensure you every indulgence that in your unfortunate situation can be consistently granted; but as it is absolutely requisite for the good order and tranquillity of the settlement that you avoid on all occasions a recital of those politicks which have produced to you the miseries a man of your feelings and abilities must undergo at this time, I hope I need not say more than that it is incumbent on me to be watchful over your conduct."

Governor Grose added that in his position he should be easily alarmed if their actions caused trouble, and that, "The letter you have just sent I cannot but consider as a very inauspicious beginning. Yourself and your services are assigned to my care, with the other convicts sent out for the purpose of cultivating the country; and it is but fair that I should inform you that you are no otherwise particularized to me than as much as has been thought necessary to excite my vigilance."

Readers may recollect that Grose had been officially warned "to keep a watchful eye" over the conduct of the Scottish martyrs, "and for their sakes, as well as for the sake of the settlement, give them clearly to understand what must be the consequence" of "any attempt hostile to peace and good order".

By the *Surprize* came another letter from the Right Honourable Henry Dundas to Governor Grose, with lists of male and female convicts on board, as well as the recruits for the New South Wales Corps, including the deserters. "None of the female convicts exceeds forty years of age," Dundas remarked, "and there can be no doubt but that they will be the means by intermarriage of rendering the men more diligent and laborious, and with greater satisfaction to themselves in proportion as the object or motive of their labour will thereby be increased and enhanced."

I have no record of the population of the Colony in October 1794, when the *Surprize* arrived, but the figures at 25th October 1795 are given in the *Historical Records of Australia*. There were then 3211 persons: this included 1362 males convicts, 546 female convicts, and 310 privates in the New South Wales Corps. The remainder were officials, settlers, free women — mostly wives of soldiers — and children.

As well as receiving a petition from Palmer, Muir, and Skirving, Lieutenant- Governor Grose also received a "Demand" by Maurice Margarot on 29th October 1794, as follows: "May it please your Honour: Brought a prisoner to this Colony in consequence of a sentence of Transportation passed against me by the Lord Justice-Clerk of the High Court of Justiciary in Scotland, and approved by His Brittanic Majesty, I, with all respect to those officers who here act in his name, claim the restoration of my freedom — Freedom, the common Birthright of Britons! — and to which I feel entitled, inasmuch as I conceive my sentence to be fulfilled on my arrival here, that sentence being Transportation and not Slavery, the latter unknown to our Laws and contrary to the British Constitution as it was established at the Revolution of 1688, which placed the present Family on the Throne for the purpose of protecting British Freedom. It would therefore not be doing Justice to my Countrymen, while cheerfully undergoing a long exile for their sakes, were I silently to suffer so great a violation of their Charters."

I have no record of any reply to this "Demand" of Margarot's. According to Palmer's *Narrative*, Margarot was not popular, in spite of Campbell's "perpetual praise" of him, "for even in New South Wales vices like his are held in execration".

On the other hand, for Palmer things "began to take a different turn", though, as he records, Campbell continued to invent "the most improbable calumnies of me". "There was no resisting the weight of evidence contained in my letters of recommendation. In many of these I was described as the reverse of what Campbell had represented me, and virtues dwelt upon, of which it becomes me to be silent. I was released from confinement by the Governor's orders, and soon after received a visit from an officer sent by him, with the most obliging expressions, and had liberty to go on shore as often as I liked till a house could be provided for me. Our sentences imply no services, they are not hinted at; the Scotch judges declared on the Bench of Justices that our sentences were fulfilled by our arrival at New South Wales, when so far from servitude being enacted we should be declared at liberty to go to any part of the world, excepting Great Britain, and they gave it as their opinion that we were entitled to such liberty." Nothwithstanding the judges' declaration, "it should seem, that the Governor of New South Wales was instructed that ourselves and services were adjudged to him, for the purpose of cultivating the land until the expiration of our sentences".

There was no further move to prosecute Palmer and Skirving for alleged conspiracy to seize the *Surprize*. Says Palmer: "By the firm tone of our petition, by the weight, possibly, of our personal characters; and somewhat also from the circumstances of Major Grose, the Lieutenant-Governor, being to leave the country on the first ship, and not wishing to embroil himself in political matters, all idea of our trial was given up."

Palmer, Skirving, and Muir had houses appointed to them, "contiguous to each other", and they had "no cause to complain of a want of civility or attention".

Wrote Captain Collins in his *Account of the English Colony in New South Wales*: "The gentlemen from Scotland took possession of their new habitations and soon declared that they found sufficient reason for thinking their situations 'on the bleak and terrible shores of New Holland' not quite so terrible as in England they had been taught to expect."

The editor of the *Historical Records of Australia* says that the Scottish Martyrs, although transported, "were not convicts of the ordinary type, differing in the fact that their services, during the term of transportation, were not assigned to the Governor, and so long as they did not attempt to leave the colony their personal freedom was assured. When the first four arrived Lieutenant-Governor Grose set apart for each individual a separate brick hut in a row on the eastern side of the Tank Stream."

This area, now the west side of O'Connell Street, was near a spring that flowed downhill to the Tank Stream. I have made many searches in the Mitchell Library, but have never been able to verify the exact location of the cottages where the martyrs lived.

News of their doings comes in a letter from Sydney Cove, dated 9th November 1794 and signed by Palmer, Muir, and Skirving, to their friend the Reverend Jeremiah Joyce (*Historical Records of New South Wales*, vol. ii). At the time it was written Joyce would still have been in prison, charged with high treason. The trio wrote: "It is with peculiar satisfaction that, through your medium, we, whose names are hereunto subscribed, communicate to the public the reasons of our separation from Mr Margarot." The letter then tells the story of Margarot's misdeeds on the journey, declaring that he "was an accessory to the wrongs they have suffered, was even an instigator of their accusation, and acted in collusion with the master of the transport. Let not Mr Margarot presume to expect to pollute the holy and immortal cause of liberty by the association of his name with those of its purest defenders. He knows well, and it is meet that the world should know, that upon the justest grounds he stands *a man rejected and expelled from our society*."

So Margarot was sent to Coventry for the rest of his days on Sydney Cove, his name anathema to his comrades of the Convention in Edinburgh.

Next letter, dated 13th December 1794, from Sydney Cove was written by Muir to an unnamed friend in London, and was printed in the *Morning Chronicle* of 29th July 1795. Says Muir: "I am perfectly well; I am pleased with my situation as much as a person can be who is for ever separated from all they loved and from all they respected; but I feel no regret, for, in the cause of the people, I consider my life and happiness as things of no value. . . . I have been constantly occupied in preparing the evidence in exculpation, and the defence of Messrs Palmer and Skirving: that affair will make a noise in Europe. Skirving, Palmer and myself live in the utmost harmony. From our Society Margarot is expelled." After expressing his thanks to local people who helped them, Muir resumed: "I have a neat little house here, and another two miles distant, at a farm across the water, which I purchased. A servant of a friend who has a taste for drawing has etched the landscape; you will see it."

My late friend, Captain J. H. Watson, an authority on Australiana, stated in the *Journal of the Royal Australian Historical Society*, vol. xiii, part i, 1927: "The only place across that water two miles distant that corresponds to this description is what is now known as Milson's Point, and the only piece of land on that side of the water which had been granted and passed to a private individual was a grant of 30 acres which had been made in February, 1794, to a convict, whose sentence had expired, named Samuel Lightfoot, and from whom Muir must have bought it, as there was no other place he could have bought. Muir called this place 'Hunter's Hill', after his home in Glasgow, which is proved by papers in the Land Titles Office so marked."

Muir's estate on Milson's Point is not to be confused with the suburb later named Hunter's Hill, several miles west on the Lane Cove River.

John Earnshaw, a Sydney historical authority on this period, published in 1959 a monograph entitled *Thomas Muir, Scottish Martyr*, a brilliant job of research. In it he says of Lightfoot's thirty acre plot: "It is described as on the 'north side of the harbour, opposite Sydney', and was centred around the small sandy beach, afterward called Cockle Beach, which then headed the bay that is situated close under the eastern side of the present northern harbour bridge pylon. On the narrow alluvial flat beyond the beach was a small hut and close around Muir was to have his domestic gardens."

Among the numerous illustrations in Collin's *Account of the English Colony in New South Wales* was "North View of Sydney Cove", on which a small house is shown in this approximate position. This could possibly be Muir's home in 1794-5.

John Earnshaw continues: "The sketch of Muir's waterside farm to which the exile refers in his letter was most probably made by a fellow Scotsman, Thomas Watling, a forger from Dumfries with some skill as an artist. His large oil painting of Sydney in 1794 now hangs in the Dixson Gallery, Sydney; he is also thought to have made the originals for many of the illustrations to the books of David Collins and Surgeon John White. The latter was a man of humane sentiment who showed much kindness to the reformers when they first arrived in the settlement. Muir the political exile and Watling the convict-artist had this in common: both had suffered sentence to this remote shore at the hands of the terrible Lord Braxfield — a bond of experience sufficient to unite most men."

I agree with John Earnshaw that from these circumstances we may be sure that "the servant of a friend" who etched the view of Muir's retreat on the north shore was none other than Watling. Alas, no trace has been found of this drawing.

Two days before Muir wrote this letter, Palmer had also bought land for himself. On 11th December 1794, for £84, he purchased 100 acres of land in the district called Bulanaming from Edward Laing, a surgeon's mate in the New South Wales Corps, who was about to depart in the *Daedalus* with Surgeon John White.

Today Newington College stands in a twenty-acre allotment in Stanmore, a suburb three miles from Sydney, on Laing's original grant. Newington College was founded on 16th July 1863 as a Wesleyan Methodist school in a house on the Parramatta River, formerly the home of John Blaxland, a pioneer who was born at Newington in Kent. On 18th January 1880 the college was removed to Stanmore.

We return to Muir's letter: "When any money is transmitted cause a considerable part of it to be laid out at the Cape or at Rio de Janiero, in rum, tobacco, sugar, etc., which are invaluable, and the only medium of exchange. We bought some rum at Oris for 18d. the gallon and can sell it for 30 shillings. In a country like this, where money is really of no value, and rum everything, you must perceive the need of my having a supply by every vessel. For a goat I should pay in money £10 sterling; now, for less than eight gallons of spirits at 18d. the gallon I can make the same purchase. . . .

"Now, my dearest friend, I must conclude; but in closing a letter to you it is like taking a farewell for ever. I pray for every blessing of Heaven upon you and your family. No day passes without you living in my thoughts. I open to you my whole soul. Others might smile, but I close this letter in tears."

Next letter from Sydney Cove was dated 15th December 1794 from Palmer to the Reverend Jeremiah Joyce. This was also published in the *Morning Chronicle* in July 1795. "I write now to shew you that I cannot forget you," Palmer said. "Mr Muir, at whose house I write (our three houses are contiguous) and honest Mr Skirving are both well, and as easy and cheerful as myself.

"The reports you have had of this country are mostly false. The soil is capital; the climate, delicious. . . . it will soon be the region of plenty, and wants only virtue and liberty to be another America. Nature possibly has done more for this than the last. I never saw a place where a man could so soon make a fortune, and that by the fairest means — agriculture. The officers have already done it, and this, in eighteen months. . . . Governor Grose reversed the whole system; he gave land not only to officers and free men, but to convicts;

he gave all convicts half of every five days, and the whole of Saturday and Sunday. By a little longer continuance of good sense, transportation will become a blessing."

Palmer continues his rhapsody: "To a philosophic mind it is a land of wonder and delight. To him it is a new creation: the beasts, the fish, the birds, the reptiles, the plants, the trees, the flowers, are all new — so beautiful and grotesque that no naturalist would believe the most faithful drawing, and it requires no uncommon skill to class them. This comes by a most valued friend."

The "most valued friend" was John White, Surgeon-General of New South Wales, who had arrived with the First Fleet in 1788, and took a great interest in the flora and fauna of the colony. As Palmer only reached Sydney on the 25th October 1794 and White departed by the *Daedalus* on 15th December their friendship was of short duration.

Before John White departs from our story he deserves a brief biography. He was born in Sussex in 1750, and after serving with distinction in the Royal Navy was appointed Surgeon-General to the Botany Bay settlement, sailing on the *Scarborough* transport with the First Fleet in 1787. While in Sydney, apart from tending the sick, John White busied himself in preparing his *Journal of a Voyage to New South Wales*, which was published in London with great success in 1790. Apart from his work in surgery and natural history, White is remembered for having fought a duel with his assistant, Dr William Balmain, during which both received slight wounds. After departing on leave in December 1794, White never returned to New South Wales. He died at Worthing, Sussex, on 20th February 1832.

Palmer's letter to Joyce continues in praise of White: "He had the courage to avow himself the friend of a man covered with infamy. He produced a character attested by some of the most respectable of our countrymen, as an argument of the falseness of the charge against me. His kindness, his feeling, his incessant plans and study to serve me, demand my acknowledgments, and will secure your approbation and applause. He has given me a home and four acres of land. I cannot read this from an inflammation of my eyes. I do not believe that you can. God bless you, my dear sir. While I have life I trust you will have the love and gratitude of your sincere friend. . . .

"P.S. Send me, if you please, seed of the early York cabbage, onions, and the everlasting pea."

Palmer apparently entrusted a copy of his *Narrative of the Sufferings of T. F. Palmer and W. Skirving* to John White to deliver to Joyce in London, since in a later letter to the Reverend Theophilus Lindsey, dated 15th September 1795, he wrote: "The whole of this narrative I have entrusted to Dr White, principal surgeon of the Settlement, who went home in the *Daedalus* in December last." There seems to have been more than one copy, because Palmer told Joyce in December 1794: "I wrote you an account of myself by the *Resolution*, Captain Locke, about a month ago, which contained a copy of the narrative of my sufferings on my passage to Botany Bay." However he received it, the narrative was published by Joyce at the price of sixpence, and in some quarters at least it had the desired effect. The *London Monthly Review* for February 1797 described it as "an affecting story of the most arbitrary and cruel treatment that, perhaps, was ever experienced by passengers, even convicts, in a transport ship: exceeding all that we have ever read of the sufferings of unhappy negro slaves in their passage from Africa to the place of their destination. Such inhumanity, such wickedness, of the truth of which we have no suspicion, loudly calls for a strict enquiry."

William Skirving also wrote to the Reverend Jeremiah Joyce in December 1794, expressing his regret for not having written sooner about the "astonishing transactions" on the *Surprize*. "You must have heard by this time of the deep plot against Mr Palmer and me. It was laid against Mr Muir, but the design of it was blown before the plot was ripe, and he escaped. The odium I incurred by aiding his escape from the plot against him, and by openly avowing my sentiments of such conduct, provoked the putting of one in his place; and I thank God that I was, being now convinced that this impolitic step was, in the providence of God, a principal hindrance to the execution of the infernal plot against the life of Mr Palmer.

"But, however this may be, blessed be God, the snare is broken, and we are escaped. Nay, we are enabled to turn and chase our adversaries, as you will see by the papers transmitted, to enable them to bring to public justice the deepest villainies and, I now believe, the most unprincipled of men."

Skirving then refers Joyce to the memorial prepared by Palmer of their sufferings on the voyage, and goes on to inform him that the Governor "appointed a good brick house to each of us, all of them adjoining; and as we would receive nothing from the stores — I mean none of us three, for you will see that we have put Margarot into Coventry — he sent to us requesting that . . . we would use the freedom to send him a list of what things we found necessary. . . . Expecting Governor Hunter every day now we are extremely anxious, flattering ourselves to know everything about our dear friends and country, which our prayer to Almighty God is that both may have escaped that impending ruin which we dreaded, even as we have escaped the plot against our lives and liberty."

Skirving's hopes of Governor Hunter's arrival were not realized for many months. That gentleman was still in wintry Plymouth Sound on 30th January 1795, on board the man-or-war *Reliance*, awaiting his departure for sunny Sydney Cove. On that date Hunter wrote to Under-Secretary King expressing his abhorrence at the news from Rio de Janeiro of the attempted mutiny of the Scottish Martyrs. He was "considering on the best mode of disposing of such infamous characters", he said. "What can their advocates in the House of Commons say in their favour after this infamous conduct? Boston seems to be such a scoundrel that I think he ought not to be allowed any of the advantages promised him, nor shall he, unless he shall appear to me to merit, by uncommon exertions in the service of the settlement, what he seems by his language and conduct in that ship to have forfeited. These are characters over whom I will watch in the strictest manner — in short, they shall be treated as they deserve; but I cannot possibly forget the language held in their various conversations. No recommendation whatever can in the smallest degree weigh with me after such language — such infamous conduct."

Hunter had obviously swallowed the tall stories of Campbell and his witnesses. Later, when he met the "infamous characters" in New South Wales, he was to modify his opinion.

CHAPTER ELEVEN

WHILE his fellow-martyrs voyaged to New South Wales, what had been happening to Joseph Gerrald, the last to be convicted, on 14th March 1794, and sentenced to fourteen years' transportation?

Wrote the Reverend William Field in *Memoirs of the Life, Writings and Opinions of the Reverend Samuel Parr*: "In April following, Mr Gerrald was removed to London, and committed to Newgate; whence in October, he was transferred to Giltspur Street prison. During the long period of his confinement, his sufferings were soothed, and his mind was cheered, by his numerous visitors, of whom some were of high rank. Various offers of money made to him he declined. It is even related that the counsel for the prosecution, at the close of his trial, apologized to him for the part which a painful duty had imposed. At the same time, he placed a purse of money on him, which, however, though destitute, Gerrald gratefully, and yet proudly refused."

Gerrald remained in prison until 2nd May 1795, when about three in the afternoon, wrote Field, "while taking his repose, which his ill-health rendered necessary, he was suddeny called; and without being permitted to return, or to take leave of his infant daughter, the companion of his imprisonment, he was conveyed to Gosport, and placed on board the *Sovereign* transport, which was already freighted with its living cargo."

Dr Field quotes a letter from Gerrald, written at Portsmouth, "on board the Hulks", on 16th May 1795.

"My dear Mr Philips," wrote Gerrald, "I know not how to express the rising sentiments of my heart, for your kindness to me. The best return I can make, is to convince you, by the virtue and energy of my conduct, that I am not unworthy of your friendship. I have repeatedly attempted to write to my ever honoured and loved friend and father, Dr Parr, but it is impossible. The tender and filial affection which I bear to him, the recollection of the many endearing scenes which we have passed together, the sacred relation

An East View of Port Jackson and Sydney Cove, taken from behind the New Barracks
By Thomas Watling

The East Side of Sydney Cove, from the Anchorage, showing the Governor's House

David Collins

John Hunter,
Governor of New South Wales

which subsists between Joseph Gerrald and that Samuel Parr, who poured into my untutored mind the elements of all, either of learning or morals, which is valuable about me; whose great instructions planted in my bosom the seeds of magnanimity, which I trust I now display, and at which persecution herself must stand abashed; all these, my friend, rush at once upon my mind, and form a conflict of feeling, an awful confusion, which I cannot describe; but which he, who is the cause, I know can feel. Tell him, my dear Mr Philips, that if ever I have spoken peevishly of his supposed neglect of me, he must, nay, I know he will, attribute it to its real cause — a love, vehement and jealous, and which, in a temper like Gerrald's, lights its torches at the fire of the furies. Tell him, in a word, that as I have hitherto lived, let the hour of dissolution come when it may, I shall die the pupil of Samuel Parr."

Dr Parr wrote to Gerrald, says Field, and also raised a small sum for him "by subscription among his friends", since he had been taken to Portsmouth "without the allowance of one moment of time for preparation, and almost without the common necessities of life. . . . The pecuniary contribution found its way, at length, to the unfortunate person for whom it was intended, but alas! there is reason to fear that the letter never reached him; and that he lived the short remainder of his days, and passed the lingering hours of dissolution, without the support and the relief, which that letter could not have failed to afford him."

The letter to Gerrald from Dr Parr which probably never reached him said: "Dear Gerrald, I hear with indignation and horror that the severe sentence, passed upon you in Scotland, will shortly be carried into execution. And remembering that I was once your master, that I have long been your friend, and that I am your fellow-creature, made so by the hand of God; and that by every law of that religion, in which I hope to live and die, I ought to be your comforter; now dear Joseph, I am for the last time writing to you. Joseph, before we meet again, that bosom which now throbs for you, and the tongue which now dictates, will be laid in the cold grave. Be it so. Yet, my dear friend, I must cherish the hope, that death is not the end of such a being as man. Some time ago, I saw your dear boy, and depend upon it, that for his sake and your's, I will show him all the kindness in my power." Parr's letter ended, "Pray write to me — God Almighty bless you, Joseph — farewell."

Says Field: "The promise that Dr Parr gave, to take charge of one of his two children, a son thus cruelly bereaved of their surviving parents, Dr Parr most faithfully performed."

On 17th May 1795 Gerrald, "On board the *Sovereign*, lying off St Helen's", wrote to his friend Gilbert Wakefield: "I should wantonly repress the warmest emotions of my heart, and feel myself guilty of a breach of moral duty, did I depart the country without bidding adieu to my respected friend, Gilbert Wakefield. The tender attentions which, during my persecution, he, a stranger to everything but my principles, unsolicitedly paid me, can never be erased from my mind."

Apologizing for the abruptness of his departure, Gerrald explains that he had received assurances, indirectly, that he would be given plenty of warning. "But they knew that I was incapable of making any submission, and therefore were determined to insult and deceive a man whom even the iron austerity of their persecution was not able to subdue. But the circle of their conduct was well rounded. That no fund of human depravity might remain untouched by them, the rankness of their duplicity was made to keep pace with the rigour of their oppression; they attemped to infuse hope only that they might enjoy the demon like satisfaction of blasting it; and I was hurried away like the vilest of malefactors, fettered and without the slightest notice, to the remote shore of the Southern Ocean, without those tender consolations of friendship which all good men willingly afford to those who want and those who deserve them. The zealous alacrity of my friends, however, has deadened the blow which ministerial malignity had aimed at my heart, and has supplied with liberality those comforts which, to a man enfeebled by long sickness, and emaciated by a close imprisonment of fourteen months, were essentially necessary to the preservation of life."

After thanking various people, Gerrald continues: "Among these friends, the revered name of Samuel Parr must ever be rememberd. Upon my past conduct, and particularly upon that part of it which marked me out as the victim of persecution, I look back with triumph and exultation. Having nothing in view but the good of mankind, my spirit feels its purity, and, therefore, must be happy. It may, indeed, be extinguished, but can never be subdued."

Gerrald, expressing himself as prepared to face his destiny with faith, concluded: "For though Justice steals along with woollen feet, she strikes at last with iron hands. During my exile I hope to be supported by your correspondence; though, even without it, I should never cease to cherish Gilbert Wakefield. May every happiness attend him."

Gerrald, a classical scholar, then quoted a Greek phrase meaning, "Concerning such whom God is slow to punish". The German poet Friedrich von Logau turned this thought into verse in the seventeenth century, and his words were translated by Longfellow in the well-known lines:

> *Though the mills of God grind slowly, yet they*
> *grind exceeding small;*
> *Though with patience He stands waiting, with*
> *exactness grinds He all.*

According to the *Dictionary of National Biography*, Gilbert Wakefield (1756–1801), scholar and controversial writer, was born at Nottingham, the son of a clergymen. After a distinguished university career at Cambridge, he held a curacy in Loverpool on behalf of prisoners brought in by privateers. He also fought against the iniquitous slave trade, Liverpool being the principal port of call for the slave ships. In 1779 Wakefield embraced unitarian doctrines and this naturally resulted in his resignation from the Church of England. After a stint at school-teaching, he wrote numerous books on many subjects and translated the New Testament (1792), becoming involved in religious controversy. He defended the French Revolution, and in 1798 attacked Richard Watson, Bishop of Llandaff, for an article the bishop had written in defence of Prime Minister Pitt, the war against France, and the new income tax. In this famous "Reply", Wakefield contended that the "poor and the labouring classes would lose nothing by a French invasion", and charged the civil and ecclesiastical system of the day with corruption. Result, Wakefield, his publisher and printer were arrested for seditious libel, and all were convicted. Wakefield occupied his two years in jail translating the classics and yarning to wealthy friends, who took round the hat and collected £5000 to help him and his family. He was released in May 1801, and died five months later of typhus fever.

Eight days after Gerrald wrote his farewell letter to Gilbert Wakefield, on 25th May 1795, the *Sovereign* sailed for Sydney Cove.

Among Thomas Fyshe Palmer's papers in Manchester College, Oxford, is a letter including an extract "from the farewell letter of Joseph Gerrald to his friend the late Newham Collingwood". This extract, written from memory by Mrs Ridyard in 1862, quotes the words, "for though Justice moves with woollen feet, she strikes at last with iron hands", so apparently Gerrald used these in more than one letter.

The letter continues: "The trial of Gerrald recalls a very painful incident in the life of Sir James Mackintosh. Gerrald had been the favourite pupil of Dr Parr, whom he had recently displeased, but who on the passing of the unjust sentence by Lord Braxfield and laid aside every angry feeling, and after vainly trying to obtain some mitigation of the sentence, raised among the friends of the Cause a considerable sum of money to help him in the land to which he was banished, which he entrusted to the care of Sir James Mackintosh to pay to him before he left England, and with it a letter of farewell, perhaps the most tender in the English language. This letter, Sir James withheld, and kept back the money, with which he paid his own debts."

According to Field's account, already quoted, the money raised by Parr did at length reach Gerrald. Unless there were two such sums, one of these stories must be wrong. The second account goes on to state that Parr was unaware that Mackintosh retained the money until after the death of Gerrald in Australia. When he found out he was justly indignant, "and went at once to London declaring he would expose the affair to the whole world. Dr Shepherd perfectly remembered the distress of the Liberal Party at the prospect of the public disgrace of so prominent a member of their party. Lords Lauderdale, Holland, and other of the leading Reformers waited on Parr to entreat him not so utterly to destroy the reputation of Mackintosh, but for a long time were unable to prevail on him to screen from disgrace this despicable and cruel crime."

At length Dr Parr consented not to publish the affair in the newspapers, but satisfied himself with writing a full account of the transaction to the leading men of the party. To Mackintosh himself he refused to write, but he expressed his opinion of him in scathing words in a letter to Mr Newham Collingwood, from whom he exacted a promise that he would read every word of it to the culprit and then leave it in his hands.

The *Dictionary of National Biography* says that Sir James Mackintosh (1765–1832) was born at Aldourie, seven miles from Inverness. He studied at King's College, Aberdeen, wrote poetry, started a debating club, and studied medicine at Edinburgh, reading papers before the Royal Medical and the Physical Society that showed "youthful audacity and power". In 1787 he went to London, where he took an interest in journalism and politics. He became friendly with Horne Tooke, Thomas Hardy, and Dr Samuel Parr, met Fox and Sheridan, and became honorary secretary to the Association of the Friends of the People, where he met Joseph Gerrald. In 1803 he accepted an offer of the recordership of Bombay and was knighted, becoming a judge in 1806. He returned to England in 1811 and died in 1832.

Late in life Parr forgave Mackintosh, says Mrs Ridyard, and recalled the copies of the letters he had writen on the subject, "with the exception of the copy he had given to Mr Parkes of Warwick, whose son, the solicitor in the House of Commons in the year 1840 allowed me to read them. It was the concluding paragraph in Gerrald's letter to Mr N. Collingwood that so deeply interested my feelings that, though I had not copied a word of it, I, by degrees, little by little, sentence by sentence, recalled it to my mind, after a visit, twenty-two years afterwards to the Court House in Edinburgh, when I remarked to my husband how much it was to be regretted that Gerrald's closing remarks in his farewell letter could not be inscribed in his monument. I had forgotten every word, though the general purport was much in my mind, but by the evening of that day I was able to remember and write down the noble and pathetic perorations of that last letter."

The letter from Mrs Ridyard ends as follows: "Many years ago when I was on a visit to Broughton Hall, Lord Nugent told me that Dr Parr first consented to meet Sir James Mackintosh at his house, desiring at the same time that no allusion should be made to the past, and that the meeting should be merely that of common acquaintances at an ordinary dinner party. . . ." After dinner the conversation turned "on the case of Quigley, an Irish priest who had recently been executed for High Treason. Mackintosh, who had hitherto been rather silent, joined strongly in the general reprobations in the conduct of Quigley, and remarked that 'nothing could have been worse', repeating emphatically that 'nothing could have been worse'."

Parr replied in steely quiet tones, "Yes, Jemmy, he might have been much worse. He was an Irishman, he might have been a Scotchman. He was a priest, he might have been a lawyer. He was a traitor. He might have been a renegade."

A sudden silence ensued, and it was with difficulty that general conversation was renewed, "but Lord Nugent said that it was to the best of his belief this was the only castigation that Parr ever inflicted on Mackintosh, ever after treating him with a good deal of friendliness".

A few weeks after Gerrald sailed on the *Sovereign*, Palmer wrote on 13th June 1795 to his friend, Doctor John Disney, in London, telling him of the troubles caused by the officer monopolists of the New South Wales Corps. The letter continues: "Mr Ellis and Mr Boston were ordered into confinement for entering a ship and endeavouring to purchase things for their use. With great respect, but firmness, they remonstrated against this invasion of the common rights of British Subjects. From that time (now many months ago) they have had no grants and no servants. Mr Boston, though sent out by the government to cure fish and make salt, has been unemployed. My men, which I bought at a monstrous rate, with a farm, have been taken from me. A message has been sent to me to pull off my hat to the officers, or I should be confined in cells and punished. Public orders have been twice given for no soldier to speak to me under the penalty of one hundred lashes. Now I never had omitted the ceremony of capping the officers, and never conversed with the soldiers."

In view of Palmer's comments in this and other letters on Boston's unemployed state, it is interesting to note that, according to Collins, he was later given a chance to show his skill in making salt. Collins writes: "From the scantiness of salt provisions, the article salt was become as scarce. There came on the *Surprize*, as a settler, a person of the name of Boston. Among other useful knowledge which we were given to understand he possessed, he offered his skill in making salt from sea-water. As it was much wanted, his offers were accepted, and, an eligible spot at Bennilong's Point, as the east point of the cove had long been named, being chosen, he began his operations, for which he had seven men allowed him, whose labour, however, only produced three or four bushels of salt in more than as many weeks." Before this, Collins records, salted meat was so scarce that it was kept for the New South Wales Corps, while the convicts were fed on rice and corn. "The effects of this ration soon appeared; several attacks were made on individuals; the house occupied by Mr Muir was broken into, and nearly all his property stolen. Some of his wearing apparel was laid in his way next day; but he still remained a considerable sufferer by this visit."

Palmer, in his letter to Disney, comments on the scarcity of beef, pork, and corn, and the high price of food (fowls five shillings each). He then describes the harmony between the natives and whites. "This was owing to the pains of Governor Phillip, to cultivate a good understanding with them. When himself was speared he would suffer no vengeance to be taken, and on no account an injury to be done to them by a white man." Unfortunately this policy had not been continued under the government of Grose and Paterson. "The natives of the Hawkesbury (the richest land possible in the world), producing 30 or 40 bushels of wheat per acre, lived on the wild yams on the banks. Cultivation has rooted out these, and poverty compelled them to steal Indian corn to support nature. The unfeeling settlers resented this by unparalleled severities. The blacks in turn speared two or three whites, but tired out, they came unarmed, and sued for peace. This, government thought to deny them, and last week sent sixty soldiers to kill and destroy all they could meet with, and drive them from the Hawkesbury. They seized a native boy who had lived with a settler, and made him discover where his parents and relations concealed themselves. They came upon them unarmed, killed five and wounded more. The dead they hang on gibbets, *in terrorem*."

The people killed were the most friendly of the blacks, and, said Palmer, had "more than once saved the life of a white man. Governor Hunter, whose arrival is so anxiously awaited, will come out with just and liberal ideas, I trust, of policy, and correct the many abuses and oppressions we groan under, as well as those of the poor natives. It seems a strange time to drive these poor wretches into famine, the almost certain consequences of driving them from their situation, when we are so near it ourselves."

Palmer ended his letter by saying that he had contracted "the malady of the country, sore eyes"; so that he had been obliged to give up writing and reading. Blisters behind the ears had given him some relief. "Some lose their sight, but in general, after the first attack, their vision is as good as ever. You may be sure I am all anxiety concerning the fate of those men, who are suffering for the welfare of others. Remember me to them, if you have the opportunity, with all the sympathy they deserve."

CHAPTER TWELVE

THE long-awaited arrival of Governor Hunter on 7th September 1795 is described by David Collins in his *Account of the English Colony in New South Wales*. "The signal was made for two sail between eight and nine o'clock in the morning. The wind being from the northward they did not reach the anchorage until late: His Majesty's ship the *Supply*, commanded by Lieutenant William Kent, getting in about sunset; and the *Reliance* with the Governor on board about eight at night. Their passage from Rio de Janeiro was long (fourteen weeks) and very rough."

Since Grose's departure the Colony had been governed by Captain William Paterson, of the New South Wales Corps, who on Christmas Day 1794, Collins tells us, had taken the oaths prescribed for the acting Governor.

A week after Hunter's arrival, on 15th September 1795, Palmer wrote to his friend the Reverend Theophilus Lindsey of the Strand, London, giving him the gossip of Sydney Town. After telling him of the alleged mutiny on the *Surprize*, Palmer continues: "When I landed, six or seven people went voluntarily to a magistrate and swore that C. [Campbell] offered them great rewards if they would swear that I and Mr Skirving hired them to murder him and the principal officers; that he held a pistol in his hand and threatened to shoot some if they did not, and to treat them as we traitors were . . . I believe I should have fallen before my inhuman tyrant had it not been for the courageous and active friendship of James Ellis and Mr Boston, the young man I wrote to you about, and his wife. They were threatened with irons, even Mrs Boston; and when Mr Boston landed, C. blasted all his prospects by accusing him of Jacobinism and drinking destruction to the King. This last was proved to be an infamous falsehood. . . ." The Bostons had also given proof of their friendship at Rio de Janeiro. The Viceroy heard of Boston's skills and "gave them every attention, kept a splendid table for them, had a man of rank to attend them, set them to work, and, when convinced of their ability, offered them any sum to set up in business, and £300 per annum each to settle in Rio. They firmly rejected the offer (though both were without a shilling) as it was their firm belief that C. would have murdered me in their absence. After such kindness it followed, of course, that we lived together and they shared what I had."

Palmer then launched forth in another attack on military monopolists who controlled all goods that came into the colony, "reselling them at 1000 per cent profit and more". Naturally the officers objected to Boston, who "by making salt and curing fish could have saved the colony from a famine. But the worst is over. They manufacture beer, vinegar, salt, soap, etc., for sale. I have a farm. But, above all, Governor Hunter who is, I hear from all hands, a good man . . . is arrived, and the despotism and infamous monopolies of the last Government are no more."

From this and other comments in his letters it is clear that Palmer had reversed the favourable opinion he expressed in December 1794 of the system introduced by Grose. The *Australian Encylcopaedia* says that Grose "was emphatically a military man, devoted to the service and putting its needs (or the needs of its personnel) above all other objects. In his view the prosperity of the settlement could only be assured by establishing complete control by the New South Wales Corps. He therefore (i) abolished the jurisdiction of the civilian magistrates except where he himself should specially direct them to exercise it; (ii) altered Phillip's system of using convict labour to grow provisions for general use and allowed settlers to employ convicts on their farms; and (iii) made liberal grants of land to all military officers who wanted it, and allowed them to pick their areas patchwork fashion, without considering the plan of roads which Phillip had constructed." Result: narrow, crooked streets, the curse of Sydney to this day.

From monopoly and the military, Palmer drifted to the Church. "The clergyman here, Mr Johnson, is a most dutiful son of the Church of England, thinking it to be the best constituted church in the world. He is a Moravian Methodist, and was bred I believe at Magdalen, Cambridge. I believe him to be a very good, pious inoffensive man."

The Reverend Richard Johnson, born in Yorkshire in 1753, had arrived in Sydney with the First Fleet in 1788 and had conducted the first church service in the shade of a great tree, supposed to be near the present Macquarie Place. After several years Johnson built a wattle-and-daub church on a spot now marked by a memorial standing on the corner of Hunter, Bligh, and Castlereagh streets, where service was first held on 25th August 1793. In 1798 this church was destroyed by fire, it was said deliberately, because compulsory attendance at Sunday service was resented by convicts. Johnson was a sensible farmer, and has been credited with growing the first oranges in the colony. He returned to England in 1800, and died there in 1827. The *Australian Encyclopaedia* says that he "had manifested faith, courage, and diligence, under conditions that were always trying and sometimes almost heartbreaking, in helping his fellow-men and tilling the soil; and thus he comes down the years not only as a distinctive pioneering clergymen but as an important figure in the agricultural history of Australia".

Back to Palmer, writing to his friend Lindsey in 1795. After stating that none of his household had heard a sermon by Johnson, he adds, "I confess I could have heard him yesterday with pleasure. It was the first Sunday after Governor Hunter's arrival. He exposed the last Government, their extortion, their despotism, their debauchery and ruin of the colony, driving it almost to famine by the sale of liquors at 1200 per cent profit. He congratulated the colony at the abolition of a military government, and the restoration of a civil one, and of the laws."

The letter ends with the information "that Mr Muir lives with me, and that he, Skirving, and I live in great cordiality; our houses in Sydney are contiguous, as also our farms in the country." The latter part of this statement can hardly be correct, unless either Muir or Palmer had acquired another property. The placing of Muir's farm near Milson's Point may be open to question, but he would not have described it as being "across the water" if it had been in the vicinity of Stanmore, where Palmer's estate was.

Next day, 16th September 1795, Palmer wrote another letter, to an unnamed friend. This letter is in the Shepherd Papers of Manchester College, Oxford. "The common disorder of the country from the time I first came on shore has so constantly afflicted my eyes that it is with great difficulty I write or read. I hope, anxiously hope, that you have heard of me long before this. I committed to the fidelity of Mr White, the principal surgeon of the settlement, by the *Daedalus* a packet of letters. To me they were more dear than life as they contained a defence of my character against the most atrocious accusations. I know, my dear friend, how incredible such an accusation must appear to you. I wish my narrative and the depositions to be published. Should it meet your eye it will faintly tell the miseries and sufferings I endured." After being preserved from such dangers Palmer felt he should not despair of overcoming those threatening him at the time he wrote, "the greatest of which is that of starvation. All the stores are exhausted, not a pound of flesh or wheat remaining."

In spite of this gloomy situation, Palmer now becomes lyrical over the "salubrious climate" and the fat cattle. "The kine, what there are of them, have the coats of race horses, and not a rib to be seen. The ground is excellent, some of it producing with the most wretched farming 40 bushels of wheat per acre, and from 50 to 80 bushels of Indian corn. If two or three thousand head of cattle were imported, and the military monopoly put an end to, I am persuaded that this land like Norfolk Island might immediately support itself. But unless changes were soon made the officers would make princely fortunes and the place would be ruined."

The letter goes on to describe the "infinite entertainment" afforded to the nature-lover. "It is certainly a new world, a new creation. Every plant, every tree, every fish and animal, bird and insect, different from the old. I believe it to be rich in minerals, especially iron, the ore of which is in immense quantities on the surface of the ground." Discussing the commercial future of the Colony, Palmer informed his friend that grape vines were thriving and tolerably good wine was produced; this would be "the staple article of commerce". Copper, coal, and fine wood might with advantage be sent to India.

"We are beginning to distil the essential oil of peppermint from the leaves of peppermint trees to send thither. If I recover my eyesight, I may attempt some experiments. But that good man, Mr ——, for whom I am filled with anxiety, forgot to send a blowpipe. Mr Skirving unfortunately broke my only thermometer. However, it is very improbable that England can afford to keep up a den of thieves that has already cost more than twelve million. It is afflicting to turn an honest mind to live where every man's hand is lifted against his neighbours, where every man is an enemy from whose depredations no vigilance can be security. The *Providence* has arrived within these few days. With heartful joy I learn by her of the acquittal of Mr Tooke." The *Providence*, Captain William Broughton, was on her way to Nootka Sound, North America, of which more later. The news of Tooke's acquittal had taken long enough to reach Sydney — about ten months.

Palmer's letter continues: "Remember me to those many friends whose kindness has alleviated my sufferings, and made my country more dear. We all enjoy perfect health." Palmer must have been the official letter-writer for the trio. No sooner did he finish one letter than he was writing the next.

On 16th October 1795 Governor Hunter wrote to an unnamed friend in Leith, Scotland: "The four gentlemen whom the activity of the magistrates of Edinburgh provided for our colony I have seen and conversed with separately since my arrival here; they seem all of them gifted in the powers of conversation. Muir was the first I saw, I thought him a sensible, modest young man, of a very retired turn . . . he said nothing on the severity of his fate, but seemed to bear his circumstances with a proper degree of resignation and fortitude."

Next customer at Government House was William Skirving. "He appeared to me to be a sensible well-informed man, not young, perhaps fifty; he is fond of farming, and has purchased a piece of ground, and makes good use of it, which will by-an-by turn to his advantage."

Governor Hunter's third visitor was Palmer. "He is said to be a turbulent, restless kind of man; it may be so, but I have seen nothing of that disposition in him since my arrival."

Last of the Martyrs to shake hands with His Excellency was Margarot. "Mr Margarot seems to be a lively, facetious, talkative man, complaining heavily of the injustice of his sentence, in which he found I could not agree with him. . . . I have to say that their general conduct is quiet, decent and orderly; if it continues so, they will not find me disposed to be harsh or distressing to them."

Despite Hunter's good intentions, Palmer was still attacking the Government as strongly as ever in a letter written soon afterwards to a friend named Paul at Dundee. After telling the oft-told story of his sufferings on the *Surprize* — adding the information that Captain Campbell "had been for near thirty years in that traffic of human misery, the slave trade" — Palmer goes on: "The Government of this land of misery and famine is a military despotism, and all the hardship, insults, robberies and mortification that you can suffer have been heaped on me. I have carefully abstained from anything drawn from the public store that they may have no pretence for my time and labour. Ellis lives with me to brew and farm. This country is a paradise, the climate is delicious and salubrious in the highest degree. The government inhabitants make it the abode of misery and wretchedness. The military officers engross everything. They alone are permitted to purchase off a ship when she arrives and they sell real necessaries to their own soldiers at a thousand per cent profit. Farewell my dear sir. With best wishes to Mrs Paul and all my good friends at Perth."

Governor Hunter had more to say about the Scottish Martyrs in October 1795. In a dispatch to the Duke of Portland dated 25th October he included a petition that Palmer, Muir, and Skirving had presented to him, with reference to the sentences imposed upon them. At that date Margarot was not on speaking terms with his fellow-martyrs, and Joseph Gerrald was still on the high seas.

Here is part of the petition, dated 14th October 1795: "Your humanity will justify our anxiety in having our state ascertained during the time we may remain in this colony. . . . The extent of our punishment is banishment. The mode of carrying the punishment into effect is transportation. The penalty imposed upon breach of the sentence is death. Already the terms of the sentence are completed. We have been banished by transportation, and there can be no higher security against our returning to Britain than the forfeiture of our lives. To all the rights of free men we are entitled, with the single instance of interdiction from one portion of the dominions of the Empire.

"Nor are we, sir, singular in our opinions concerning the interpretation of our sentences. That, after having reached the shores of this island, we were to be bereaved of our freedom, and our persons subjected to an imprisonment of fourteen years, never entered into the conceptions of those who tried us. On the contrary, we have the uncontradicted and solemn testimony of a peer of the realm in Parliament, declaring that the President of the High Court of Justiciary has publickly acknowledged our claim to that freedom which we now demand."

The Martyrs were referring to a speech made in Parliament by the Earl of Lauderdale, in which he quoted Lord Justice Braxfield as saying "that in sentencing these persons to fourteen years' transportation, in consequence of which they were to be sent to Botany Bay, it was not in his contemplation that they should be prevented from going to any other, provided they did not return here, or that they should be kept in servitude and subjected to control".

In the same petition the Martyrs quoted Sir George MacKenzie, a distinguished writer upon the criminal law of Scotland, who said, "With us no judge can confine a man whom he banisheth, to any place without his jurisdiction over other countries, and so cannot make any acts or pronounce any sentences relative to them."

Governor Hunter, in the dispatch enclosing this petition, wrote: "I have examined with care and consideration the sentences of these people. I have perused their arguments in favour of and against these sentences, and I am obliged to confess, my Lord, that I cannot feel myself justifiable in forcibly detaining them against their consent. I am the more inclined to this opinion in considering the manner in which they have been sent out. It has been customary to have the services of other convicts assigned over to the Governor ... but this has not been the case with respect to these men. They appear to have been particularly cautious of not giving the public any claim upon their labour, for they have not accepted any provisions from the public store since their arrival. They have lived quiet, retired, and as much at their ease as men in their circumstances can be supposed to be; yet they do not appear satisfied with their situation here considered as compulsory. They can have no other cause of dislike. Although they have it not in their power to return to any part of Great Britain but at the risk of life, they probably might have a desire to pass their time in Ireland. I hope I may receive His Majesty's instructions upon this subject."

While Palmer was berating the military monopolists of Sydney Cove, and waxing optimistic over the climate and agriculture of the Colony, his good friend John Boston was in hot water because he let his prize pig wander. It was like this.

On 29th October 1795 Quartermaster Laycock, who had had an argument with John Boston over money matters, sent Private William Faithfull of the New South Wales Corps to shoot a pig belonging to Boston which was trespassing in the garden of Captain Foveaux. Unfortunately, Faithfull shot the best pig in the garden as Boston arrived on the scene. The irate owner verbally attacked Private Faithfull, who responded by striking Boston on the head with his musket.

Boston retaliated by suing William Faithfull, Quartermaster Laycock, and two onlookers, Lieutenant McKellar and Private Eaddy. Boston claimed £500 damages.

The court, consisting of Judge-Advocate Collins, Dr Balmain, and Captain George Johnston, after listening for seven days to both sides of the case, gave a verdict for Boston against Faithfull and Laycock, and awarded Boston twenty shillings from each of them. The onlookers, McKellar and Eaddy were found not guilty.

An appeal against this decision by Faithfull and Laycock to Governor Hunter was dismissed by him, with the remark, that "the assault complained of has been fully proved, and I do not only confirm the verdict already found by the Court in which this cause was tried, but I must add that I have thought it a lenient one".

At last, on 5th November 1795, Joseph Gerrald arrived in Sydney on the *Sovereign* to join his fellow-Martyrs. But he was not to share their exile for long. Five months later Palmer told the sad story of his last days in a letter to an unnamed friend, dated 23rd April 1796: "Alas, Joseph Gerrald has fallen the victim of ministerial malignity. He was in such a state that none but — could think of sending him such a voyage. The lowest ruffian would have more lenity showed him. The summer was unusually hot and the great variation of the climate in four months after his landing, put a period to his existence. The surgeon of the *Reliance*, the worthy Dr Bass, who arrived from

Norfolk Island a fortnight before his death, in spite of all obloquy (for much attends the even speaking to us) attended him twice a day."

Surgeon George Bass had arrived at Port Jackson on H.M.S. *Reliance*, with Governor Hunter, on 7th September 1795. He departed for Norfolk Island with his ship on 21st January 1796, returning to Sydney on 5th March 1796. Joseph Gerrald died eleven days later.

George Bass was born in Lincolnshire on 3rd February 1771. As a youth he studied hard and joined the Navy as surgeon's mate. After the death of Joseph Gerrald, Bass made many explorations with his friend Lieutenant Matthew Flinders, during which they discovered and named Bass Strait and circumnavigated Van Diemen's Land. On 5th February 1803 Bass sailed in the *Venus* on a trading voyage to South America. He never returned, nor was the *Venus* ever heard from again.

Back to Palmer's letter of 23rd April 1796 to his English friend: "Before this Gerrald could get no medical assistance whatever, except the servant lad of the hospital. B—— the principal surgeon, and at that time the only one, would not, in spite of my repeated calls, my entreaties, even threats, do his duty. During a three months' illness, the greatest part of the time attended with danger, I could extort from him only three visits. In one of them he took away his medicines under the pretence that they were not proper, but I could never get him to trouble himself to send any other. Gerrald was at my house the last two months and lay in my rooms. I attended him night and day, and the attention of my friends who live with me was equal to mine. Some few hours before his death, calling me to his bedside, *'I die,'* said he, *'in the best of causes and, as you witness, without repining.'*"

"B—— the principal surgeon", who refused to give medical assistance to Gerrald, was William Balmain, born in Perthshire, Scotland, in 1762. He entered the Royal Navy in 1780, and reached Port Jackson with the First Fleet in January 1788. He was appointed assistant to Surgeon-General John White, and the two men became mortal enemies, fighting a duel, as noted in an earlier chapter. Dr White left the Colony in 1794 and Balmain became Principal Surgeon in 1795. He departed for England in 1801 and died there two years later.

Governor Hunter, in his dispatch to the Duke of Portland dated 30th April 1796, also gives an account of Gerrald's illness and death. "When the *Sovereign* storeship arrived, I found Mr Joseph Gerrald had been sent in that ship. He was landed here in a very declining state of health, which rendered it necessary that he should reside in some quiet and retired situation. For this purpose application was made to me for permission for his purchasing a small house and garden (then to be sold) in the neighbourhood of Sydney, but so retired as suited the weakly state he was in. Permission was immediately granted for his residing in any place that might be convenient to his health. Here he saw his friends, and was visited by the Surgeon, but he was soon pronounced to be in rapid consumption, of which he died on the 16th day of March last."

Palmer says of Gerrald's grave: "He was buried in a garden forming part of a little plot, which he had purchased at Farm Cove, in Port Jackson. The inscription on his tomb records that 'he died a martyr to the liberties of his country, March 16, 1796, in the thirty-fifth year of his age'."

Visitors to Farm Cove will see that it is now a horticultural paradise, where a tiny stream nourishes glorious trees and gardens, as it lazily drifts into the salt waters of Farm Cove. Near by, a brass tablet states: "In these gardens began the agriculture and horticulture of a continent. The first grain in Australia was established on this site with seeds and plants brought by the First Fleet in 1788."

Captain David Collins recorded Gerrald's death in his Account of the *English Colony in New South Wales*. "On the 5th November 1795 arrived Mr Joseph Gerrald, a prisoner, in a very weak and impaired state of health. In this gentleman, the gifts of nature matured by education (because he misapplied them) could not save him landing an exile on a barbarous shore; where the few who were civilized must pity while they admired him. At three in the morning, 10th March 1796, Mr Gerrald breathed his last, glorying in being a martyr to the cause which he termed that of freedom, and considering as an honor that exile, which brought him to an untimely grave."

Because Collins said that Gerrald died on 10th March and Palmer gives the date as 16th March, I secured a copy of the death certificate from the Registrar-General. This reads: "Mr Joseph Gerrald, buried on the 16th March, 1796. Convict Seditionist. A man apparently of great understanding. Buried at his own request in his own garden. St Phillip's Church of England, Sydney."

At that time I had not read much about Gerrald and was not planning a book on the Scottish Martyrs. But when I read the words "Convict Seditionist" I saw red. In the course of writing threescore books, I've scrutinized dozens of death certificates, including those of Ned Kelly, Daniel Morgan, Ben Hall, and other bushrangers of the last century. Murderers all — but it was never disclosed on their death certificates, while here was a man being followed into eternity with a passport reading "Convict Seditionist". So I began a dossier on him. After five years I had bought and read half a hundredweight of books about the Scottish Martyrs, and had read millions — yes, millions — of words about them in the Public and Mitchell Libraries. And that's how this book came to be written.

After this short digression, we'll return to Sydney Town in 1796 — a fateful year for the Scottish Martyrs. Both Hunter and Palmer, in their letters telling of Gerrald's death, report the departure of two more of the company — Muir by an American ship and Skirving, like Gerrald, by the final escape of death.

Palmer, in his letter of 23rd April, after describing Gerrald's last days, continues. "Within three days of his death poor Mr Skirving died of the same trouble. He had had the disorder a month before he complained. Indeed complaints would have been useless as B—— paid him one single visit. The excellent Mr Bass from the time he knew of it attended him twice a day. He removed from his house to camp next door to mine some weeks before Gerrald died, giving every attention. In the month of February last Mr Muir made his escape in the *Otter*. He is to visit the Friendly Isles, to take a cargo of skins at Nootka Sound, to stay some time at the Philippines, to proceed to China, and then to Boston, a voyage of two years. I told him I thought I should be at home before him. He went in excellent health and spirits, as his constitution is of iron. With Margarot I can have no intercourse, so that I am left alone with none to associate with but my friends Boston and Ellis."

Said Governor Hunter in the dispatch already quoted: "An American ship named the *Otter* commanded by Ebenezer Dorr, and belonging to Boston, having touched at this port to refresh his ship's company, and to have some repairs done to the ship, being bound on a voyage to the north-west coast of America and China, after having been treated here with much civility, and assisted in her repairs as far as it was in our power to forward them, he, contrary to a very pointed article in the Port Orders, which he had received on his arrival, carried from hence several people, for whose embarkation he had not obtained any permission, and, amongst the number, Mr Thomas Muir."

The story of Muir's escape is a long one, and we'll defer it to the next chapter.

The Governor continued: "Mr William Skirving, a very decent, quiet, and industrious man, who had purchased a farm already cleared, and was indefatigable in his attentions to its improvement, just as the labour of the harvest was near over, was seized with a violent dysentery, of which he died on the 19th of the same month. There, therefore, remains of the five persons who were sent out under that particular sentence, only two, Mr Fyshe Palmer and Mr Margarot, who live quiet and retired."

The Registrar-General's certificate states: "William Skirving, buried on 19th March 1796, Convict Seditionist, but a man of respectable moral conduct. St Phillip's Church, Sydney."

An unnamed writer, in *Tait's Edinburgh Magazine* in January 1837, wrote a twenty-page article on "The Memoirs and Trials of the Political Martyrs of Scotland, Persecuted During the Years 1793-4-5". After a lengthy description of the trial, in which, the author says, Skirving "acted as his own counsel and conducted his case with great ability and acuteness", the article continues: "On the voyage to Botany Bay, and from the colony, after eleven months' residence, we find him writing to his wife in these terms: 'My increasing love for you constrains me already to begin writing to you; but I shall keep my letter open while I may not lose the first opportunity of transmitting it. My unshaken faith in God our Saviour, that He is and will continue to be the husband of my widow, and the Father of my fatherless, while the designs of His providence require the continuation of our separation, continues my support in this very unpleasant voyage. I trust your experience of this grace support your comforts and invigorates your faith and hope in the same Almighty power and love.' "

The quoted letter continues with news of Skirving's farm: " 'I am already an heritor and freeholder in New South Wales; I have purchased a farm, crop, and work already done upon it, valued above £80; I have also got upon it man, woman and beast. I am not however in the slave trade, be assured, but shall treat them as brethren if they behave well. I have also the servant allowed me by the Governor, and a lad of the name of Moor, belonging to Edinburgh, a free man, who was left here by accident some time ago, whom I found in a very destitute condition. In remembrance of you, I have given the name of New Strathruddie to this far-away farm, and, I trust, if I get any tolerable assistance sent me, to make it soon of more value than the old.' "

Governor Hunter, speaking of the Martyrs in his letter of 30th April to the Duke of Portland, continues: "Those who are now gone have been often heard to complain of the want of that attention from their friends in England which they had been led to expect, but of which they had not since their arrival here received any proof whatever. They for some time continued to live independent of the public store, and appeared to have little doubt, thro' the assistance of those friends, in whom they appeared to have much confidence, that they would be enabled to live without the aid of Government. They have, however, from the disappointment of expected supplies, which they looked for by some of the several ships which had lately arrived here, been under the necessity of requesting that I would order them provision from the public store, which they now receive."

Palmer was certainly dissatisfied with conditions in New South Wales, but he seems to have blamed the local authorities and the military monopolists rather than neglect by his friends in England. In his letter of 23rd April 1796, already quoted, he writes: "My heart would reproach me were I capable of neglecting you who have been so attentive to me. I have written to you divers times but, I have reason to think that every one of my letters not sent by a private hand would have been stopped on your side of the water. When I lived in ease surrounded by every comfort, had a prophet told me what I should undergo in three short years I should have thought it far beyond my strength and ability to bear. But there is an elasticity in the mind that makes it rise again and bears it buoyant over surrounding difficulties. I did not expect to escape alive from the dangers of Campbell's ship, and the snares by which I believe Ministry tried to destroy me.

"When my friends Ellis and Boston remonstrated against that oppressive monopoly of the officers which reduced to indigence every one but themselves, the whole rage of the plunderers was directed against me, the presumed adviser of it. Helpless and totally in their power I experienced all the affronts and insolence they could heap upon me, and was alarmed at the threats and violence of the conspiracy against me. My two friends punished (and me together with them) by denying them every assistance promised in England."

Palmer's letter ends with a plea for no publicity. "You will remember, my dear sir, the wretched dependent situation I live in here, at the mercy of a despot whose will is law. Let not one syllable of this letter be published as coming from me, not at a time when by it arrival here it may heap more miseries on my head. Farewell. Remember me most affectionately to those to whom it is my constant ardent aspiration to return."

In a letter written on 5th May 1796 to the Reverend Jeremiah Joyce in London, Palmer made similar accusations. First, however, he mentioned that he had "received Dr Priestley's answer to Paine and your letter concerning his reception there, with a Nankeen jacket and trousers that fit me exactly". Joseph Priestley was a chemist who had discovered oxygen, and was also a dissenting clergyman who had espoused the unpopular cause of the American republicans and, later, the French Revolution. His unorthodox writings attracted numerous kindred souls, previously mentioned in this narrative, including Thomas Hardy, the Reverend Jeremiah Joyce, and the Reverend

Ebenezer Dorr, Junior, Captain of the *Otter*
From a painting in the possession of the California Historical Society

Old Windmill, Government Domain, Sydney

An Early Sketch of New South Wales Aborigines

T. F. Palmer. He emigrated to the United States in 1794, where he died about ten years later.

Back to Palmer, writing to his friend Joyce. "The persecution for political opinion is not confined to Great Britain, but extends to her remotest connections. They are all aristocrats here from ignorance, and being out of the way, or desire, of knowledge. Governor Hunter is a furious one, and sees with no friendly eyes those of opposite principles. This my friends Boston and Ellis and I woefully experience. He had defeated or discouraged every attempt of theirs to benefit the colony or themselves. We are told by a person high in office and high in his confidence that it is his intention to do so in order to drive them into the woods or a farm; or from the country. With talents capable of the most beneficial exertion in this colony they are doomed to starve as far as he can make them as useless characters. I never go into company, and consequently have no inducement (were I so weak) to speak on politics." Palmer then discusses the recent death of "poor Gerrald. He died in my arms on the 16th March. I never knew a man of greater talents. To have a person of his great understanding and virtue at my elbow was a comfort comprehensible."

Palmer then stated that he was "enclosing the inscription for Gerrald's tomb, which at a favourable opportunity I mean to place there. I enclose likewise the opinion of the excellent Mr Bass, surgeon of the *Reliance*, on the view of Gerrald's body. This most worthy man in defiance of all aristocrats and all obloquy or hazard attended the sick patients regularly twice a day. Alas, he came only from Norfolk Island one fortnight before the death of his friend Gerrald. Balmain the surgeon could not be prevailed upon to attend them. He never once saw Mr Skirving. Remember me affectionately to Mrs Lindsey (whose spectacles I constantly use), and Dr and Mrs Disney. I hope, my dear sir, to see you again in this world."

When news of the deaths of Skirving and Gerrald was received the grief of their friends and families was distressing. I wonder what were the feelings — if they had any — of Lord Braxfield and the other benign bastards who sat on the bench at Edinburgh and had sent them to their death?

Palmer's proposed inscription for the tombstone of Joseph Gerrald read: "Here lies Joseph Gerrald, Barrister of the Supreme Court of Judicature in Pennsylvania, condemned by the Court of Justiciary in Scotland (in defiance of the law of the land) to fourteen years' transportation beyond seas for meeting at Edinburgh, 1793, a Convention of delegates from the popular societies of Great Britain to obtain a reform in the Commons House of Parliament. When bailed out of prison between his capture and trial he first learned the sentences of his several associates, and tho' perfectly sensible that the corrupt court would pronounce the same on him, tho' entreated by his friends who offered to pay the penalty of his bail not to stand trial, he lent a deaf ear to their affection and returned to the public trial. Having suffered many months the rigours of a loathesome prison, tantalized to the last by the Ministry with hopes of liberty, broken in health, and emaciated by a consumption caused by the foul air he breathed, altho' almost unable to walk, he was hurried away in the dead of night, without a moment's warning, loaded with irons, and sent by a flagitious apostate (who ten years before had trodden in

97

the same steps and counterfeited the same virtues), a *Condemned Felon* to New South Wales."

The "flagitious apostate" referred to by Palmer was William Pitt, who had formerly advocated parliamentary reform.

"Gerrald was a man of singular endowments, of deep sagacity, great application, and most retentive memory. The Grecian and Roman authors were at his tongue's end, and he was fluent besides in the French, German, Spanish and Italian languages. He was deeply versed in Metaphysical, moral and political knowledge, and, as the illustrious Godwin observes, 'from his various information the wisest might have been content to learn'.

"From genius, and from these and other stores, his eloquence was (as his hardened judges involuntarily exclaimed) irresistible. He could convince the reason by weight of argument and call up at command to his assistance every emotion of the human heart. He was too, says Godwin 'placable and generous to an extreme'. The magnanimity of his spirit and the purtiy of his sense of honour could only be understood by those who made them the subject of personal observation."

Continued Palmer: "Torn from the bosom of that polished and learned society of which his gay spirits and great acquirements made him the delight and ornament; most inhumanely sentenced to that of robbers, ruffians and the offscourings of mankind, he lingered through two years of this society, four months of them only in this climate, fatal to his enfeebled constitution, and expired on the 16th March 1796, aged thirty-five, *A Martyr to the Liberties of His Country*. Reader, learn and imitate his virtues!"

I have not been able to find the source of Palmer's quotation from Godwin, but Godwin's letter to Gerrald, quoted in an earlier chapter, shows his high regard for him.

On 16th September 1796 Palmer wrote again to his friend the Reverend T. Lindsey in London, "You know not, my friend, what a benefactor you are to us three" — meaning himself, Boston and Ellis. He thanked Lindsey for the gift of a substitute for hops. "We brew for our living, sell our beer for considerable profit, which is in high estimation."

Palmer than complained of the "despotic caprice" of a party that flourished by "universal and pernicious use" of spirit. "My heart bleeds over the distress of so many of my countrymen. I must conjure you to send me out nothing more but to reserve it for those who stand in so much need of it. The newspaper reviews is all that I want. I must insist upon it. I shall really be unhappy if this is not attended to. As to my health, it is tolerable, but the climate undermines most constitutions. Farewell, my dear friend, with affection and gratitude. I seal this packet with my arms as the last letter was broken into."

CHAPTER THIRTEEN

We now return to the story of Thomas Muir and his unauthorized departure
from Sydney, which was recorded by Hunter and Palmer in letters quoted in
the previous chapter. The story of Muir's escape is clouded with complications,
especially since so many erroneous narratives have been written of his
adventures. We'll start with some plain facts supplied by John Cumpston
in his *Shipping Arrivals and Departures 1788–1825*, published in a limited
edition in 1963. This record, which took the author years to compile, lists
the arrival in Sydney of the storeship *Ceres* on 23rd January 1796, Master,
Thomas Hedley, from England, Rio, Amsterdam Island. She brought a
cargo of beef and pork. One day later, on 24th January 1796, comes the arrival
of ship *Otter*, Ebenezer Dorr, from Boston, to refresh.

The *Ceres*, John Earnshaw informs us, brought not only stores, but news
and letters from home. While making the long trip across the Indian Ocean
she had called at Amsterdam Island and there picked up four men, two
French and two English, who had been landed as a sealing party from the
French brig *Emélie* more than three years previously. It appears that the
Emélie, after landing her party, was seized by the British man-of-war *Lion*
and taken to China. So the four marooned men on the remote island were
thrown on their own resources. "Their leader was a young Frenchman, Pierre
Francois Péron, a man of courage, resource, and varied accomplishments. . . .
He kept his companions at work gathering sealskins. When their clothes wore
out coverings were fashioned out of the skins while the flesh of the animals
furnished their chief sustenance."

John Earnshaw found that in all published works on Muir there was a
haitus caused by the failure to discover any record of the *Otter's* voyage
across the Pacific. He felt that among the material in the Mitchell Library
there must be some reference to it, and after a search of several months it was
discovered in a rare work entitled *Mémoires du Capitaine Péron sur ses
Voyages*, published in Paris in 1824.

A biographical sketch of Péron states that he was born in Lambe Selec,
Finistère, on 6th February 1769, and served in the Merchant Marine, becoming

a captain before his retirement in 1804. Péron and a friend, Bernard, spent several years writing Péron's *Mémoires*, but the publisher "suppressed more than one third of it". In 1826 he was elected First Deputy Mayor of Saumur. The date of his death is unknown, nor have his original diaries and manuscripts ever been found.

We return to Amsterdam Island, where by various means Péron kept his mates alive through the long, bleak, sub-Antarctic winters until rescued by the *Ceres* in December 1796. Says John Earnshaw: "For some unknown reason Captain Hadley could not or would not load the sealskins, but carried away the castaways, leaving the product of their three years' toil and privation."

In Sydney Judge-Advocate David Collins noted the arrival of the *Ceres*: "The introduction of a stranger among us had ever been an object of some moment; for every attention was considered as due to him who had left the civilized world to visit those so far removed from it. . . One of the Frenchmen, M. Parron, apparently deserved a better thing of society than his companions supplied. He kept an accurate journal of his proceedings with some well-drawn views of the spot on which he was so long confined . . . they had, in the hope of their own or some other vessel arriving to take them off, collected and cured several thousands of seal-skins, which, however, they were compelled to abandon."

Now comes a most amazing coincidence, and I must confess my gratitude to John Earnshaw for his historical delvings into days long since gone, and his hearty enthusiasm in supplying material for my story and translating the relevant passages of Péron's *Mémoires*.

Says John: "Collins's pen was hardly dry from recording this news [the arrival of the *Ceres* with Péron] when on the following day, 24th January 1796, the Boston vessel, *Otter*, Captain Ebenezer Dorr, came into port. It was soon learned that Dorr had called at Amsterdam Island a few weeks previously and picked up a fine store of cured sealskins. . . . We can have little doubt that the Boston skipper had offered a pious prayer for such a providential windfall — he did what any other man would have done who sailed those lonely waters. It was only his misfortune that the owner of the skins should await his arrival at the next port of call."

Péron lost no time in calling on Dorr to recover his sealskins. "After having eluded the main point for a while, Mr Dorr said he considered himself very fortunate to have been sent by Providence to the spot and put my skins in a safe place, and while I was waiting to realize their value he offered me a position on his ship as first officer for his trip to the North West Coast of America and China and the return to Boston. I accepted his offer. At Sydney Cove the officers who heard of my mishap showed great interest in me."

Collins says that while at Sydney Dorr sold "2 hogsheads of Jamaica rum, 3 pipes of Madeira, 68 quarter casks of Lisbon wine, 4½ chests of bohea tea, and two hogsheads of molasses".

Péron states in his *Mémoires* that on 18th February 1796, in accordance with his arrangements with Dorr, he left Port Jackson in the *Otter*. The ship set a course to the east, the intention being to go north of New Zealand. She had a crew of fifteen seamen.

Several months later, on 15th July 1796, Thomas Muir, then living in Monterey as a guest of the Governor, Don Diego Borica, wrote to General George Washington, President of the United States, asking for sanctuary. After describing the arrival of the *Otter* in Port Jackson in January, Muir continues: "The Captain agreed to give me a passage to Boston, provided I could effectuate my escape from that port without danger to myself. Upon the evening before his departure, I pushed out into the sea, in a small boat, with two servants. About the middle of next day, we were received into the ship, some distance from land. This needless to observe, that in an emergency so critical, and to me so momentous, I could not provide myself with any necessaries for the voyage."

A variation of this story appeared later in a book published in Paris in 1798 under the title *Histoire de la tyrannie du Gouvernement Anglais exercée envers le célèbre Thomas Muir, Ecossais, etc.* The publisher claimed that this was Muir's own story, as told to a Citizen Mazois of Bordeaux. To my knowledge there is only one copy of this book in Australia, and this is in the Mitchell Library. It is No. 276 in Sir John Ferguson's *Bibliography of Australia*.

According to this version, Muir had lost all hope of returning to Europe before the arrival of the *Otter*, and "devoted himself to the cultivation of a little patch of land with the assistance of two faithful servants who followed him, or to reading works which he had been able to bring with him, and very frequently to catching fish which were very abundant in this country, providing an easier subsistence for a man of his standing than rural occupations".

The entrance to "the bay of this prison" was carefully guarded by two frigates, and every ship on berthing was strictly searched to ensure that the new-comers had brought "nothing which could interfere with their confinement or the peace of the garrison, such as weapons". After being searched, the *Otter* was allowed to enter. Muir, according to the Mazois version of his story, "had barely sighted the strange vessel when he burned with a desire to board the ship, and without divulging his identity hear the news from Europe, and perhaps his family". He was able to do this, because he was the possessor of a fishing boat, and such an occupation gave him liberty to come and go from the roadstead, and sometimes even to leave the harbour. "It happened that the Captain of this vessel was a Scotchman, living for a long time in America, where he had heard of the reputation and misfortune of our convict. The Captain, without knowing he spoke to Muir himself, asked news of him, and spoke of his family, giving him much proof of his esteem and pity, and his desire to serve him."

Muir then asked to be admitted to the Captain's cabin and speak to him privately. This account gives a rather French flavour to the meeting of the two Scots. "Well, my dear compatriot," said Muir, throwing himself into the Captain's arms. "I am the unfortunate person in whom it seems you take such a great interest, I who moisten you with my tears. Give my unfortunate father the embrace I may give you, give it to all true friends, and let those tears which fall upon your breast rekindle there the love of liberty in sufficient strength to spread it amongst our brothers."

The Captain offered to assist Muir to escape. "I will run every risk, even of taking your place, to remove you from your tyrants, and mine, alas!"

"I will not have a gallant man like you imperilled," replied Muir. "I accept your offer, but this is the plan we will have to adopt, so that all danger rests with me, and not with you. . . . The frigates which searched you on your arrival will be much stricter at your departure. You told me that this will be in four days' time. In this season the fog is thick at night, and does not lift until noon. Give me a compass, and I shall set off twelve hours before you in my boat. Follow the same course and perhaps you will find me on the vast ocean out of sight of land, and if you should not find me, then I shall have perished of a death much sweeter than the life which I lead here."

The comments on the weather here do not inspire much confidence in the writer's accuracy. Fogs that do not lift till noon are not frequent in Sydney at any time of the year, least of all in summer. Certainly nobody could predict one with such assurance four days ahead.

According to this account, Muir and his two servants put to sea at the time arranged, and with the help of their compass they followed the agreed route, sometimes sailing, sometimes rowing. Next morning the land seemed so far off they were sure they could not be seen. But their troubles were not over. The *Otter* did not appear; she had not been able to leave on the day planned, getting under way only the next morning. The wind was strong and the sea heavy, and Muir and his companions had to row for twenty-four hours, with hardly any respite, to keep to the route which the *Otter* was to follow. "Their strength was exhausted, land was no longer in sight, nor was the American vessel, and they lay down in the boat, overcome with cold and lack of sleep. By one o'clock of the second day the sun had restored a little of Muir's strength. He lifts his head out of the boat. 'God be praised,' he shouted, 'I see our rescuer on the horizon! Friends, have courage and row nearer to make it easier for them to see our little selves. . . .' The exhortation was unavailing; their strength was exhausted; all that Thomas Muir could do was to tie a shirt to the end of an oar, and lift it into the air, fixing it at the bow of the boat. While this action was taking place, the American followed the agreed course and took down his sails, to slow down his speed."

But the unfortunate convicts, without being aware of it, had been driven more than three leagues off course, and it would have been the end if a lookout who had been scanning the horizon had not miraculously seen this tiny point in the mighty ocean. In less than an hour "they hoisted on board the unfortunate men, prostrated with the heat, and almost lifeless. Care, kind words, fresh food, and above all the sacred love of freedom, gave them back their former health in a few days."

From John Earnshaw's odyssey of Thomas Muir, I learn that the *Otter* was built in Massachusetts in 1795. A three-master of 168 tons, she was divided into two decks with a square stern. She was principally owned by the Dorr family, and Ebenezer Dorr, junior, was her captain on the visit to Port Jackson. Peter Mackenzie, in his *Life of Thomas Muir*, says that the main purpose of the voyage was to rescue Muir. According to his story, some generous citizens in the United States "where Muir was revered as a Martyr in the cause of Freedom", shared the expense of having the *Otter* fitted out in New York and dispatched to Sydney, under the command of "Captain Dawes", with "the bold project of rescuing Muir at all hazards". Mackenzie's account of this part of Muir's adventures, however, is not reliable, as we shall see later.

Muir and his two companions were not the only convicts to leave Sydney on the *Otter*. Péron says that five (or possibly six) convicts left the ship at the Friendly Islands, and other records show that there were still eight on board when she reached California.

Muir's departure was noted by Collins in his *Account*. "On the morning of the 18th February, the *Otter*, Capain Dorr, sailed for the north-west coast of America. In her went Mr Muir and several other convicts whose sentences of transportation were not expired. Mr Muir conceived that in withdrawing (though clandestinely) from this country, he was only asserting his freedom; and meant, if he should arrive in safety, to enjoy what he deemed himself to have regained of it in America, until the time should come when he might return to his country with credit and comfort. He purposed practising at the American bar as an advocate; a point of information which he left in a letter. In his country he chiefly passed his time in literary ease and retirement, living out of the town at a little spot of ground which he had purchased for the purpose of seclusion."

Palmer, writing to his friend Dr John Disney on 14th August 1797, informed him that Muir's effects had been sold by the Provost-Marshal to satisfy his creditors.

We return to Péron on the *Otter*, now safely away from Sydney. "On the 2nd March, after a change in the weather, the sea became suddenly still like ice, and of a whitish colour; it was covered with phosphorescent matter known to naturalists as jelly-fish, and to seamen as Spanish bonnets. In spite of the fact that the weather was very overcast, there was a light around the ship so bright that one could read the smallest characters. . . . On the 7th March at two o'clock in the morning we crossed the Tropic of Capricorn."

The *Otter* was in the vicinity of the Tongan or Friendly Islands. This group had been discovered by the Dutch navigators, Schouten and Le Maire, in 1616, and had been visited by Abel Tasman in 1643, by Wallis in 1767, and by Cook in 1773 and 1774.

On 8th March 1796, writes Péron, the *Otter* was about three leagues from Rotterdam Island (Polynesian name Anamooka). "We could see a great number of canoes coming towards us. Then five Indians came on board. . . . One of them told us he was a chieftain, and offered us cooked fish wrapped in coconut leaves." Under his guidance the *Otter* passed north of Anamooka, and at three o'clock was met by another fleet of canoes, carrying an abundance of fruit. While searching for a place to anchor, the ship's company kept up "a very active bartering" with the natives, and before land the decks were loaded with six kinds of banana, watermelons, oranges, yams, sweet potatoes, pineapples, coconuts, breadfruit, sugar-cane, and shaddocks. "When night came we fired a cannon; the natives understood the signal, took to their canoes and went back to the island."

Péron continues his narrative: "There were more than one thousand tall and vigorous natives who were renowned for their adroitness and their tendency to steal anything. In case they made an attack, we brought all the swords and guns on deck, and our ten cannons were charged and run out. At sunrise we fired a cannon, and at this signal the sea became covered with canoes; and it was a race as to who should reach us first." A hundred canoes swarmed round the *Otter*, and bartering began again.

Another day the *Otter* was in a sea of islands, "twenty-six spread all over the horizon", as the mariners sought a way out of "Porto-du-Labyrinthe", as Péron called it. The chief of one island "gave us a pig weighing fifty pounds for some scissors, and one of our men deserted in one of the canoes. He most probably gave in to the hospitality and also perhaps to the attractions of the women, of whom none appeared to be cruel."

Near the island of Tongataboo the natives offered fine pearls for trade, then "six big fat pigs", for which the white man gave two axes, knives, scissors, nails, a borer; "This munificence greatly pleased them". Five of the convicts from Port Jackson "left us furtively to go and establish themselves on Er-oo-Wee".

On the night of 18th March the *Otter* left the Friendly Islands, and a few days later "passed Savage Island to the north-west at a distance of seven leagues". Savage Island, or Niue, is one of the Samoan Group, discovered and named by Captain Cook in 1774.

On 3rd April, at about three in the afternoon, we noticed a small island about five leagues away, and a little further along two others of the same size." Next morning, "we sailed close inshore and saw two men following us on foot; others appeared on hillocks and under trees, waving mats and pieces of materials. Taking this as a signal to go ashore, we went to the lee of the island, steering east", where a wide bay opened before the mariners.

Wrote Péron: "Four men and myself, with Mr Muir, our passenger from Port Jackson, entered the ship's boat. I directed it into a village that we had seen through the trees." The boat was stopped by a coral ledge, and Péron "lifted the oars and by signs enticed some natives towards us". After some hesitation, "six of them came armed with spears and clubs, but at a short distance away five of them stopped, and the sixth, holding a club in one hand and a branch of coconut palm in the other came forward. Supposing the branch to be an hospitable sign, I got out of the boat with Mr Muir and stood on the coral ledge."

With the sailors ready to fire in case of an attack, Péron went towards the natives, extending his hand as a sign of goodwill. Alas, they failed to understand his amicable gesture, as he showed them fruit, then scissors, as a sign that he wished to swap steel goods for fruit. They accepted the presents, but when Péron made signs that he wished to visit their village they did not savvy, and began screaming, shouting, and waving their weapons. "Pointing to our boats, they made signs that we should leave at once. Mr Muir, thinking that they had not quite understood, began pleading with them, and tried to explain that we did not have any weapons by throwing up his arms." This was the signal for the natives to run away, looking backward to see if the white invaders were following them. Then the sailors clambered into their boat, and at this some of the natives who were in canoes took courage and paddled behind them to within pistol-range of the *Otter*.

Again Péron rowed towards them. "Whether by this time they were more assured or not, they waited, and received me with goodwill. I exchanged coconuts, stone axes, mats, ropes and even the materials they were wearing for our goods, and before they left us they invited us to go ashore."

These people were obviously unused to the sight of white skins and European clothes. "They were ignorant of our tools and the objects with which we bartered. Everything united to convince us that we had the right to attribute to ourselves the honour of having discovered three new islands; and in this conviction I gave them the name of the 'Iles de la Loutre' [Otter], which was the name of our vessel. In order to distinguish them we named the eastern one 'Péron and Muir', the one in the north 'Dorr' after our Captain, and the name of 'Brown' was given to the third after one of our officers."

Péron now took sights of the island, as a reminder to future mariners that his name, his ship, and his comrades' names were perpetuated in this tiny group of coral atolls.

Dr J. C. Beaglehole tells us in his noteworthy *Exploration of the Pacific* that in 1765 Commodore Byron, heading westward after passing the Society Islands, saw "a group of islands, fertile and beautiful, and swarming with people, but defended in every direction by rocks and breakers". Byron thought this group, in latitude 10°15′, were part of the elusive Solomon Islands, and he called them the "Islands of Danger". It is probable that they were the islands described by Péron.

John Earnshaw considers that, from the position given by Péron, the three islands can be identified as those named Motu Ko, Pukapuka, and Motu Kotowa on the modern chart. Although the *Otter* was not the first vessel to sight this group of islands, Péron and Muir were probably the first Europeans to land there. Today, Pukapuka is included in the New Zealand mandate of the Cook Islands, the group that Cook named the Hervey Islands in 1773. It is seven hundred and twenty miles north-west of Rarotonga.

Leaving the islands behind, the *Otter* headed north-east towards the continent of North America. On 29th April 1796 she crossed the Tropic of Cancer, and on 12th May Péron noted a flight of birds going towards the east. A day later other birds, coming from the east, flew in a north-westerly direction.

The mariners saw on 29th May, "in daylight, the summits of American mountains over the horizon. We were then about forty miles from land." At that distance huge masses of peaks, tablelands and crests, most of them covered in snow, rose in tiers, one behind the other. As they drew near the entrance of the Strait of Juan de Fuca, which separates the southern end of Vancouver Island from the mainland, "the scenery became more pleasant to the eye, trees covered with green and bushy twigs spread from the water's edge to the top of the mountains". Juan de Fuca, a Greek pilot, discovered the strait in 1592. Captain Meares, who reconnoitered it in 1788, was assaulted by the natives and forced to go back. Vancouver was luckier in 1792.

On 30th May, while the *Otter* was sailing along the western shore, a canoe came alongside. "In it were nine swarthy Indians, of rather small size, whose clothes consisted of a piece of cloth, fastened round their necks by two leather straps, opened in the front, and hanging to the middle of their legs in the back. Their heads were covered with small plaits which were like many rays diverging from the same centre, almost like those worn by our opera devils."

Péron was unfavourably impressed by the "coarseness of their manners". Another canoe arrived, and the whites swapped the Indians a fathom of blue cloth for an otter skin. Péron later bought a fifty-pound turbot from some fishermen.

The sea-otter trade became known to British sailors when Captain Cook and Captain King visited this region in 1778, in search of a sea road round North America from the Pacific to the Atlantic Ocean.

The search for the supposed passage had been going on for over a century. So valuable would its discovery be to British shipping, it was thought, that an Act was passed "for giving a public reward to such person or persons, His Majesty's subject or subjects, as shall discover a north-west passage through Hudson's Streights, to the western and southern ocean of America". This reward of £20,000 — a huge sum for those days — was to go to the owners of the ship or ships "first finding out and sailing through the said passage".

Henry Hudson, an English navigator, made four voyages from Holland and England to the Arctic regions in the region of latitude 40 degrees north, in search of a short route to China, between the years 1607 and 1610. On his last journey in the ship *Discovery* of 55 tons he entered the huge bay that now bears his name. The explorers were ice-locked until the spring of 1611, when some of the crew accused Hudson of wrongly withholding rations, and turned him adrift with his son and seven others. No more was heard of them.

Cook was hoping to find an entrance from the west. After discovering the Hawaiian Islands on 18th January 1778, the *Discovery* headed north-east until the coast of America was reached. Sailing north to latitude 70 degrees near Bering Strait, the expedition was halted by pack ice. Back to Hawaii to thaw out, where on 14th February 1779 the world's greatest explorer was killed and eaten by the natives. Later navigators tried to pierce the passage from both the north-west and the north-east, but it was not until 1944 that Inspector Henry A. Larsen of the Royal North Mounted Police, in the 80-ton *St Roch*, did the job. When I interviewed him at Ottawa he told me of his many attempts to get through. Finally it was decided to make a dash through in one season, east to west. In 1944 this was accomplished.

Cook mistakenly thought Vancouver Island was the mainland of America. A thriving trade began in otter skins with Chinese merchants in Canton, and soon sailing ships from England and the United States were busy killing seals for skins which brought high prices. Then the Spaniards got in for their share, and established a settlement at Nootka Sound. This caused trouble.

Back to Péron: "Two canoes coming from the village of Out-cha-chel advanced towards us, each of them carried eleven fat and dumpy Indians. As they left the shore they started singing a war-song in a strong and sonorous voice and beating time with their paddles against the side of their canoes. When they arrived at fifty fathoms from the ship, they stopped singing, and all standing at the same time unfastened their blue cloth garments from their necks. Thus naked, they took up their oars again and made towards us in silence and great haste."

When the Indians reached the *Otter*, "one of them, with a truculent face and a strong voice said, *'Can-zi-ca-gan'*, which we thought was a polite greeting". The sailors politely repeated, *"Can-zi-ca-gan"*, and the Indian made a speech. But as the sailors did not understand him, Péron made signs offering blue cloth for otter pelts.

The Indians had no pelts and paddled away, to be replaced by others. When the sailors insisted on pelts they, too, departed in frustration. Another canoe-load arrived, and the owners made signs that there was a large village on the south side of the strait, where there were plenty of pelts. After wooding and watering, the men of the *Otter* explored the bay, then fired a gun to report their arrival.

"At nine o'clock a canoe was seen, coming from the sea and carrying four men and three children, wearing bear or stag skins, or gunny cloth. Their faces were as black as those of our chimney sweeps, the smell of their bodies unbearable; they sold us three salmon and disappeared towards the mouth of the river.

"On the same day," wrote Péron, "I got on board the dinghy with Mr Muir and four good rowers, with the intention of visiting the river. Fifty steps from the river we came across a hut belonging to five Indians. One came towards us, and led us to an old man sitting in front of the hut. With many gestures, he urged us to go in, and immediately unrolled several pelts."

This hut was square about sixty feet long by twenty feet wide, and eight feet in height. In the middle of the room was a large fire. The only furniture was scooped blocks of wood on which the visitors sat, a mattress, blankets, and animal pelts. Says Péron: "Putrid meats, rancid fats, tainted flesh, the bear meat cooking in the fire place, the public conveniences — all that was higgledy-piggledy in the room they lived in, so these poor devils' clothes and skin were impregnated with an unbearable stench."

Scattered around the hut were mussel, oyster and scallop shells. Outside, in a meadow, was a partly constructed canoe made of hard wood, with a grain like walnut, four feet in diameter and twenty-five feet in length. "I was unable to make them explain," wrote Péron, "how they could have moved such a heavy load, or how they could launch it into the sea." Péron was also impressed by a forest of "enormous oaks and pine-trees, more than an hundred feet high".

When the *Otter* sailed on 8th June two canoes approached the ship and several Indians climbed aboard. One stole a knife. His mate watched a sailor being shaved, after which he demanded similar treatment. "The barber, happy to do so, washed the Indian's face and shaved off his beard. This greatly amused his compatriots."

Next day, near the mouth of the Strait of Juan de Fuca, they came in sight of a big village, from which a huge number of canoes, carrying men, women and children approached the *Otter*. The chieftain persuaded the white men to come to their village, named Tatascon. Some wore bear, otter and beaver skins; others wore old clothes, old coats and bonnets. Several wore top-hats and had their hair done in a club. "A few showed us some English heavy rifles and made us understand they had no more powder."

In the distance they saw a number of natives, two to a canoe. "Instead of using nets to catch fish, they used rods fourteen feet long, at the end of which had been fitted pieces of wood shaped like a rake. They were about six inches long, an inch apart, and so on, half-way up the rod. Each fisher plunged this instrument in the water and quickly drew it out, bringing with it a lot of herrings. Some, using dried animal guts and wooden hooks, were catching fifty- to sixty-pound turbots and other heavy fish."

Péron was impressed at the Indians' skill in drawing; on most of their canoes they had represented fish, birds, and ground game, using a kind of limestone.

"On 10th June we steered towards Nootka, a bay lying on the western side of North America, where we wanted to buy food from the Spanish. Some beautiful trees grow here. The people are short, fat and beardless. The English have a great skin business here."

The chief of a large village came aboard on 16th June, a man about fifty years old, thick-set, with a big head. "His name was Out-cha-chel, and there was something ferocious depicted in his face. I took the opportunity to go ashore; Mr Muir wanted to come with me. It was decided with Captain Dorr that the Indian would be kept as a hostage."

On shore more than three hundred persons of all sexes and ages made the white men welcome, shouting *"Vacache"*, meaning "Good day", to which Péron and Muir replied, *"Vacache"*. After a lot of hugging from the Indians, and a flirtation with the wives of the chieftain, Out-cha-chel suddenly arrived in the hut.

"Mr Muir and I remained bewildered; the thought came to us that Mr Dorr wanted to sacrifice our lives by abandoning us to these savage people's mercy. As it was dangerous to show fear, I paid Out-cha-chel great compliments, telling him how happy he was to have such charming wives. He stopped me abruptly and told me that all these women belonged to him, that the Indians in the village were his subjects and that when he went to war he was always the victor. The chief then opened a big sea-chest, and brought out a man's head, which he held by the hair."

To Péron's horror, when the chief saw his emotion, he returned the head, and drew out another, while "Mr Muir muttered that it was possible he would put our heads next to his".

Péron remarked that the people of this twenty-seven-hut village were very keen on brandy, treacle, and biscuits, but since the *Otter*'s company were short of food, they could not do much to win popularity in this way.

Péron and Muir were allowed to return to the ship with their heads still attached, though later, on the shore of a small island near by, Péron says, "I saw a corpse the sea had thrown back, and whose head was missing. It occurred to me that it might very well have been one of the so-called enemies over whom Out-cha-chel had triumphed." Next day, when the *Otter* was about to depart, the dinghy was sent to collect the hawsers left behind. Out-cha-chel and the Indians surrounded it in their canoes and, taking hold of the sailors, tried to drag them ashore. In this dangerous situation the white men kept their heads and fought off their attackers with oars and knives. "Mr Muir and I congratulated each other for having got out of the hands of Out-cha-chel safe and happy."

CHAPTER FOURTEEN

AT MIDDAY on 22nd June 1796 the *Otter* arrived at Nootka, where a ship was
anchored inside the western head, which formed a long line of steep and
bare rocks. This proved to be a Spanish naval vessel, the *Sutil*, commanded
by Don José Tovar. Tovar, says Péron, "sent us one of his officers to guide us
into the harbour which he called Friend's Creek. This officer told us that after
discussions between England and Spain, the latter power had resolved to
evacuate this settlement and that their mission was to watch the way the
English behaved in these quarters."

The Spaniards and the English had been eyeing each other with suspicion,
and sometimes coming to blows, in this region ever since Drake singed the
King of Spain's beard. There had been a clash at Nootka Sound nine years
before the *Otter* arrived. The trouble began with arguments between seal-
hunters, especially when British traders established a fortified trading-post at
Nootka Sound. When the Spanish Viceroy of Mexico heard about this he
sent the Spanish warships *Princessa* and *San Carlos*, commanded by Don José
Martinez, to investigate the unauthorized occupation by the British of what
the Spaniards claimed to be their territory. This was in 1787.

At Nootka they found three British ships, with an armed trading-post on
shore. Don Martinez seized the ships, confiscated their cargoes, imprisoned the
crews, demolished the trading-post, and erected a fortification in its place
which he named San Lorenzo. One of the English skippers, Captain Meares,
after being released from custody, returned to England and on 30th April
1789 petitioned Parliament to obtain redress from Spain for this act of
violence. William Pitt, Prime Minister, promptly demanded satisfaction
from the King of Spain, threatening war if this were not given.

Negotiations began, Spain climbed down, and signed the Nootka Convention Agreement in London on 28th October 1790, permitting the British
to trade on the disputed coast north of San Francisco, until a better agreement
could be made. Captain George Vancouver, who had sailed as a midshipman
with Cook on his last voyage, was put in command of a British expedition sent

to the Pacific to negotiate with the Spaniards on the spot. His ship, the *Discovery*, was accompanied by the *Chatham*, under Lieutenant William Broughton, and later by the supply ship *Daedalus*. Vancouver met the Spanish envoy, Don Juan Quadra, at a rendezvous in Nootka Sound in September 1792. After a harmonious meeting the two leaders bestowed their joint names on the large island where their meeting took place. The name "Quadra or Vancouver Island" appeared on charts for many years, until Quadra's name was dropped.

They failed, however, to agree in the interpretation of their instructions, and, after a second meeting at Monterey, they decided to refer them to their respective governments in London and Madrid.

Vancouver sent Broughton to report to His Majesty's Government in London; the Spanish authorities allowed him to travel across country to save the long journey by sea round South America.

It was now decided to send the *Daedalus* to Sydney Cove with livestock for that settlement. Says Vancouver: "Our carpenters fitted up commodious stalls on the *Daedalus* for live cattle; Senor Quadra having with his accustomed liberality, offered me any number for the service of His Majesty's infant colony in New South Wales. Twelve cows, with six bulls, and the like number of ewes and rams, were received on board the *Daedalus*." Not all the stock survived the voyage, but Captain Thomas Rowley, one of the pioneer breeders of Merino sheep in New South Wales, purchased his first Spanish ram from this consignment.

Nootka was finally ceded to Britain by Spain, but the Viceroy of New Spain, the Marquis de Branciforte, still kept a vigilant eye on what was going on along the coast. He wrote from Mexico City to his superior in Madrid, His Excellency the Prince of Pas, on 27th September 1796: "Among those auxiliary defence and security measures which I have resolved to take for the benefit of our institutions in upper California, one consisted of dispatching every six months, a small vessel from the port of San Blas, to watch foreign ships arriving at these coasts."

The schooner *Sutil* was the first ship chosen to fulfil this patrol, and she left San Blas on 16th March 1796. Her captain, Don José Tovar, pilot of the Royal Armada, was instructed to investigate all foreign ships in the North American coastal area around Nootka Sound, and to convey news of them to his immediate chief, the Governor of Upper California, living in the Presidency of Monterey.

The *Sutil* struck bad weather, and Tovar, reporting his voyage to the Viceroy in August 1796, states that though he sighted a frigate on 28th May, he could not recognize her, and was prevented by a dense fog from taking any further action. On 16th June the *Sutil* reached Nootka Sound where Tovar learnt from the Indians that "Captain Broughton, in charge of a war frigate, and another of two masts (her supply tender), left the above port for about ten days, saying he would return shortly."

Broughton, after Vancouver had sent him home with dispatches, had again been sent to the Pacific, under secret orders, in command of the sloop *Providence* and her tender. He had reached Port Jackson in August 1795. At the time of Broughton's visit Palmer, Muir, Skirving, and Margarot were living in their cottages fronting the Tank Stream only a few hundred yards from where the *Providence* was anchored in Sydney Cove. Probably Broughton was aware of their presence, but he does not mention them in his *Voyage of Discovery to the North Pacific Ocean,* the account of the wanderings of the *Providence* and her tender from 1795 to 1798. Broughton, after leaving Sydney in October, had called at Nootka Sound on 17th March 1796, where he collected correspondence left for him by Vancouver and learnt that "the Spaniards had delivered up the port".

The two British ships hovered about the coast of North America taking observations, surveying, and fishing until June. When the *Sutil* arrived at Nootka they had gone to Monterey, preparatory to sailing for the south-west of South America, where Broughton had been ordered to make a survey. Don Tovar states in his report that he was preparing to leave Nootka on 19th June when "an American frigate called *El Otro*, Boston", arrived. Péron, as we have seen, gives the date of the *Otter's* arrival as 22nd June. Tovar's report continues: "The Captain, whose name was Dour [Dorr] came on board and showed me a passport issued by the Spanish Consul residing in America, for the free trade in hides and skins, and although it carried the crest of Spain's coat of arms I could not read it, as it was a mixture of both languages."

The skippers swapped yarns, during which Captain Dorr gave Tovar some startling news. "He told me that he had reached New Holland and there talked with an English captain named Barba, who is in charge of a brigantine. And that the said captain had told him that he had orders from England to engage in hostile action against our nation, and also that he thought the said Captain Dorr was carrying documents which were of the same tenor."

In search of Captain Barba, I fossicked through the pages of John Cumpston's *Shipping Arrivals and Departures 1788–1825,* in and out of Sydney. I found that the brigantine *Arthur*, Captain Barber, arrived in Sydney on 1st January 1796 from Calcutta, with a cargo of "beef, pork, and calico, on speculation", and departed on 3rd April for Bengal. But Broughton would have left Sydney before this ship arrived. My impression is that Dorr's tale was propaganda. He wanted Tovar and the *Sutil* out of the area, so that he could purchase skins at his own price.

Furthermore, wrote Tovar to his chief, José Quin (a pilot-aspirant whom he carried on board), "informed me that a captain of a small English frigate named *Juan Adamson*, had told him that two English frigates had left Sydney, one of forty-eight guns, and the other carrying twenty-two guns, for the purpose of taking possession of, and forming an establishment at Nutka, and further that the adjutant of another captain called Bron, on the *Infanta Carlota*, had learnt that two trading vessels were coming from England to form a sort of establishment in fifty-four degrees forty minutes, for negotiating in hides and skins."

Strange rumours! The *Providence*, 400 tons, carried only sixteen guns, and her supply tender, eighty tons, presumably carried fewer still. And Nootka, in latitude 49 degrees 33 minutes, was over three hundred miles south of the supposed new settlement.

Captain Dorr then asked Tovar whither he was bound. "I replied 'Bucarelli', to which he said that he was sorry to see such a small craft as mine with such a small crew to go about these ports and mix with Indians, as they were going to kill three of his sailors in the port of Clonyucuat, despite the fact that he had an imposing vessel in their eyes."

Captain Dorr then "generously" offered Pilot Tovar to convoy him to Bucarelli, "also, as he was short of food, being burdened with thirty-five men, stowaways from New Holland, he would give me five sailors who would be pleased to embark with me". As Don Tovar had five sick men, and no doctor on board, he accepted Captain Dorr's offer. When the five, presumably some of the *Otter*'s stowaways, were transferred to the *Sutil* they told Captain Tovar that they would like to work permanently with the Spaniards. The Don replied that he would put their request before his chief in New Spain.

They were not the only ones to join the *Sutil*. Thomas Muir, no doubt alarmed by the news that H.M.S. *Providence* was in the vicinity, also asked for a passage. Says Earnshaw: "While both vessels were slowly working out of harbour Muir's belongings were transferred to the *Sutil*. In these circumstances there was little opportunity to say a last farewell to Péron and his shipmates on the *Otter*. They never met again. As the vessels drew apart we may wonder if Muir did not feel a stab of some deeper sentiment at the parting with Jane, the convict girl, with whom as we may fondly imagine, he had shared deeper ties than just those of a fellow convict and voyager." We shall hear more of Jane later.

Péron would no doubt have parted from his friend with regret, and his tribute to him is worth repeating: "Among the deportees on the *Otter* there was one of whom I shall always keep a warm memory. Mr Muir . . . had been condemned with Palmer in England with a few others for having wanted to overthrow the Government. He was an enthusiastic partisan of the French Revolution and wanted to produce another based on Liberty and Equality. Mr Muir was a man of great talent. His unselfishness and loyalty won my esteem and that of others who knew him in his misfortune."

Soon after their departure from Nootka bad weather separated the two ships, and the *Sutil* made for Monterey alone. Tovar was probably beginning to feel uneasy by now at having taken Muir and the others on board, since there was a strict viceregal edict against the entry of foreigners, and especially Protestants, into New Spain.

Explaining the matter later to the Viceroy, in the report already quoted, Tovar wrote: "I bring to your notice that Don Tomas Moro [Thomas Muir], of the American ship *El Otro*, Boston, while in the port of Nutca, requested me to offer him passage to proceed via New Spain to the States of America, to go with General Washington. This individual, as far as I was able to understand him, is a high-ranking gentleman from Scotland who has been persecuted by the English Government for defending his mother country and the Christian States of Ireland until his banishment from the Isles; but being able to go to other parts of the world, and finding himself in New Holland, he took the opportunity of embarking in the said vessel." Don Tovar then explained to his chief that to save Muir a long journey round the Cape of Good Hope, he had acceded to Muir's petition and consented to his passage.

The *Sutil* arrived at Monterey on 5th July 1796, fifteen days after the departure of H.M.S. *Providence*. Although Muir was an illegal immigrant, he

Resolution and *Discovery* in Nootka Sound, April 1778
From a water-colour by John Webber, Admiralty Library

Providence and *Assistant* in Adventure Bay

An Indian of Monterey
By an Artist of Malaspina's Expedition

was received by the Governor of Alta California, Don Diego Borica, and his wife with great kindness, for which, says John Earnshaw, he "expressed his undying gratitude, and for the first time in over three years he was able to enjoy the amenities of polished social contact as a free man. To Borica, the worldly and intelligent army officer, cut off from events in this distant territory, the arrival of a cultured and easy-tongued traveller must have been a veritable godsend, and we cannot doubt that Muir, with little else but his wits to offer, used every resource to impress his host."

The Governor, however, had an official duty to report the arrival of foreigners in the country. He wrote to the Viceroy at Mexico on 13th July, and after referring to Dorr's stories about British designs against Spain, which he did not believe, he proceeded to the subject of the foreigners brought to Monterey.

"Your Excellency, with the object of being able to inform you of the circumstances regarding the said Scottish Intellectual, Don Thomas Muir, I suggested that he write down everything concerning himself (translating the extract from a printed trial which he showed me) and I dispatch to your Superior Hand the original of same, with his portrait which he also handed to me, saying that his followers in England had sent it to him, where they were thinking of erecting a marble statue to him for his firmness and energy shown in defence of the rights of the Scottish people who had nominated him their deputy."

Readers will recollect that earlier in the narrative our friend Thomas Hardy described meeting Muir on the *Surprize* at Portsmouth and getting a copy of Muir's portrait by the sculptor Mr Banks. A copy of this print, reproduced in this book, was given to me by John Earnshaw. My friendly researcher, Cavan Hogue, made a search for a copy in the Archives of Mexico City without success.

Governor Borica also passed on to the Viceroy Muir's account of his stay in Paris during the great revolution of 1792–3: "He gives very concise information of what occurred and paints in very vivid colours the characters of the principal personalities, such as Mirabeau, Condorcet, La Fayette, Robispierre, Danton, L'Egalité and others, appearing no less informed about the political situation in England. He is proceeding in the *Sutil* to San Blas, hoping to be allowed to continue his voyage until he is able to put himself under the protection of Washington, President of the United States, awaiting the development of a revolution in the English Ministry which he forecasts will take place in a short time."

Governor Borica's letter to the Viceroy also informed him of the arrival of the *Providence* early in June and of her stay of fourteen days wooding, watering, and victualling.

CHAPTER FIFTEEN

Muir spent a fortnight as the Governor's guest, while the *Sutil* was being repaired, and the time must have passed pleasantly. His future was still uncertain, but he might well have felt that the worst of his troubles were over. In any case, just to be living comfortably ashore must have been bliss after the hardships inevitable in a long sea voyage in those days. That part of California was a beautiful and fertile region, and no doubt Muir, like many another seafarer before him, enjoyed the abundance of fresh food it produced.

The Spanish settlements ruled by the Governor were mainly missions, most of which had been founded through the efforts of Padre Junipero Serra, known as the Conquistador of the Cross. This energetic missionary had been sent from Mexico by the Viceroy in 1767 to convert the Indians of California and establish Spanish ownership of the land, which had been claimed for centuries without much effect. La Pérouse visited Monterey in 1786 on the voyage that later took him into Botany Bay a few days after the First Fleet, and he found the missions flourishing. His account gives the impression that they ruled their converts with an iron hand. There are seven hours allotted to labour in the day, two hours to prayers, and four to five on Sundays and festivals, which are dedicated to rest and divine worship. Corporal punishments are inflicted on the Indians of both sexes who neglect pious exercises. ... In a word, from the moment a convert is baptized, he becomes the same as if he had pronounced eternal vows: if he make his escape for the purpose of returning to his relations in the villages, they cause him to be summoned to return three times; and if he refuse, they claim the authority of the governor, who sends soldiers to force him away from his family, and conduct him to the missions, where he is condemned to receive a number of lashes with the whip."

Besides looking after the souls of the Indians, the priests "have constituted themselves the guardians of the women's virtue. An hour after supper they have the care of shutting up, under lock and key, all those whose husbands are absent, as well as the young girls above nine years of age. During the day they are entrusted to the superintendence of the matrons. So many precautions are still not sufficient, and we have seen men in the stocks, and women in irons, for having deceived the vigilance of their female Arguses, who have not been sufficiently sharp-sighted."

The Journal of La Pérouse is filled with vivid descriptions of the Indian way of life, their games, their deer-stalking, and their search for otter skins, which previously "bore no higher value than two hares' skins".

Another comparatively recent visitor to Monterey, who was also to visit Muir's late but not lamented place of residence, New South Wales, was Captain Alexandro Malaspina, an Italian by birth and a Spaniard by adoption. He was in command of a Spanish expedition on a voyage of discovery round the world(with the object of drawing a maritime atlas and examining the resources of the remote Spanish dominions in the East Indies, which had been discovered by Ferdinand Magellan nearly two centuries previously. Information about Malaspina's expedition is scarce, and I am deeply indebted to Edith C. Galbraith, whose excellent article on the subject was published in the *California Historical Society Quarterly* for October 1924.

Two corvettes had been built for the expedition; one was named *Desubierta*, meaning *Discovery*, and commanded by Malaspina, while his second-in-command, Bustamente, was allotted the *Atrevida*, meaning Intrepid. On board were scientists, botanists, astronomers, cartographers, hydrographers, mineralogists, doctors, and artists. Each warship carried a crew of 102, of all ranks. Malaspina's expedition cleared the port of Cadiz on 30th July 1789. After rounding Cape Horn, the ships sailed up the South American coast, where they called at many ports, collecting plants and mineral specimens and setting up observatories on shore to determine calculations of latitude and longitude, while the artists recorded the lives and customs of the people.

Parting company, the two ships met months later at Acapulco, a Pacific port in New Spain, or Mexico, and sailed north again on a fruitless search for the North-west Passage, making a long survey of the rocky coasts of Nootka Sound, still a Spanish possession. The Spaniards circumnavigated Vancouver Island, proving that it was not part of the mainland.

On 11th September 1791 the corvettes dropped anchor in the bay of Monterey. There they remained for about a fortnight, receiving generous help from the missionaries in their collecting and other activities. The next year was spent wandering about the Pacific, and on 13th March 1793 they reached Sydney.

David Collins gives a vivid account of their doings in his *Account of the English Colony in New South Wales*. He comments on the splendid construction of the vessels, which were well manned, and had "a botanist and a limner on board each vessel". The "limners" worked eagerly during their stay, depicting on canvas a record of convicts and black men and women, as well as scenes of the countryside. Copies of these outstanding records of early Sydney can be seen in the Mitchell Library, Sydney. Malaspina requested permission from Governor Grose to erect an observatory, which was granted, and "they chose the point of the cove on which a small brick hut had been built for Bennelong by Governor Phillip, making use of the hut to secure their instruments".

Alas, after Malaspina returned to Spain he fell out of favour at court and was unjustly imprisoned, while his great expedition never received the recognition it deserved.

If Muir had heard Malaspina's full story during his stay at Monterey he would no doubt have had a fellow-feeling for him as another victim of injustice. He might also have taken warning that all Spanish authorities were not necessarily as kind as his host, Don Diego Borica. Eight letters that he wrote from Monterey express only optimism, but in fact they never reached those to whom they were written. The Viceroy intercepted them and, after having translations made, forwarded them to Spain. They are now in the Archives of the Indies in Seville. John Earnshaw published them for the first time in the Appendix to his monograph on Muir.

The first of these letters, dated 15th July 1796, was addressed to General George Washington, President of the United States. In it Muir relates the story of his trial at Edinburgh, his exile to New Holland and his escape from Port Jackson by the *Otter*. Then comes the story of his journey across the Pacific to Nootka Sound, and his passage on the Spanish vessel to Monterey. "In a few days we sail for San Blas, where I will remain, waiting the permission of the Viceroy of Mexico to pass through the country. Sir, I have claimed the protection of your name. I hasten to Philadelphia to solicit it in person. . . . I have likewise presumed to draw upon you for what expenses may attend my journey. Needless to observe that these bills will be joyfully reimbursed in Europe."

Muir's letter, too long to quote in full, ends: "From my infancy I have considered myself your pupil, and it is my glory, that in a land, permitted, almost to be visited by none, the name of General Washington presents me everywhere, respects and attention."

In this letter Muir also says: "With this I have written to Dr Priestley; I know not the place of his residence. I have likewise written to Mr Millar, an advocate at the same bar, my colleague in principal and in action, who, I have been told in New Holland, has retired from persecution into the sanctuary of that constitution of which you were founder and at present the defender. Mr Millar is the son of the celebrated professor at Glasgow under whose legal tuition I was educated. Your goodness will forward these letters to these Gentlemen."

Muir's second letter from Monterey was to James Maitland, Earl of Lauderdale, who had championed Muir's cause in Parliament. After narrating his exile to Botany Bay, and his escape to America, Muir continues: "In Philadelphia I will find in General Washington a friend, a protector, and a father. My heart overflows with gratitude to the Spanish Nation. . . . If in future I cannot be useful to the narrow spot I called my country, I may at least be useful in a more enlarged circle. A life devoted to science, and consecrated to private virtue, may not be wasted in vain, for the interests of mankind. Tell your friends, tell your brother, Colonel Maitland, tell Messrs Sheridan, Tierney, Erskine, etc., that I anticipate the day when restored to polished society, I can indulge with freedom and with certainty my recollections. . . . In the course of five months, I will have the satisfaction of writing from Philadelphia."

Muir's third letter was to Charles, Earl of Stanhope, wherein he repeats the story of his imprisonment, his exile, his escape, and of his intention to visit General Washington in America. "Deign then, my Lord, to receive in your hands the renewal of my homage, and the pledge of my faith, and believe me, that my future conduct will not disgrace the past, that my mind, firm and erect, rises superior to affliction, and that when I descend into the tomb, my enemies will be unable to impeach my consistency. Convey my congratulations to our excellent friend Joyce and by him to his colleagues. Tell them that with a sacred sensibility, I enjoyed their triumph, but not their triumph, but the triumph of *Constitutional rights and of eternal Justice.*"

The fourth letter was to Messrs Lindsey and Shields, who Muir addressed as "My dearest friends". After a vivid description of his escape from Port Jackson, and his other adventures, which readers now know by heart, the wandering Scot outlined his plans: "I flatter myself I shall obtain a passport from the Viceroy of Mexico. I shall ever speak in terms of the highest esteem and affection of the treatment I have received from the Spanish Nation. The nobleman who commands the province in which I am, has acted as a friend and father. In a few days we sail for San Blas, where I shall remain till I obtain permission from the Viceroy to proceed to Mexico, Vera Cruz and the Havannah. Write me under cover to General Washington — Dr Priestley of course I will visit. Hitherto I have seen nothing but the hand of God exerted in my favour, and my mind is filled with profound gratitude. Palmer is well, Skirving but poorly, and Gerrald alas, I left him at the point of death. He urged my departure. I have now the prospect of being of solid service to my Colleagues — I know their wants — I can inform their situation."

Dr Joseph Priestley, the man of science who discovered oxygen, has already been mentioned in Palmer's correspondence. A pioneer of religious reform, always a dissenter, Priestley in September 1792 was made a citizen of France, and elected a member of the national Convention. He accepted citizenship but declined election to the Convention. On 14th July 1791 he was invited to a public meeting in his home town of Birmingham, to commemorate the fall of the Bastille, two years earlier.

Priestley refused, but that evening a mob raided his home, smashed his chemical apparatus, fired his home and wrecked his library of rare books. As a result, Joseph Priestley, after preaching a farewell sermon, emigrated to America on 7th April 1794, where he settled in the village of Northumberland, Pennsylvania. It was Muir's hope to resume his friendship with Priestley after his arrival there.

Letter Number Five from Monterey, written on 14th July 1796 (Bastille Day), was to Charles James Fox, the brilliant Whig member of the House of Commons, "An opportunity occurred," said Muir, "upon 19th February of my vindicating my freedom, that freedom to which my right in Parliament was admitted, the moment I should set my foot upon that shore, but that freedom which, without my exertions and the providence of God, I never could have ascertained in that remote region as long as Ministers remained in power."

Muir then narrated the story of his exile, escape, and arrival at Monterey. "My reception from the Nobleman who commands the Province has been such as will ever live in my memory. If in the midst of exertions I should ultimately sink, deign, sir, to cause to exist forever, in the recollection of the English nation, whenever the gratitude of that nation, emancipated from the vilest tyranny of the vilest of Ministers, may be acceptable to a man of honour and a friend of humanity. Let it be known to them that in Don Diego Borica, poor, unknown, and exiled, I found a benefactor whose unsolicited kindness will suffuse my eyes with tears until the last moments of life. . . . Remove the anxiety of my friends. Tell them I hope to live to make some exertions still more strenuous than the past for the salvation of my country. If however the hour for those should be past — in America, in the bosom of the good and of the learned, my future days will glide on, consecrated to science and to private virtue. In whatever part of this globe I may be doomed to wander or to reside, for you my sentiments of esteem and of admiration are unchangeably the same."

It was now time for poor homesick Muir to write to his parents. Letter Number Six begins: "My dear Pappa and Mamma, You will be surprised and happy to have a letter from me dated from this place. After a passage of four months from New Holland we arrived in Nootka Sound. I there found a ship belonging to the King of Spain preparing to proceed to San Blas. Before I could have arrived in the American ship at Philadelphia it would have taken eighteen months and I ran the greatest danger of being stopped in India. I propose to travel overland through Spanish America to General Washington where I will receive the kindest attention."

Muir then outlined his plan to go south to San Blas in Mexico, with Pilot Tovar in the *Sutil*, a journey of twenty days, thence overland to Vera Cruz on the east coast of Mexico, where he would catch a ship to Havana and Philadelphia.

"The Governor," Muir added, "a nobleman of high rank, has shown me such civilities as could not be believed. Every refreshment has been sent aboard for me. Could you imagine, that even the Governor's lady, with her own hand, could have employed herself in making some portable soups for me during the remainder of my voyage. . . . By the time I get to Philadelphia I shall have completed a voyage around the world. I will now be able to be useful to myself to you and mankind. . . .

"Rejoice my dear Pappa and Mamma and bless God that I am again at liberty and in the midst of a good and kind and humane people. Write me everything under cover to General Washington."

Letter Number Seven was to the Reverend Joseph Priestley. Muir was aware that Dr Priestley had left England in April 1794, and was now living in Pennsylvania. "I deeply regret I was hurried away from London a few hours before you and Mr Lindsey did me the honour of calling upon me at the place of my confinement. I have, by the Divine blessing, at last established my legal, my unquestionable rights, of going from New Holland to any place I might choose, excepting Great Britain. This I have effectuated, not without exertion, not without danger, and you will perceive with the circuit of the globe. I have detailed the particulars in my letter to General Washington. I am now hastening, through the Spanish territories in America, to Philadelphia. I hope with the protection of God, to be there in the course of six months. The situation of my colleagues, in that forlorn dismal and inhospitable region, is mournful."

Muir then spoke of the illness of Skirving, and the good health of Palmer. "Gerrald, alas, I left upon the bed of death. Of Margarot, I can speak with little certainty, but I believe he is greatly to be pitied." The letter ended with his hopes of reaching America, "when I shall rejoin the benefactors of mankind. Much yet I may have to endure, and I cannot raise the cup, lest it should be dashed from my lips."

The last letter from Monterey was to John Millar, junior. "Poor Gerrald told me in New Holland, that you too have been added to the numbers of the victims of an atrocious ministry, that in voluntary exile you and your family have been obliged to retire to America, and forced to begin the world anew. May God grant you happiness according to your utmost wishes. I have broken my chains with much exertion and danger and I have vindicated that freedom which never again will I resign but with life."

Muir then describes New Holland, and his fellow-martyrs — Skirving, Palmer and Gerrald, the last of whom he "left on the bed of death. He urged me to this enterprise. My youth, my situation, demanded superior exertions. I now have the prospect of being of service to my colleagues. . . . My life since I left you has been a romance. I have literally circumnavigated the globe. If I publish my voyages and travels, as I think I will, I smile, when I think that a man of the gown must make his debut to the world, as a Navigator."

After again eulogizing the glorious Spanish nation and his illustrious host, Borica, Muir expresses his hopes of meeting in America the friends of his happy days in Edinburgh. "The idea of Reunion with those whom I love and esteem, will animate my vigour, as I ponder upon the immense way which yet remains before me."

From the *Dictionary of National Biography* I learn that Muir's schoolmate, John Millar, junior, a promising young man, went to the Bar, and published a book upon the law relating to insurances in 1787. He married the daughter of Dr Cullen. Ill-health and the unpopularity of the Whiggism he inherited from his father induced him to emigrate in the spring of 1795 to America, where he died soon afterwards from a sunstroke.

At last the *Sutil* was ready to depart, and on 21st July, with Muir on board, she up-anchored and sailed south, reaching San Blas on 4th August. Here Pilot Tovar had to make his report to the Viceroy. His account of his voyage to Nootka and of how he came to take "Don Tomas Moro" on board there has already been quoted. He went on to explain that he had become dissatisfied with Muir's story. "He had embarked without clothes, or money, or jewels, or any article which could be worth ten pesos; the trunk and mattress which he carried had been given to him by the captain of the vessel, and although he told me that the latter was supposed to keep two hundred pesos for him, and that he could not send these to him because of being separated, this being an evident untruth, first because the said captain is a man of independent means, the owner of many vessels, and who has done a large amount of business in New Holland, and secondly, having dispatched to him trunk and mattress whilst he and I were under sail, it is obvious that he would have sent him the money at the same time; so I am convinced of having been cheated through that sincere feeling of pity that I had for him." Pilot Tovar concluded his report by saying that Muir had "written to His Excellency the Viceroy, asking for his passport for Vera Cruz, which the Governor of Monterey had dispatched". The report was dated "12th August 1796, San Blas", and ended with the pious hope, "May our Lord protect your life for many years."

But the Viceroy of Mexico took a dim view of Don Tovar's imprudence. In a lengthy report to his chief in Madrid, he stated: "Pilot Tovar, though having sufficient professional knowledge as a sailor, lacks capabilities and insight regarding political and state affairs, and he was mistaken in allowing the commander of the Boston vessel to help five English sailors, escapees from Botany Bay, under the pretext of replacing his sick crew, and also Thomas Muir, a Scotsman who, according to him, had been banished to New Holland following Parliamentary revolutions in which he had played the principal role."

Branciforte now refers to Muir's prolific letter-writing in Monterey. "This individual wrote two letters to me, one from Monterey, 17th July, and the other one on his arrival at San Blas, of 17th August, in which he states the reason of his capture and asks for permission and assistance to proceed through this Kingdom to the States of America and under the protection of President Washington."

Branciforte now gets down to business. "By virtue of, and justified by Laws and Royal Orders kindly given to me by Your Excellency in regard to foreigners entering this dominion. I ordered the five sailors and Thomas Muir to be conducted to this capital without outward signs of being under arrest but placing them under the Orders of Don Salvadore Fidalgo, Frigate Captain, and of Don Andreas de Salazar, lieutenant of the same class of ships, in order to have them attended to, looked after and watched, as I have in mind to send them to Vera Cruz and have them transported from there to Spain, consigned to the Special Judge who is in charge of arrivals and at the disposal of Your Excellency. I have considered this to be convenient without consenting to the requests of the Scotsman to be transferred to the United Provinces of America, his conduct being unknown to me and . . . the very fact of his banishment, which he confesses, gives reason for his becoming harmful if protected by Washington."

Apart from the possible trouble Muir might cause in international relations, it was natural that Branciforte, a Spanish nobleman, would not wish to assist revolutionaries like Muir and Washington to get together.

Branciforte continued: "Having kept translations of the above-mentioned two letters which Muir wrote to me, and of eight other writings to various persons befriended by him and in whom he trusts, I beg to send such originals to Your Excellency in the enclosed parcel, number two, together with his portrait and a memorandum book in print. This was the portrait sent by Borica, and mentioned earlier by Hardy.

"For the transport of these foreigners by land and sea, some expenses might arise, as I gave orders to assist them in their necessities and with some distinction in regard to Muir, without omitting, however, to economize on their expenses; trusting Your Excellency will submit this to His Majesty so as to obtain his approval of those small expenses."

Poor old Pilot Tovar now gets dunked in the soup. Says Branciforte: "The Western Navy Commander of San Blas has put Pilot Tovar under arrest for having allowed the Scotsman to be interned at Tepic; I gave my approval and have ordered legal proceedings to be taken against him for this fault and for having transported foreigners in contradiction to Royal decrees, in order to have a report made to the King. Tovar will be kept under arrest until Your Excellency shall convey to me the Supreme Decision of His Majesty."

Tepic was a tiny town, twenty-two miles from San Blas, and about one thousand feet about sea level. Tovar had increased his crimes by transporting Muir there from fever-riddled San Blas.

More from Branciforte on Tovar: "I do not believe that the pilot's action implies any other crime than that of stupidity and ignorance which made him an easy prey by being seduced by Muir's alertness and cunning and that of the commander of the Boston vessel in burdening him with some individuals, perhaps outcasts for their actions and banished to Botany Bay, which is the Siberia of the English." This letter, signed by the Marquis of Branciforte to the Prince of La Paz in Madrid, and dated 27 September 1796, ends with the kind salutation: "May God protect Your Excellency for many years."

Muir had no choice but to go where the Viceroy directed. He reached Mexico City on 12th October and Vera Cruz ten days later. At this point let's take a look at Peter Mackenzie's biography of Muir, of Muir's journey from Nootka Sound. There, according to Mackenzie, the *Otter* struck a chain of rocks and went to pieces. "Every soul on board perished except Mr Muir and two sailors", who, after "wandering for some days in a state of great bodily and mental distress", were captured by a tribe of Indians. "Mr Muir was soon separated from his companions, but contrary to his own foreboding, the Indians treated him with singular kindness."

Muir lived with the Indians for about three weeks ,"until he contrived his escape. He had no human being to direct his course. The stars of heaven were his only guides. And in the most abject and forlorn condition he travelled the whole of the western coast of North America, a distance of upwards of four thousand miles without meeting any interruption. When Muir laid himself down to repose, by night or by day, in the open air or under the shade, he always recommended his soul to the merciful protection of his Maker. He at last reached the city of Panama, the first civilized place since he left Sydney."

I can't stand any more of Mackenzie's meanderings; his hero mooching four thousand miles through deserts, crossing creeks, climbing the Sierras of California, dodging wild Indians, and wilder Mexicans, while clambering over cactus with bare feet. What a tale!

CHAPTER SIXTEEN

BEFORE we embark for Europe with Thomas Muir, we'll return for a time
to Monterey, where on 27th October 1796 there was news of the arrival of
some old friends of his. It is recorded by a diarist whose name is unknown,
but who was presumably a government official in Monterey. His entry for
that day reads: "A soldier arrived at the Presidente from the Carmelite
Mission with news of a boat having landed five Englishmen. The Governor
sent me there immediately, where I found only the captain of the frigate
Boston, who showed me his passports signed by the Consul of Spain and the
President of Congress. I took them to show to the Governor and then returned
to the captain who promised to come to the port for provisions, as he was
very short."

On 30th October the frigate berthed. "Her captain Don Juan Dorr asked
to be allowed to present his respects to the Governor. The frigate is called
Otter Boston, carries twenty-six people and, according to reports, only six
guns."

Since parting with the *Sutil* off Nootka, John Earnshaw tells us, Captain
Dorr had made his way north, trading for sea-otter skins with varying success.
By September he had reached the Queen Charlotte Islands, then shortage of
food forced him to turn south to California, though to do this he had to brave
the Spanish intedict against foreign vessels. By the time the *Otter* reached
Monterey they had only a little fat and biscuits left.

Péron was still with the *Otter*, and in his narrative he tells of the Governor's
kindness and affability. "I always remember with emotion the kind interest
he showed me. Mr Muir . . . having preceded us to Monterey, had told him
I had been abandoned on Amsterdam Island, my misfortunes, and the nature
of my relations with Mr Dorr." But, says Péron, the Governor's kindness did
not get the reward it deserved from Dorr.

The anonymous diary takes up the story: "*November 5.* The provisions were sent to the American frigate from the Presidente. Some of the Englishmen being missing, one corporal and twelve soldiers went to look for them. Five were found and returned to the beach." Then, two days later: "Received news of an Englishman having been left behind. A sergeant and eight soldiers found him, and although the boat was sailing it picked him up. When the boat was out of sight five Englishmen presented themselves. After sunset a soldier arrived at the Presidente from the Carmelite Mission (three miles away) with news of the English captain having landed at that beach five sailors and a woman."

Next day the five men and the woman were brought to the Presidio. With one voice all said that the captain of the frigate with a pair of pistols compelled them to leave and take the boat, saying, "To Monterey!"

A lengthy correspondence now began between Governor Borica in Monterey and Viceroy Branciforte in Mexico City. After describing the arrival of the *Otter* in Monterey, the Governor states that Dorr was given cattle, flour, beans, mutton fat, lard and vegetables, all of which he paid for with drafts. The report continues: "Captain Dorr asked permission to land some English sailors who had boarded their ship without permit when in an English port. Such permission was denied, and to avoid trouble every one was compelled to go back on board on the day prior to sailing. The Captain, however, forgetting the hospitality that he had received, on that same night landed five men out of sight of the batteries and the landing guard. They presented themselves next morning after the frigate had left the inlet."

On the night of 7th November, wrote Borica, the *Otter* again cruised along the coast and landed five men and one woman, "the captain forcing them with a pair of pistols in his hands to go ashore". The Governor would never have believed that Captain Dorr was "capable of doing a thing so foreign to a good man", otherwise he would have taken measures to prevent it, though without maritime forces at his disposal he could have guarded only a limited portion of the coast.

Captain Dorr, having successfully replenished his food supplies and reduced the number of mouths to eat them, sailed for the Hawaiian Islands, thence to Canton in the following year. Here, says John Earnshaw, Péron left the *Otter* after an argument with Dorr over the sale of his sealskins, and joined the Boston vessel *Grand Turk*, which sailed for her home port on 23rd March 1797, arriving in Boston in December of that year. Péron now instituted a successful suit against Dorr for moneys due from the sale of his sealskins. The case lasted nearly a year, Péron writes in his *Mémoires*, and "the issue made me bless the noble and beautiful institution of the jury, which in a remote country protects the foreigner as well as the residents . . . the time I spent in that hospitable land is the happiest of my life." During the next few years Péron made further voyages to southern waters in the *Sally* of Boston, before retiring from the sea to his native land in 1804.

John Earnshaw has made an intensive search in the National Archives of Mexico City for records of the castaways left by the *Otter* at Monterey. He has found that there were eight convicts, including a woman, and three seamen who had sailed with the *Otter* when she left Boston in August 1795.

John is puzzled over the woman, described as Jane Lambert, a convict who escaped on the *Otter* from Sydney. One of the three seamen from Boston was Andrew Lambert, ship's carpenter. Was Jane smuggled aboard the *Otter* in Sydney as a guest of Lambert's or was she Muir's servant who escaped with him, to be abandoned when he hurriedly left the *Otter* in Nootka Sound to join the *Sutil*?

In the Mitchell Library, Sydney, is the Indent Register of the *Surprize*, which lists the names of all convicts who were transported on her from England. I searched this Register for women named Jane.

There was a Jane Wiggins, alias Young, sentenced at London on 12th December 1792 for seven years.

There was Jane Wilson, alias Scanlan, sentenced at Surrey on 2nd October 1792 for seven years.

There was Jane Huggins, sentenced at Middlesex on 11th September 1793 for life.

It is important to remember that these three Janes were convicts on the *Surprize*, the transport that carried Muir and his fellow-martyrs from England in 1794. Did one of these three escape with Muir from Botany Bay, and later call herself Jane Lambert?

Says John Earnshaw: "In the National Archives of Mexico City are over two hundred documents which tell of the sedulous care with which the Spanish authorities recorded the weary pilgrimage of Andrew and Jane Lambert through their dominions. For almost a year the little company of eleven English and Americans remained at Monterey in the tolerant charge of Diego Borica, who was so satisfied with their behaviour and diligence at their various trades that he wished to retain their services."

In October 1797 they were sent in the frigate *Concepcion* to San Blas, where they languished for four months while awaiting the long march across Mexico to Vera Cruz.

Says Earnshaw: "A petition in English, still preserved, tells of their poverty and wretchedness, and asks that they be allowed to work for the necessities of life. At last in March 1798 orders arrived for their journey across Mexico, but by then the little band was reduced to nine." One had died from malaria, and one escaped by boat to South America.

Three months later the nine wayfarers arrived at Vera Cruz, where six were repatriated to their homeland. But Jane Lambert was terrified of being returned to England, which meant being sent back to Botany Bay to complete her sentence. Andrew and Jane Lambert petitioned the Viceroy, to be allowed to stay in New Spain and to be instructed in the Catholic religion. With them was Peter Pritchard, a convict from Sydney.

Says Earnshaw: "The two men worked in the King's shipyard at Vera Cruz, but soon the enervating climate brought them to their beds, and Jane was forced to beg alms from door to door to provide them with food. Again the ever considerate Viceroy allowed the couple to move to the more salubrious climate of Mexico City while Pritchard went to Havana." In September 1802 the Spanish authorities, "apparently tiring of their six years' surveillance of these two humble foreigners, decided that they must sail for Spain within two months".

Comments John Earnshaw: "We may now wonder whether Jane ever reached London to astound her friends with fabulous tales of far-off lands, or, as the now legal Mrs Lambert, she returned with her husband to spend her days in some quiet New England village."

We return to Thomas Muir, whom we left at Vera Cruz, waiting to be transported to Spain. Travel was risky, since Spain had declared war on Britain on 5th October 1796. Muir was sent by warship to Havana, where he was imprisoned for several months, before leaving for Spain on the *Ninfa*. Nearing Cadiz on 26th April 1797, the *Ninfa* and the *Santa Elena* were pursued and attacked by British ships, and the *Ninfa* was captured, after a fierce battle during which Muir was wounded and lost his eye.

We are indebted to William James for the English version of this event, as told in his five-volume *Naval History of Great Britain*, published in 1822.

"At six o'clock in the morning of 26th April 1797, the British 74-gun ship *Irresistible*, Captain George Martin, and 36-gun frigate *Emerald*, Captain Velterers Cornwall Berkely, being on a cruise of the coast of Spain, fell in with and chased two Spanish frigates, The *Santa Elena* and *Ninfa* of 36 guns and 320 men each. On discovering by what superior force they were pursued, the two frigates ran for and anchored in Conil Bay near Trafalgar."

After skilfully rounding dangerous rocks, the British ships, "at half past two in the afternoon, followed them, and a smart action ensued; which at four o'clock terminated in the capture of the Spanish ships. The *Santa Elena*, after she had struck, cut her cable and drove on shore, her crew effecting their escape. This frigate was afterwards got off, but in too damaged a state to be kept afloat; she accordingly went down. Part of the *Ninfa*'s crew also escaped to the shore. The loss sustained by the two frigates was 18 men killed and 30 wounded. The *Irresistible* had one man killed and one wounded: the *Emerald* escaped without a casualty. The *Ninfa* (built in 1794, measuring 890 tons), under the name of the *Hamadryad*, was taken into the British service."

Rumours of Muir's presence on the *Ninfa* reached Scotland after the battle. The *Caledonian Mercury*, reporting the action, quoted Captain Martin from the *Orion*: "By a letter just out of Cadiz we understand Mr Muir is not dead, but badly wounded in the face. He says he made his escape from the frigate after we boarded her, where he saw some of his townsmen."

As we might expect, the best yarn comes from Peter Mackenzie's *Life of Thomas Muir*. Mackenzie first quotes an officer of the *Irresistible*, whose story of the action appeared in the *Edinburgh Advertiser* of June 1797.

"On the 26th inst., lying off shore," wrote the officer, "saw two strange ships standing for the harbour, made sail after them with the *Emerald* frigate in company, and after a chase of eight hours they got an anchor in one of their own ports. We brought them to action at two in the afternoon, and continued a glorious action till four, when the Spanish colours were struck on board, and on shore, and under their own towns and harbours. Our opponents were two of the finest frigates in the Spanish service, and two of the richest ships taken during this war. A Viceroy and his suite, and a number of general officers were on board. I am sorry to say that after they struck, the finest frigate ran on shore. We got her off at 12 at night, but from the shot she received she sank at 3 in the morning, with all her riches. We arrived here with our other prize, and are landing our prisoners. Among the sufferers on the Spanish side is Mr Thomas Muir who made so wonderful an escape from Botany Bay to Havannah. He was one of five killed on board the *Nymph* (*Ninfa*) by the last shot fired by us. The officer at whose side he fell, is now at my hand, and says Muir behaved with courage to the last."

Peter Mackenzies goes on: "But see what follows: when the action was over the officer and crew of the *Irresistible* boarded the frigate to take possession of her as their prize. On looking at the dead and dying, one of our officers was struck at the unusual position in which one of them lay. His hands were clasped in an attitude of prayer, with a small book enclosed in them. His face presented a horrid spectacle, as one of his eyes was literally carried away, with the bone and lower part of the cheek, and the blood about him was deep."

Some of the sailors, believing him to be dead, "were now in the act of lifting him up to throw him overboard, when he uttered a deep sigh, and the book fell from his hands. The British officer snatched it up, and on glancing at the first page, he found it was the Bible, with the name of Thomas Muir written upon it."

Naturally the officer was astonished. "Thomas Muir was his early school-fellow. He had heard part of his history, but to find him in this deplorable situation was incredible and heart-rending. Without breathing his name, for that might have betrayed his unhappy countryman, who might perchance survive, the officer took out his handkerchief and wiped the gore from the mangled face of Mr Muir."

The kindly British officer, and ex-schoolmate, now tied up the wounded man's forehead, "and after performing these kind and Christian offices, he enjoined the sailors to carry him gently on board a skiff to the shore hospital, where good nursing proved Muir's salvation."

Readers can please themselves what they believe. At any rate, Muir was not taken prisoner, and he recovered from his wounds in a Spanish hospital.

While in hospital, John Earnshaw says, Muir wrote to Thomas Paine, author of *The Rights of Man*, who was then in Paris. This letter is now in the National Library of Scotland. "I greatly rejoiced when I heard you were still in Paris. I flatter myself to be there in the course of this winter and to have the opportunity of cultivating that friendship I value so highly. Since that evening I parted with you in the Palais Royal my life has been composed of many agitated and uncommon scenes. These I will have the happiness of relating to you in a few months."

Muir had no doubt met Paine on his visit to Paris in January 1793, after his liberation on bail and before his trial. Paine's life in France since then had not been all glory. He had fallen out with Robespierre, and had been imprisoned from December 1793 to November 1794. Foreseeing trouble when a motion was passed to exclude foreigners from the Convention, he had hastened to finish the last part of *The Age of Reason*, writing the last words only six hours before his arrest.

"Contrary to every hope," Muir continued, "I have almost recovered from my wounds. The Directory has manifested to me the most flattering attention.

The Spaniards detain me because I am a Scotchman, but I have no doubt that the interposition of the Directory, will operate for my freedom. Remember me in the most affectionate manner to all your friends, who are the friends of liberty and of human happiness."

Eventually Muir was allowed to leave Spain for France. At Bordeaux his arrival was the signal for popular rejoicing and a public celebration. The story is told in a book already quoted — a small brochure with a large title, *Histoire de la tyrannie du Gouvernement Anglais exercée envers le célèbre Thomas Muir, Ecossais.* As we have seen, this book claims to give Muir's story as he told it to "Citizen Mazois, merchant of Bordeaux, one of the patriots who received Muir on his arrival in this city; this Citizen has guaranteed the accuracy of the details collected in conversation with the celebrated Scotchman".

According to this account, Muir remained in Bordeaux for several days in November 1797. "The patriots of Bordeaux welcomed, treated and received him as a martyr of liberty. . . . His wounds disfigured him, the left side of his face had dropped one inch. The Government will surely aid him in this misfortune and in the present circumstance will know how to draw from him all the information necessary."

From Bordeaux Muir proceeded to Paris, where his approach, Earnshaw tells us, had been heralded in the *Gazette Nationale* (2nd December 1797) by a "eulogistic article written by the artist David, a prominent figure in the Revolution. . . . The Directory appears to have relieved his wants and for the time being Muir entered in the life of the city and basked in the adulation offered him. During the early part of 1798 Muir enjoyed many of the comforts of civilized life that had been so long denied him."

We learn something of Muir's life in Paris from an article, "Two Glasgow Merchants in the French Revolution", by Dr H. W. Meikle, published in the *Scottish Historical Review*, January 1911. John and Benjamin Sword of Glasgow visited Paris in 1797, in search of profitable investment. "During their sojourn in the capital they called on Thomas Paine, not from any knowledge of him they said, but merely out of curiosity. Paine informed them that Thomas Muir was in Paris, and they paid him a visit, having known him as a student in the University of Glasgow. Muir appeared to live in style and kept a carriage. . . . He explained that the loss of one eye, and the imperfect vision of the other, necessitated his keeping a carriage."

During an evening spent by the Sword brothers in the company of Paine and Muir, "a long discussion ensued on religion, which Paine reprobated, while Muir endeavoured to defend it. Benjamin Sword even affirmed that Muir was intoxicated on that occasion. This led to the breaking up of the party."

Living in Paris at this time was the Irish patriot General Theobald Wolfe Tone, seeking French co-operation in his scheme for a landing of United Irishmen and French troops in Ireland. His journal records his visits to influential men for his purpose; for example, the entry for 23rd December 1797 says: "Called this evening on Buonaparte. He lives in the greatest simplicity, his house is small, but neat, and all the furniture and ornaments in the most classical taste."

The journal also lists a number of fellow-exiles in Paris, including "Napper Tandy, Ashley, an Englishman, formerly secretary to the Corresponding Society, and one of those who was tried with Thomas Hardy in London for high treason". Tone adds, "We all do very well, except Napper Tandy, who is not behaving very well."

James Napper Tandy, a member of the United Irishmen, after raising a small army of patriots, which was suppressed, had been sent to prison. When discharged Tandy had fled to America, and later to Paris. Tone's journal continues: "Napper Tandy had of late a coadjutor in the famous Thomas Muir, who arrived in Paris, and has inserted two or three very foolish articles, relating to the United Irishmen, in the Paris papers; in consequence of which, at a meeting of the United Irishmen, now in Paris, with the exception of Tandy, it was settled that Lowry, Orr, Lewines, and myself, should wait upon Muir, and after thanking him for his good intentions, entreat him not to introduce our business into any publications which he might think proper to make."

The four Irishmen waited on Muir a few days later, "but of all the vain, obstinate blockheads that ever I met, I never saw his equal," wrote Tone. "I could scarcely conceive such a degree of self-sufficiency to exist. He told us soundly that he knew as much of our country as we did, and would venture to say he had as much the confidence of the United Irishmen as we had; that he had no doubt we were respectable individuals, but could only know us as such, having shown him no powers of written authority to prove that we had any mission."

Muir also told the United Irish delegation "that he seldom acted without due reflection, and when he had once taken his party, it was impossible to change him; and that as to what he had written relative to the United Irish-men, he had the sanction of, he would say the most respectable individual of that body, who had, and deserved to have, their entire confidence and approbation, and whose authority he must and did consider as justifying every syllable he had advanced".

The delegates presumed "this most respectable individual" to be Tandy, and they were not impressed. After a discussion of nearly three hours, Tone continues, "we gave Mr Muir notice that he had neither licence nor authority to speak in the name of the people of Ireland; and that if we saw any similar productions to those of which we complained, we should take measures that would conduce neither to his ease nor respectability; for that we could not suffer the public to be longer abused. The fact is, Muir and Tandy are puffing one another here for the private advantage. This conversation has given the *coup de grâce* to Tandy with his countrymen here, and he is now in a manner completely in Coventry. He deserves it."

A few months later, in September 1798, the French-Irish expedition departed from France. Its ships were blockaded in Lough Swilly by a British fleet of nine warships and forced to surrender. Tone was recognized, captured, and taken to Dublin, where a court martial sentenced him to death. Tone, who had been given French military rank as an Adjutant-General, asked to be shot as a soldier, but this was refused.

According to his son's narrative, he could see and hear the soldiers erecting

The Presidio at Monterey
By an Artist of Malaspina's Expedition

La Pérouse at Monterey

Convicts at Sydney, 1793
By an Artist of Malaspina's Expedition

the gallows for him, and, "having secreted a penknife, he inflicted a deep wound across his neck". He died from this wound a few days later on 19th November 1798.

Napper Tandy, who had also landed in Ireland, was more fortunate. He, too, was put on trial at Dublin, where he was defended by Curran. "Delays were thrown in the way of his condemnation, and in the meantime Napoleon claimed him as a French General and designated an English prisoner of equal rank as a hostage for his safety. Tandy was exchanged, and spent the remainder of his days at Bordeaux."

A century after Napper Tandy's death in 1803, we kids at St Benedict's School, Sydney, taught by Irish Marist Brothers, used to sing:

"I met with Napper Tandy and he took me by the hand,
And he said, 'How's poor ould Ireland, and how does she stand?'
'She's the most distressful country, that ever yet was seen.
For they're hanging men and women for the wearing of the Green.'"

We return to Paris, where we left Muir riding in his carriage as a star boarder of the French Government. By May of 1798, says John Earnshaw, "the first flush of his welcome had faded, the problems of money became insistent, his wounds oppressed him and he sought for some quiet niche for future security. To the 'Citizens Directors' he appealed for help."

Muir's letter, dated 20th May 1798, now in the French Archives, says: ". . . Nevertheless, I am very unhappy — I eat your bread without being of any use to the Republic. If my physical strength had come up to my inclinations I should have requested the honour of fighting your enemies on the frontiers — but alas! that is impossible!"

He explains that although his property in Scotland is small, he has expectations from his aged parents, "who mourn for me night and day. . . . I have arranged all the materials of my travels and the events of my exile, at present there remains nothing to do but set them in order. They will be a work of two quarto volumes — this work is most eagerly awaited in England. I shall get three thousand pounds sterling for the copyright from London booksellers." Muir then suggests that the manuscript be forwarded to a Hamburg agent nominated by the French government who would receive the expected three thousand pounds to their account. "On the grounds of this proposal he asked the Directory to grant him a small estate from the public domain to the value of one hundred and fifty thousand francs, which he promises to repay." But, says John Earnshaw, "Muir's brief moment is past. His petition lay in the ministry for months until some official dismissed the poor wanderer's earthly affairs with a laconic note on the margin: 'Since then Muir has died.'"

Dr H. W. Meikle, whose article on the Sword brothers was quoted earlier, published another article, "The Death of Thomas Muir", in the *Scottish Historical Review* in October 1948. In this he states that there had always been a doubt as to the date of Muir's death, and lists various authorities who give different dates. Seeking the truth, Meikle visited Chantilly, twenty miles from Paris, and "through the kindness of the Mayor of Chantilly procured an official extract from the Registrar of Deaths", which stated that Muir died on 26th January 1799. Dr Meikle also quotes the substance of a statement made by three neighbours of the dead man, that "at 6 a.m. a foreigner died in this commune, known to them casually, who called himself Thomas Muir; that they knew neither his place of birth, nationality nor age; that the above-mentioned Citizen Lepauvre delivered his newspapers which had come through the mails addressed to him under the name stated above; that he had found there only the boy, La Bussine, a child of twelve years of age, who informed him first of the death."

Muir was in the thirty-fourth year of his age when his odyssey ended. He could truly boast, "I have encompassed the world." Says Henry Meikle: "The cemetery where Muir would be buried has now been built over. Only the monuments of those who had a *concession perpetuelle* were transferred to the existing cemetery, and there is now no record of Muir's grave."

His burial place is forgotten, like Thomas Paine's, but the words he spoke to Lord Justice Braxfield before being banished to Botany Bay for fourteen years are still remembered: "Were I to be led this moment from the bar to the scaffold, I should feel the same calmness and serenity which I now do. My mind tells me that I have acted agreeably to my conscience and that I have engaged in a good, a just, and a glorious cause — a cause which sooner or later must and will prevail, and by a timely reform, save this country from destruction."

Over thirty years later the first Reform Bill was passed, and Muir's prophecy was fulfilled.

CHAPTER SEVENTEEN

WE'VE followed the footsteps of Thomas Muir from Port Jackson to his death-place near Paris, and now return to the shores of Sydney Cove, where the Reverend Thomas Fyshe Palmer shared his tiny brick home, on the banks of the Tank Stream, with his friends Mr and Mrs Boston, and his devoted disciple, James Ellis of Dundee.

Their neighbours were Mr and Mrs Maurice Margarot, but their names were taboo in the Palmer household since the treachery of Margarot to his comrades on the *Surprize*.

After the Scottish judges had banished and sentenced Palmer to seven years in Botany Bay, he appeared to spend his time writing to friends in England and Scotland, usually narrating his sufferings on the *Surprize* at the hands of Captain Campbell. The last letter quoted from Palmer to the Reverend Jeremiah Joyce was dated 5th May 1796, and included Palmer's proposed inscription on the headstone of Joseph Gerrald. The deaths of Gerrald and Skirving are mentioned again in a later letter written from Sydney by Palmer, on 14th August 1797, to Samuel Whitbread of Southill, Bedfordshire. Thanks to the Archivist of Bedford, England, I have a copy of this. In it Palmer also refers to the petition the Martyrs presented to Governor Hunter for a sympathetic review of their case and for permission to leave Australia. "On the arrival of Governor Hunter, Messrs Muir, Skirving, and myself delivered to him the enclosed Memorial, which he transmitted to the Secretary of State. He has had an answer to it by the last ships which came from the Cape, and yesterday he favoured us with the contents. He tells me that he had instructions from the Secretary of State to detain us in this place until the expiration of our sentences, which are accompanied with the opinion of the Crown lawyer that it is legal for him to do so. He tells me also that the opinion of the Lord Justice Clerk and the Lord Advocate and of the Scots judges could not be sent by the same conveyance as at the time of sailing they were all in the country.

"You will doubtless observe the duplicity of Ministry. To obviate the odium caused by the illegality of our sentences their creatures at Edinburgh declare that our sentences are completed on our arrival and that we are at liberty to go to any part of the world except Great Britain, at the same time they give their servants here the most preremptory orders to keep us in custody at New South Wales."

Palmer reckoned that he was warranted in saying that "this custody has already been the death of two of us. Mr Skirving on his death bed declared to me that he never recovered from the starvation of short allowance in the year 1795, and Mr Gerrald's death was hastened if not occasioned by the quick vicissitudes and strong heat of this climate unsupportable by his feeble constitution."

Palmer continues: "Mine is greatly impaired. I hear the same of Mr Margarot. Now if the Scots lawyers and the Lord Justice Clerk (I believe I might add Judge Blackstone) be rightly founded in their opinions that we are at liberty to depart when we please, the detention of us appears to me to be little more than a cold-blooded proof of murder. And this by the express order of Ministry."

The letter concludes with the suggestion that if Whitbread found "a proper opportunity" he might bring the matter before Parliament — "but this must be left to your own judgment on which I have the highest confidence. Accept, sir, my deepest thanks for your zealous and able endeavours to serve me. I believe the whole Kingdom joins me in gratitude for your great exertions to . . . restore the violated rights of Britons."

Samuel Whitbread was born in Bedfordshire in 1758. He studied at Eton and Cambridge, after which he travelled around Europe with a tutor, then went to work in his father's brewery. In 1789 he married the daughter of Sir Charles (later Earl) Grey and the following year was elected the Whig member for Bedfordshire. He now became a proponent of negro emancipation, the extension of civil and religious rights, and an advocate of national education. In 1793 he was crusading for parliamentary reform, a minimum wage, and peace with the French at any price. As the years rolled on, he became more embroiled in parliamentary matters, attacking abuses of all kinds. Says the *Dictionary of National Biography*: "Whitbread died by his own hand on 6th July 1815, having cut his throat. . . . At the inquest the jury found that he was in a deranged state of mind at the time the act was committed: his friend Mr Wilcher gave evidence that his despondency was due to belief that his public life was extinct. . . . In the opinion of a good judge of character, Whitbread 'was made up of the elements of opposition'. . . . Lord Byron considered him the Demosthenes of bad taste and vulgar vehemence, but strong and English."

On 14th August 1797 Palmer also wrote to the Reverend Dr Disney. Palmer's letter did not reach his clerical friend until 11th February 1799. This letter is of historical interest, because Palmer mentions his efforts to earn a living for himself, his protégé Ellis, and the Boston family. The letter begins with thanks to Disney and the English friends who had not forgotten him.

"I received three pamphlets with the *Morning Chronicles* to April. We have read over and over our stock of books, therefore it would be charity to send any celebrated pamphlets that our friends have done with. Your noble gift of the Encyclopaedia has been of infinite use and entertainment, and has instructed us in arts necessary to a livelihood. An interested and powerful monopoly of trading officers, who have the art to persuade an old man to do just what they please, have thrown every impediment possible to our getting an honest one. But in spite of all, we have weathered our point."

The "old man" referred to was Captain John Hunter, second Governor of New South Wales. Born in 1737, he had served over forty exhausting years at sea, and was unable to cope with the military officers who controlled the courts, the convicts, the produce of the land and also the rum, more valuable than money.

Back to Palmer: "In a great measure owing to the help of your Encyclopaedia, we have built and navigated a little vessel. We meant it for fishing, but as we could not have any encouragement for what was so evidently for the public good, we have made it a mercantile vessel, and trade from hence to Norfolk Island, a thousand miles distant."

A footnote to Palmer's letter to Disney says: "As many volumes of the Scotch *Encyclopaedia* as were then published, were presented to Mr Palmer, by the joint contribution of a few friends, before his departure from England." From the 1961 edition of the *Encyclopaedia Britannica* I learn that the first and second editions were published in Edinburgh in 1768 and 1776, followed by a third edition in 1788. It was issued in weekly number as one shilling each. By 1797, when it was completed, eighteen volumes had been issued, containing 14,579 pages and 542 illustrations. This "Dictionary of Arts and Sciences" must have been a treasure trove for the literature-starved Scottish Martyrs.

After reading Palmer's reference to building a small mercantile vessel for trading to Norfolk Island, I visited the Public Library in search of the early Scottish editions of the *Encyclopaedia*. Unfortunately the Library did not have these, but they did have a similar version printed in Dublin in the year 1796, two years after the Martyrs had reached Sydney.

The shipbuilding article was most informative; after tracing the history of shipbuilding for two thousand years it proceeded to practical instructions on how to build a ship, dealing with problems and requirements of length, breadth and height, the keel, the sternpost, the rudder and scores of other necessary items. With these instructions were a list of drawings: ships with one mast, ships with two masts, ships with square-rigged sails, and ships with fore and aft, or leg-of-mutton sails. With such assistance Palmer and his pals completed their vessel for trading to Norfolk Island. "To be sure," says the clergyman-cum-mariner in his letter to Disney, "we are obligated to sail without a licence or certificate (which the governor, poor man, positively refuses), and are liable to be hanged as pirates by anybody that chuses to give himself that trouble. I hope we shall not return to Europe poorer than we came."

The fact that no licence was granted may explain why there is no mention of "Boston and Company", meaning the partnership of Boston, Palmer, and

Ellis, before 1799 in Cumpston's *Shipping Arrivals and Departures*, though they were apparently trading as owners in 1797. They first appear as owners of the schooner *Martha*, which may have been the vessel they built with the help of the *Encyclopaedia Britannica*. Her first arrival entry in the list reads: "*Martha*, schooner, 14th December 1799, 30½ tons. Master William Reed. Owners, Reed, Boston and Co. Registered 1799. From Bass Strait. Cargo 1000/1300 seal skins, 30 tierces seal oil."

She departed on 6th March 1800. "bound southward, oil, seal skins; sealing Cape Barren Island. Gang from *Nautilus* — Norfolk Island. Articles for sale."

Later in the year the *Martha* ran into trouble. In August 1800 she is recorded as having been "driven aground in Little Manly Bay and bottom beaten out, refloated with casks and taken to Sydney for repairs."

Captain David Collins, in his *Account of the English Colony in New South Wales*, gives fuller details: "The *Martha*, having been allowed to go to Hunter's river for coals at the beginning of the month, on her return, having anchored in some very bad weather in the north part of the harbour, Little Manly Bay, was by the parting of her cable driven on to a reef where her bottom was beat out. With assistance of the officers and crew of the *Buffalo*, she was got off, and being floated with casks, was brought up to Sydney, where her damage was found not to be irreparable. By the Master's account it appeared, that he had not been in the river, but in a salt water inlet, about five leagues to the southward of the river, having a small island at its entrance. He was conducted by some natives to a port at a small distance from the mouth, where he found abundance of coal."

From this I gather that the salt-water inlet which the *Martha* had entered was Lake Macquarie, where the village of Swansea now stands. After getting samples of coal from the natives, Captain Reed, or Reid, headed south and was wrecked in Little Manly. I cannot find any further record of the *Martha* after she was refloated in Sydney Harbour.

Palmer, after stating that Skirving blamed food shortages as the cause of his death, continues. "This brought a rupture on me, and otherwise disordered my frame. The extreme vicissitudes of the climate are rather possibly too much for a broken-down old man like me." Palmer, born in 1747, was then aged fifty, and hardly an old man. He resumes his letter: "To the young and the robust they are nothing, who lie in the woods without harm. My fellow-sufferers laugh at me, but I have no scruple in saying it is the finest country I ever saw. An honest and active governor, who could administer an equal government, might soon make it the region of plenty. At present the settler is obliged from necessity, to sell his wheat at 3s. a bushel, to an avaricious huckster, who turns it in to the stores at 10s. per bushel."

Giving several instances of military extortion, Palmer then writes: "We have laid out what would sell here for £300, on a farm, and we never could have interest to turn only forty bushels in to the store, from the time we have been on the island. By these means the colony is ruined. All the necessaries are double the price they were when we landed. Every farmer and settler is only a tenant at rack rent to the officers. All of them keep huckster's shops, where you may buy from a dram to a puncheon of spirits, from a skeign to a pound of thread. I cannot affirm it to be with — I hope that it has been without the governor's knowledge — but the most extortionate shop in the colony has been that of Government House. They sell indigo at this moment for its weight in silver."

From the huckster-like goings on at Government House, Palmer proceeds to tell the sad story of "the wreck of the *Sydney Cove*, bound from Bengal to this place, wrecked on the coast in lat. 41° 47'. The mate and others left the wreck in the long boat in the tempestuous winter season, and this was wrecked on the coast. But the super-cargo and two others, after many hardships arrived safe."

These three survivors told Palmer that the *Sydney Cove* was wrecked near an archipelago of islands, "with a strong tide and current from east to west, and vice versa; from which a rational conjecture may be formed that there is a passage right through the island. Should this conjecture be true, and this passage navigable, the passage to India would be considerably shortened."

The conjecture was proved true by Lieutenant Matthew Flinders and Surgeon George Bass, who left Sydney on 7th October 1798 in the 25-ton sloop *Norfolk* and discovered a passage between Australia and Van Diemen's Land, which they then circumnavigated. Governor Hunter, delighted with their discovery, named the strait in honour of Bass.

The *Sydney Cove* was wrecked in Bass Strait on 8th February 1797, while bound from India to Port Jackson. Seventeen men in a boat reached Cape Everard on what is now the Victorian coast, where the boat was wrecked. They then set out on foot for Sydney, hundreds of miles away over rugged and unexplored country. Says the *Australian Encyclopaedia*: "Only three of the men survived that exhausting journey." These reached Wattamolla, about twenty miles south of Sydney, where they were picked up by a fishing boat. "Two vessels were sent from Sydney to rescue the remainder of the company of the *Sydney Cove*, but one of these was lost with all on board."

Palmer describes the fate of two other members of the ship's company, the mate and the carpenter, who met their end not far from Lake Illawarra. "The mate, an amiable man, walked till exhausted. The carpenter, churlish and avaricious and without sense, seized fish from the natives, gave them nothing in return and offended them so much, that the first mate . . . fell a victim to the carpenter's folly and they both perished. My most worthy friend, Dr Bass, surgeon of the *Reliance*, went out on purpose to find these two. He found only their bones. He returned only yesterday, but what is more important, he discovered a seam of coal, seven miles long, a great part of which is above ground. He has brought home three bags; it burns capitally, some of which the Governor sends by ship (the *Britannia*) to Sir Joseph Banks. The coal is only twenty yards from the sea, and about 45 miles distant from Sydney."

Bass's own more accurate report describes the coal seam as beginning about twenty miles south of Botany Bay and being within hand's reach of anyone passing the foot of the steep cliffs in a boat. His voyage to Coal Cliff, as it was called, was between 5th and 13th August 1797.

In this letter to Disney Palmer also talks of the country north of Sydney, where the natives "are larger and more numerous than here. Seven convicts lived five years among them. I have repeatedly conversed with them. They were received and supported with singular kindness and hospitality. If these people are to be believed, they took the whites to be the ghosts of their departed friends, whom death had made white. They enquired after their fathers, mothers, and how they employed themselves. I believe this account, because when Captain Broughton of the *Providence* sloop of war took these convicts away, the natives brought two dead young men on board, begging Captain Broughton to bring them back in a year or two."

The *Providence*, as we have already noted, arrived in Sydney from England in August 1796, on her way to Nootka Sound. As she approached Sydney gales drove her northward, and she took refuge in Port Stephens. There her crew found four convicts living with the aborigines; they had escaped from Sydney in a small boat nearly six years earlier. Collins gives their names as Tarwood, Lee, Connoway, and Watson, and describes them as "miserable, naked, dirty, and smoak-dried" when they were discovered. They returned to Sydney on the *Providence*.

"Two or three natives of my acquaintance have begun to cultivate the ground and with a little attention on the part of government, they might soon be civilized," Palmer continued. "Ellis and I stayed with them a week, and we promised to return to hoe the ground and plant it for them. But I am now too infirm. It is singular that no dialect, or rather language, reaches above forty miles extent, some not half so far, so that a native of one district is unintelligible to another. They are as free as the air they breathe, and pay respect only to bravery and talents. They have no chief or priests. They have a discipline by which every member of the commonwealth is coerced into good order."

For slight offences, a few spears were thrown at the offender, "which he may ward off with his shield — if he can". For serious offences, "these spears must not only be thrown, but broken. If the offender is wounded, and justice be satisfied, nothing can equal their care and kindness to the wounded person."

Palmer's letter also tells Disney of the arrival of a deal box addressed to Muir, who had escaped in the *Otter*. "I opened it before the Governor: this was given to the provost-marshal to be sold for the benefit of his creditors."

Palmer's next — and last — letter from Sydney, dated 10th September 1799, was to his "dear friend, J. T. Rutt", whom it reached on 3rd April 1800. Palmer thanked Mr Rutt for a letter dated 28th September 1798, which arrived by the transport *Hillsborough*. "Of 300 convicts put on board, ninety-seven died before they reached Sydney harbour, and ten since. They were whipped, confined in pestilential air, and starved. The captain H—— would not allow them a swab to clean the place. I saw their filth. In consequence, the jail fever made its appearance. Eight had died in one night at the Cape of Good Hope. It is painful to relate the barbarity, the tyranny, the murderous starvation of this wretch."

Captain H——, commander of the Death Ship *Hillsborough*, was William Hingston. She left Portsmouth with 300 male prisoners on 23rd December 1798, reaching Port Jackson on 29th July 1799, after a journey of 218 days, the worst transport voyage ever recorded. The story has been told in my book, *Bound for Botany Bay*.

136

Back to Palmer's letter to his friend Mr Rutt. "I was very pleased with Wakefield's pamphlet. I sent a servant with it to a friend some miles distant, who was robbed of it because it was tied in a handkerchief. I must beg you, therefore, to send me another." This was a pamphlet written by Gilbert Wakefield, mentioned previously as a sincere friend of Joseph Gerrald's.

"Mr and Mrs Boston and two children, Ellis and myself have always lived together." When the Boston family joined the *Surprize* in England they had three children. Evidently one of them had died.

Wrote Palmer to Rutt: "We have engaged in many schemes to make a living. Among the rest, brewing and farming, and what every officer civil and military does here, buying goods on board a ship and selling them on shore. We built a vessel at great expense to trade between this place and Norfolk Island, and a very beneficial trade it was, but the Governor of Norfolk Island (Captain T———), being a trader himself, found that it interfered with his profits, and raised the strongest clamours against the enormous price we sold at. We sold liquor at 25s. a gallon, and he at that time £5. At last he would not suffer us to land it at all, notwithstanding we had Governor Hunter's permit."

Captain T——— was Captain John Townson, who had relieved Philip Gidley King as Lieutenant-Governor in October 1796. Townson ruled Norfolk Island until 12th November 1799, after which he returned to Sydney.

Back to Palmer. "We suppose the crew on this rose and seized the spirits, for we never more heard of captain or ship. We would have made our fortune soon. I am ashamed to say how much we lost. We were not disheartened. We set to and built another at great expense, loaded her with a cargo that would make good returns, and sent her to Norfolk. We had previously made a good quantity of salt to cure the cheap pork of Norfolk Island, and to put it into the stores here where it is so much wanted. She has been gone now five months."

As Palmer's letter is dated 10th September 1799, it means that his unnamed boat would have left Sydney in April or May 1799, but I cannot find any record of a ship owned by Palmer or Boston about this period. Palmer fears for the safety of his second vessel. "The gales have been dreadful, and we have every reason to fear that she is lost likewise, so that we have to begin again. As there is little chance of my being able to draw anything out of the company's stock to enable me to get home, I must take another method."

Palmer had discovered that "the cerated glass of antimony with ipecac-uanha, will cure the most inveterate fluxes of this country in a day or two. So little attention is paid to the sick, that I am obliged to doctor some, although I know that I do it with a rope around my neck. I would not change my residence for a week without these medicines, so very subject am I to this disorder. I know that I should have been dead but for them. I give seven or eight grains of cerated antimony, and alternately small doses of ipecac-uanha. Oh had I known of this remedy at Spithead what misery and wear and tear of constitution I should have escaped. Possibly Gerrald and Skirving might now have been alive! Pray tell this to Dr Hamilton and Blake."

Palmer's last letter from Sydney Cove ends with a request to Mr Rutt to "recommend me to those worthy friends, Lindsey, Tooke, Disney, and all who are pleased to interest themselves about me. Your obliged and affectionate, T. F. Palmer."

The *Dictionary of National Biography* says that John Towill Rutt (1760–1841), politician and man of letters, born in London, was the only son of George Rutt, at first a druggist in Cheapside, and afterwards a wholesale drug merchant. Young John studied hard, and "his teacher recommended his parents to send him to the University, but they were strict nonconformists, and would not accept his advice." So John entered his father's business, and worked hard, but became more interested in literature and the common weal than in making money.

Like many of those who corresponded with Palmer and Muir, Rutt joined the Society for Constitutional Information, sided with the French Revolutionaries, and became an active member of the Society of the Friends of the People, to which Lord Grey, Erskine and other prominent Whigs belonged. "The sufferings of the Scottish reformers, Muir, Palmer, and Skirving, excited his warmest sympathy; he visited the convicts in the hulks, when awaiting orders to sail, and sent papers and pamphlets to them in Port Jackson."

John Rutt gradually changed his religious convictions and, like Palmer, became a Unitarian. By 1796 he was a leading member of the Gravel Pit congregation at Hackney, of which Belsham was the pastor. He became firm friends with Gilbert Wakefield, helping him during the riots at Birmingham, went bail for him, and helped him after his incarceration in Dorchester Jail. Rutt published a small volume of poetry entitled *The Sympathy of Priests, Addressed to T. F. Palmer at Port Jackson*. He died at Bexley on 3rd March, 1841.

Into the picture again comes George Mealmaker, weaver of Dundee. We last heard of him at Palmer's trial, on 12th September 1793, when the indictment read, in part: "during the month of July 1793, having been present at a meeting held in Dundee, which meeting denominated itself *A Society of the Friends of Liberty*, the said Thomas Fyshe Palmer did put into the hands of George Mealmaker, weaver in Dundee, a manuscript or writing, of a wicked or seditious nature, in the form of an address to their Friends and Fellow Citizens; and feloniously written or composed by the said Thomas Fyshe Palmer".

One of the Judges had stated that in his opinion, "Mr Palmer was not the author of the handbill which caused the trouble. Mealmaker composed and wrote it, and the fact is proved as well by his testimony, as by the other evidence."

Nevertheless, Palmer was banished to Botany Bay for seven years, while Mealmaker went free. Mealmaker quietened down for many months, until 1797, when societies of United Irishmen, United Scotsmen, and United Englishmen spread over Great Britain, which resulted a year later in what was called the Irish Rebellion of 1798.

Our learned friend Lord Cockburn, in his *Examination of the Trials for Sedition in Scotland*, said of these united societies, "they were unquestionably of a criminal and dangerous character. They acted by secret meetings, affiliated branches, and unlawful oaths; and however innocent individual members might be, the views of the leaders certainly went beyond any reform, even Universal Suffrage and annual parliament."

Parliament in Westminster decided to check these unlawful associations, and on 19th July 1797, "the Act of the 37th George III cap.123, was passed. The principal object and enactment of this statute was to prevent the taking or administering of certain oaths or engagements, which acts it was provided should be punished by transportation for any period not exceeding seven years."

This Act did not frighten Mealmaker, who blithely went his way, haranguing audiences at meetings, well aware that informers were listening and noting statements by him considered to be of a seditious character. And so it was, on 10th January 1798, that "George Mealmaker, weaver in Dundee, present prisoner in the Tolbooth of Edinburgh", was indicted "at the instance of Robert Dundas, Esquire, of Arniston, his Majesty's advocate for his Majesty's interest, for the crime of sedition".

The charges are too long to be fully listed, so I'll content myself with the main ones.

In the year 1797 "a number of seditious and evil disposed persons did, in various parts of Scotland form themselves into an association denominated *The Society of United Scotsmen*. . . . George Mealmaker is a leading member and in the year 1796 or 1797 did administer oaths at Dundee . . . did wickedly, and feloniously circulate various seditious and inflammatory papers the general tendency of which was, to excite a spirit of disloyalty to the King: in particular a pamphlet intitled *The Moral and Political Catechism of Man, or a Dialogue between a Citizen of the World, and an inhabitant of Britain,* which was composed and written by the said George Mealmaker."

After addresses were made by counsel for the Crown and counsel for the prisoner, the Judges found that there was a case against Mealmaker, and the prosecutor began his task. The first witness, John Aitken, a weaver, took the oath, and gave evidence "that he once paid a penny, which he understood was collected to pay the expenses of the delegates".

Witness Aitken also knew the signs of the Society of United Scotsmen, which were "to join the two hands, mixing the fingers, and still keeping them so, turn the hands with palms out — answered by putting one hand on the back of the other, and mixing the fingers. The words used were, I love sight — I hate light."

Witnesses included David Douglas from Cupar. David got confused, and so annoyed the judges, who growled "that this witness has been guilty of gross prevarication and concealing the truth".

So into prison at the Tolbooth went David, therein to be detained till he be again brought before this court". For three days the court sat, taking evidence, especially from Mealmaker, who made three sworn declarations that "he does not know any association of persons that goes under the name of the United Scotsmen". He also refused to answer several questions, denied that he knew John Aitken, and denied many other charges directed against him.

At three o'clock of the morning of 12th January 1798, after Mealmaker had been on trial for nearly three days, the jury were ordered to return their verdict at two o'clock that afternoon. Fifteen good men and true, fourteen of them bankers and merchants, entered the box, "and having considered the criminal libel pursued at the instance of his Majesty's advocate against George Mealmaker, they all in one voice find George Mealmaker guilty of the crimes libelled".

The Lords Commissioners of Justiciary, having considered the verdict, "ordered that the said George Mealmaker be transported beyond the seas for the space of fourteen years, and that if after being transported he shall be found at large within any part of Great Britain or Ireland during the said fourteen years without some lawful cause, he shall suffer death".

After sentence was pronounced, the prisoner addressed the court in a few words. Here is the substance: "He thought his sentence hard, considering that it had only been proved against him that he had published the *Catechism of Man*, which he solemnly declared was merely intended as simple or abstract political propositions, and with no view to injure the country. He said that he was to be another victim to the pursuit of parliamentary reform, but he could easily submit, and go to that distant country, where others had gone before him. He did not fear it. His wife and children would still be provided for, as they had been before; and the young Mealmakers would be fed by that God who feeds the ravens. As to the court, he had nothing to say, but he thought the jury had acted very hastily, for if he was rightly informed, they had only taken half an hour to consider his case. They knew best whether their conscience said they had done him justice; but there was a day coming, when they could be brought before a jury where there was no partial government, and where the secrets of the heart were known. He begged now to take leave of them all."

CHAPTER EIGHTEEN

ON THE trail of boats owned by the Palmer-Boston-Ellis Syndicate, I checked the pages of John Cumpston's *Arrivals and Departures*, and noticed the following arrival: *"El Plumier*, 2nd December 1799, captured 7th July 1799, off the Maria Islands when bound from California to Lima by whalers *Barbara, Betsy* and *Resolution*. Condemned as prize, Sydney, 7th December, 1799."

From other sources I knew that *El Plumier* later played an important part in Palmer's life. Her story may be read in the second volume of the *Historical Records of Australia*, in a letter from Governor Hunter to the Duke of Portland, dated 3rd January 1800. "On the second of December last a Spanish merchant ship entered this port from the west coast of America. She was captured near the coast of California by three whalers who had letters of marque, and ill-fitted for any more distant voyage they availed themselves of this settlement, and sent her hither, where she has been. tried by a court of Vice-Admiralty and condemned as lawful prize."

Governor Hunter also stated that *El Plumier*'s cargo consisted of spirits, wine and other articles, produced in Peru. Because the British Government had failed to supply spirituous liquors, sorely needed in the Colony, the Governor stated that it was his intention to purchase these spirits and supply them to the settlers at a reasonable rate to thwart the military monopolists who charged four guineas a gallon "for an adulterated spirit".

Also in Cumpston's records for December 1799 is the entry, already quoted, giving the arrival of the schooner *Martha* on 14th December from Bass Strait with oil and sealskins, her Master being William Reed, her owners, Reed, Boston and Co.

Herbert J. Rumsey's *Pioneers of Sydney Cove* lists many First-fleeters, including "William Reid, *Sirius*, Seaman. He received a grant of what was known as the Eastern Boundary, Parramatta, on 30th March 1791."

On 16th October 1791 Governor Phillip reported: "Reid has 12½ Acres cultivated on the creek leading to Parramatta. He is to be supported and clothed from the Public Stores for 18 months, to have a hut built for him, and to receive the necessary quantity of seed-grain and implements of husbandry required for growing the ground for the first year: 2 sow pigs, 1 cock, 6 hens, and assistance in clearing two acres of land."

William Reid, or Reed, next appeared in Cumpston's shipping list as master of the Colonial schooner *Francis*, 44 tons, in 1798. The *Francis* had been sailing to Bass Strait for seal-oil and skins, and to Norfolk Island with stores. So he had seafaring experience to contribute when he joined forces with Palmer, Boston, and Ellis.

Records about the doings of Boston and Ellis in Sydney Cove are scarce, I did find a petition in the *Historical Records of New South Wales*, dated 13th January 1800, signed by eighteen people, asking Governor Hunter's permission to purchase goods "for ourselves and familys, as well as for the cultivating of our farms, and carrying on other useful avocations". They stated that they now had an opportunity of purchasing articles from the ship *Minerva*. One of the desired articles was "13 pipes of rum at 7s per gallon". Two of the signatories to this petition were James Ellis and John Boston. I have not found any record of a reply.

The doings of the Palmer, Boston, and Ellis Syndicate are also referred to in the *Journal of a Voyage in the Missionary Ship Duff*, by William Smith, published in 1813.

William Smith arrived in the Pacific Ocean in the year 1796, on the *Duff*, owned by the London Missionary Society, master, Captain James Wilson. The missioners had their ups and downs in the islands of Tahiti, as various native factions fought each other. Then the Tahitians expelled most of the English missionaries from Tahiti, including William Smith. They sailed on the *Nautilus* for Norfolk Island, which was reached on 22nd April 1798, but were unable to land because of stormy weather. So the *Nautilus* headed for Port Jackson.

John Cumpston reports the arrival of the "brig *Nautilus*, Captain Charles Bishop, from Otaheite with missionaries and a cargo of pork", on 14th May 1798. Governor Hunter made the missionaries welcome and "offered them the usual grant of land which the government gives to freemen".

Land grants listed in the second volume of the *Historical Records of Australia* include one to "William Smith, Missionary from Otaheite, 100 acres, Prospect Hill". Smith, not keen on farming, presented himself to Robert Campbell, whose barque *Hunter* had arrived in the colony on 10th June 1798, soon after the *Nautilus* dropped anchor with Smith and his comrades. The *Hunter* was loaded with trade goods, but the military monopolists controlling the colony refused to buy from Campbell, except on their terms, which were low. Campbell rejected their offer and decided to return to India on the transport *Barwell*, which left Sydney on 17th August 1798. Before leaving, Campbell appointed missionary Smith as his agent, with instructions to transfer the cargo from the *Hunter* into a store on the west side of Circular Quay and sell it on better terms.

The *Hunter* sailed from Sydney on 20th August 1798, reports Cumpston. She was bound for the River Thames on the north island of New Zealand, seeking spars for the Calcutta market.

Wrote Smith: "Mr Campbell instructed me to sell the remainder of the cargo and collect his debts. He gave me a power of attorney, and expressed his intentions of returning to the colony in nine months, but he did not return for seventeen months." Smith made many sales during his employer's absence, and also had some bad luck. One day, he said, he was invited to a party in the country, after which he returned to Campbell's store in Sydney Cove and found that it had been plundered. A large portion of the loot was found "in a pig-sty, covered with filth". The thieves were discovered and secured. "They had made free with the rum bottle, to which was attributed their detection. An inspection of the stock was made and there appeared a deficiency of between two and three hundred pounds."

William Smith also narrates stories of the missionaries' endeavours to farm near Sydney, and the murder of missioner Samuel Clode, who was axed in July 1798 by a soldier, Jones, and two accomplices. "By an order of the Governor, the house where the murder was committed was burnt to ashes; a temporary gallows was erected on the spot, and these three inhuman wretches were taken out of prison, and conveyed in a cart to the place where they were launched into eternity, more execrated than pitied by a multitude of spectators."

At last the overdue *Hunter* arrived from India on 14th February 1800. When Mr Campbell entered his house at what is now Circular Quay, his nose, he claimed, was "saluted with the smell of Spanish liquor which had been accidentally spilled on the floor. The house was more like a grog-shop than the residence of an East-India merchant." Worse still, Campbell took stock and found a large amount of money missing.

A suit was brought before a civil court in Sydney, and Smith found himself "in the hands of an inexorable creditor, who showed a determination to confine the poor debtor till the utmost farthing was paid. The Provost-Marshal received his warrant to commit me to prison where one of the tenants observed that 'when I had counted all the stones, bars and bolts of the prison-house I might then expect to be liberated'."

After being confined for about three weeks in the debtors' prison, Smith heard that some merchants, Messrs Boston, Palmer, and Ellis, had purchased a ship called the *Plumo* (*El Plumier*), "which had been taken from the Spaniards and brought to this port for sale". After refitting the vessel, they intended to "proceed to New Zealand for a cargo of spars, which they designed to ship to the Cape of Good Hope". Feeling sorry for Smith, they offered him a passage if he could escape. They suggested that he should make his way "to Jarvis's Bay, about 80 miles south, as a place of refuge till the vessel was ready in about three weeks".

This voyage was in fact to be Palmer's long-hoped-for departure from the Colony. His seven years' sentence had expired. The records show that on 17th March 1800 he sold the hundred acres of land he had purchased in December 1794 to Ebor Bunker, for £90. Bunker, an American, had arrived in Port Jackson on 28th August 1791 as master of the *William and Ann*, a convict transport. He later went whaling, married — it is said thrice — had a family, and died at Liverpool on 27th September 1836.

Following the suggestion of his new friends, William Smith escaped from prison, found a boat he had built four months previously, and set off for Jervis Bay, but rough seas forced him to seek sanctuary in an inlet twenty miles south of Sydney. With him were two Irish political prisoners, Desmond and Riley, both transported for their part in the Rebellion of 1798.

When a ship finally appeared it was not *El Plumier*, but a government vessel, which chased the escapees, and Smith was captured. "Poor old Patrick Riley," wrote Smith, "determined to perish rather than be taken prisoner, succeeded through amazing difficulties in passing to Botany Bay. He arrived safe at a distant settlement, where he was secreted by a friend, and ultimately sailed in the *Plumo*."

As for William Smith, his friend and jailer the Provost-Marshal "did not recognize me from my Robinson Crusoe appearance, having a long beard, an emaciated body, and clothed only in a red flannel shirt".

Governor Hunter then appealed to Campbell to release Smith, but Campbell was inexorable. "I was remanded to my old quarters in the prison, which I found very comfortable. A few days previously, the ship *Royal Admiral* had arrived with convicts, also ten missionaries destined to join the brethren at Otaheite, commanded by Captain W. Wilson, late first officer of the *Duff*. Wilson had in the *Duff*'s voyage manifested great friendship toward me."

According to a letter from Captain William Wilson to Governor King, the *Royal Admiral* arrived on 21st November 1800 at Sydney Cove, "with convicts and stores on account of Government" .

Three hundred convicts had joined the *Royal Admiral* in England on the 23rd May 1800. Listed on her convict indent was "George Mealmaker, age 31, sentenced Edinburgh Court of Justiciary on 12th January 1798, 14 years".

Said Captain Wilson: "I am sorry to state to your Excellency that in consequence of a fever, which showed its malignant effects at a very early period of the voyage, forty-three of the convicts have died on the passage, also one convict's wife."

Five days later Governor King stated in a General Order that: "The *Royal Admiral* arrived here the 20th instant, having lost forty-nine convicts of the jail fever in her passage. Many of those who were landed from her are in such a weak state that I do not think much labour will be got from them for some time, altho' it is but common justice to the master to observe that no complaint has been made of any improper treatment."

Says William Smith: "The arrival of Captain Wilson was a very interesting event. A detail of the circumstances which led to my unpleasant situation would be expected; and as it was reported that I had appropriated my employer's property towards the purchase and fitting the *Plumo*, I had to labour against these prejudices. They were inquisitive in investigating this subject; and the interview terminated to their satisfaction. They found, which was confirmed by other testimony, that there was no foundation for crediting such reports; perceiving they had only originated in suspicion."

Captain Wilson later wrote to Smith in prison, and asked him if he had

Thomas Muir,
after losing his eye.

Part of the Petition of "Eleven English People" abandoned at Monterey by Ebenezer Dorr

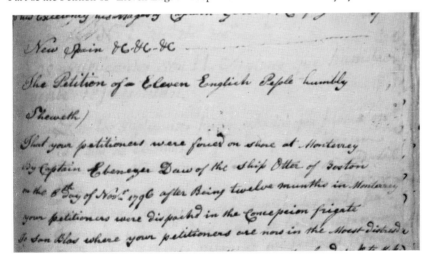

The Watering Place at Tinian, Ladrones Islands:
Anson's Camp

Aguana from the Reef
From Haswell's account of his voyage to Guam

been "ensnared by any of the owners of the *Plumo* to advance them money, furnish materials", or in any way assist them. This Smith denied, and with this assurance Captain Wilson started a list "and generously subscribed fifty pounds sterling. It was then presented to the missionaries, who subscribed thirty pounds, and to the officers of the ship who added twenty-two pounds, making the total collection one hundred and two pounds."

The kind Captain also took the list among the colonists, who cheerfully subscribed, "and in two days the deficiency was procured, and paid to my prosecutor, who gave a receipt in full".

So Campbell got his pound of flesh and William Smith was freed. Better still, he was given a job as "purser on the *Royal Admiral*, which allowed twenty-five shillings a month" and commissions. Says William Smith: "The ship's concerns being finished, we sailed from Port Jackson about the end of December 1800, towards New Zealand, hoping to obtain a cargo of timber for the China Market." Smith had a bad memory. The *Historical Records of Australia* lists "the departure on 28th March 1801 of the ship *Royal Admiral*, William Wilson, master, 923 tons, 24 guns, 98 crew, bound for China".

Says Smith: "The passage from Port Jackson was propitious, weather pleasant until our arrival at New Zealand. In making the land, we were prevented from coming to an anchor for two days by contrary winds." And they were contrary, with tempestuous gales which all but wrecked them on the shore, until, "in the most critical moment the wind suddenly changed a point in our favour, by which we were enabled to clear the rocks. At sunset the wind subsided, and became a calm."

The religious author then quoted the words of the psalmist as appropriate to the situation: "They that go down to the sea in ships, that do business in great waters; these see the works of the Lord, and his wonders in the deep."

The *Royal Admiral* at last reached a haven in the River Thames, where they came to anchor in seven fathoms of water. From some Maoris the storm-tossed mariners learnt that there was "good timber country to the south where we should find an abundance of trees, and also that a ship was there. This was a gratifying part of the intelligence, as we had no doubt that it was the *Plumo*, which had sailed a few days previous to us. We made sail, and shortly after came in sight of the *Plumo*. In boarding her, to my great pleasure, saw my old friend and companion in distress, Patrick Riley, who was much gratified to see me."

John Cumpston's *Arrivals and Departures* lists "*El Plumier*, William Reid, Master, sailed 5th January 1801 for Cape of Good Hope". Apparently she had not been ready to sail as early as her owners expected when they offered to help Smith escape.

Continues Smith: "The previous arrival of this ship expedited our business; they having explored part of the country, and had found a field of fine trees about twenty miles from their vessel. They had made little progress towards cutting timber, owing to a serious accident their ship had sustained by being driven on a sandbank, breaking eight of her larboard timbers, which rendered it necessary that all hands should be employed for a long time to repair the damages."

After refreshment on the *Plumo*, Smith's party, aided by Maoris, found the stand of timber, and there erected "two huts for the habitation of the captain, the officers, myself and stores, and about thirty men". Trees were good, average height 90 to 120 feet, which took plenty of hard work cutting down and squaring them, until "we discovered that a present of an axe or a red cloak of flannel, were great inducements to the natives to lend a helping hand".

Then the natives began pilfering, so "Captain Wilson determined to put a stop to these stealings, and to recover the stolen articles. He succeeded, though the measures adopted were hazardous." Two Maori chiefs were imprisoned, informed of the consequences should they attempt to escape, and that they would not be liberated until the stolen articles were returned.

This news was given to the natives, who to the number of eight hundred assembled at break of day next morning, armed with spears and clubs, determined to rescue their chiefs. They halted about fifty yards from our bamboo fort. As our number consisted of only thirty men, armed with muskets and cutlasses, having also two swivel guns mounted on posts, and surrounded by a fence seven feet high, the captain resolved to withstand an assault. Every man was at his post, with the guns double-shotted, in expectation of the dreaded moment."

Somehow or other sanity prevailed, the stolen goods were returned, the chiefs were liberated, and concord reigned.

Smith's narrative is full of interesting sidelights of their stay in the Thames River. Once while seeking a lost pinnace he saw a party of Maoris, not less than "four to five thousand, assembled for the purpose of making war upon another tribe. They were frightful in appearance, singularly dressed in war habits, and painted in a ludicrous manner. They were armed with spears about fifteen feet in length, and clubs."

No mention is made of trouble with the Maoris in the Log and Journal of the *Royal Admiral*, from which, thanks to the Trustees of the Alexander Turnbull Library in Wellington, I am able to quote a few extracts.

According to this record, the ship arrived off the islands known as Three Kings near the North Island of New Zealand on Monday, 13th April, and after eight days of heavy seas and squalls "came to in the River Thames in eleven fathoms. At six got down top gallant yards and masts upon deck; hoisted out the pinnace and longboats; several canoes came alongside; received fish and vegetables from them for nails."

On 27th April, "At seven a.m. sent seven armed men in search of four prisoners (who had secreted themselves on board at Port Jackson) that had made their escape in a boat alongside." The prisoners were captured the following day.

For the next two or three weeks the spar-gathering went on. The entry for 7th May records: "At noon received one spar 78 feet long by 18 inches in diameter." On 9th May "Natives arrived with six spars"; on 13th May "Raft arrived with 4 long spars and 6 short spars"; next day "the pinnace returned with 5 spars", and a day later "a spar 28 feet long was brought alongside."

Bad weather, heavy swells and squally rain delayed the work for a time, but it was resumed on 22nd May. Chief spar-getter was Captain Wilson, who lived ashore, evidently instructing the natives in the art of using steel axes to fell and lop trees.

On 12th June the Journal records: "At 8 a.m. hoisted out the cutter and sent her on shore with 2nd officer to enquire after the captain and the three boats. At 2 p.m. she returned and we were informed that the captain and the boats were employed in getting the *Plomer* off shore" — another name for *El Plumier* or *Plumo*. Captain Wilson and his crew in the pinnace now ran aground, and ten men with blocks and tackles were sent to her.

On 16th June 1801 "the Captain arrived having a spar for a jib boom. Got the pinnace and cutter in and everything ready for sea. The *Plomer's* boat also arrived with oars, having lost a large canoe full of timbers for boats, oar and plank. We have the unfortunate news of the loss of the longboat with the mast, sails, and rigging. Several of the boat's crew and extra hands that were employed came on board very sick and unfit for duty owing to the badness of the weather and long exertions in the mud trying to get the boat off. At 10 a.m. weighed anchor and set double-reefed topsails and foresail; fresh breeze from the south east."

And so the *Royal Admiral* "under double-reefed top-sails and foresail, with light airs, variable to ye south-east bore up the passage" into the Pacific Ocean, heading for Otaheite. William Smith was full of regret at leaving "friend Patrick Riley and my other friends behind". He begged Captain Wilson to take Riley along, but Wilson was loath to do this, since Riley was an escaped convict, and H.M.S. *Porpoise* was "expected to be at Otaheite on our arrival". So Riley stayed behind with Palmer, Boston, and Ellis on *El Plumier*, still seeking her cargo of spars.

CHAPTER NINETEEN

Voyage of "El Plumier" — Captain Wilson's Letter — Prisoners of the Spaniards at Guam — Boston, Ellis, Reid Reach Manila — Palmer Dies at Guam — Dampier and Anson at the Ladrones — Palmer Buried in Unhallowed Ground — Bones Taken to Boston — Haswell's Journal — Voyage of the "Lydia" — Arrival at Guam — Journey of "El Plumier" — Indians on Guam — John Boston at Manila — Captain Balch — Mystery of Palmer's Burial — John Harris at Norfolk Island — First Policeman — His Rows with Governor King — Captain Mellon's Tale — Ship "Duke of Portland" — Strange Story of Elizabeth Morey — John Boston in Sydney — Sails in "Union" — Pendleton and Boston Murdered by Cannibals — Death of James Ellis.

NEARLY three years passed without news of the Boston, Palmer, and Ellis syndicate.

Then came a report in the *Sydney Gazette* of 12th May 1804, which said: "The following particulars relative to the persons who left Sydney in the ship *Plomer* in the beginning of 1801, we extract from a letter received by a gentleman from Captain Wilson of the *Royal Admiral*: Harris, who took passage per the *Plomer*, is lately arrived in London, and gives an interesting account of that vessel's progress after she left New South Wales."

According to this account, the *Plomer* (or *El Plumier*) arrived in New Zealand on 2nd March 1801 and sailed agaon on 20th August "for Tongataboo, whence being unable to procure supplies, she sailed again to the Fever Islands, and there got upon a reef entering the harbour's mouth. She was considerably damaged, part of her after keel being knocked off and her rudder unhung; so that before they could leave, bulkheads were erected in the after hold and tightened with clay, in order to cut off the fractured parts."

The Sydney-siders then headed for Macao, in China, but the vessel was very leaky. "Having suffered incredibly for want of provisions, they put into Guam Bay on the 12th January 1802, in hopes of procuring succour, but to their great mortification, the ship was made a prize, and themselves detained as prisoners. From hence Messrs Palmer, Harris, Puckey, and some of the crew sailed the 20th January 1803, Messrs Boston, Ellis, Read, and the others of the ship's company having left it sooner by a Spanish vessel bound for Manila, which had remained only a few hours in the Bay. Mr Palmer was deeply affected at missing the first opportunity; and having exposed himself in a leady boat, with a fruitless desire of overtaking her, contracted a severe cold, and shortly after paid the debt to nature."

This account is confusing. If Palmer contracted his last illness in trying to overtake the first vessel, and then sailed in the second, he was presumably

148

already ill when he left Guam, and would probably have died on the voyage. But other accounts state that he died in Guam.

Back to the *Sydney Gazette*. "Mr Boston, when arrived at Manila, engaged with some of the monied people in the concern of a distillery, and has been very successful; Mr Ellis is with him; and Captain Read has the command of a Spanish vessel out of Manila. Their mate, Butler, and his wife, got to Copenhagen; Puckey died on his passage from Manila to Europe; Mr Boston's children are both dead as is Mulligan also; so that Harris and his son are the only persons among the number who have reached England."

Another version of the *El Plumier* tragedy is contained in *The Journal of William Lockerby*, a sandalwood trader in the Fijian Islands during the years 1808–90. The Appendix to Lockerby's *Journal*, which was published by the Hakluyt Society in 1925, contains numerous extracts from periodicals dealing with the South Seas in the early part of the nineteenth century.

The *Monthly Magazine* for 1st February 1804 gives the story as already told of the arrival of the starving sailors on *El Plumier* at Guam. "Upon coming to anchor on January the 10th, 1802, the Spanish Governor, in reply to their solicitations for provisions, assured them that unless they departed in two hours he would detain them as prisoners of war; for to the enemies of his country he could give no support."

Necessity obliged them to submit to the hard terms offered. "They were taken prisoners and a guard put into their ship. Messrs Palmer, Ellis, Boston, Reed, and Harris, Senior and Junior, lived with the Governor, and were treated with hospitality. During their stay, which appears to have been a year and a half, Mr Palmer was seized with dysentery, a disease with which he has been afflicted since he left England, but for which he conceived he had discovered an infallible remedy in cerated glass of antimony and ipecacuanha."

The author of this story, after wondering whether Palmer's medicine was any good, ends his letter: "Palmer lingered under the disorder till the beginning of June 1802, when a mortification took place which terminated his valuable life on the second day of that month. His effects and papers he bequeathed to Mr James Ellis, who now resides at Manila and, with Mr Boston, is carrying on a large distillery under the protection of the Spanish Governor."

The year given for Palmer's death in this article, 1802, must be a mistake for 1803, since the author states that *El Plumier* reached Guam in January 1802, and their stay on the island "appears to have been a year and a half."

So death came to Thomas Fyshe Palmer, the dedicated scholar from Bedfordshire, in the fifty-fifth year of his age, far from his homeland in the remote isles of the Ladrones.

These islands, the Ladrones or Marianas, had been visited by many voyagers since their discovery by Magellan in 1521, often, like Palmer and his friends, in search of provisions. William Dampier came more than once; of his visit in 1710, with Woodes Rogers, he wrote: "The necessity of stopping at these islands to get refreshments was very great, our sea store being almost exhausted." Generous supplies were provided on this occasion by the local Spanish authorities, but when Anson arrived in 1742 Britain and Spain were at war, and he landed on the island of Tinian, which was then almost uninhabited, and hoped the Spaniards on near-by Guam would not learn of his presence. His expedition was in desperate straits, with over a hundred men down with scurvy, and it was vital to get them ashore for a time, so they could eat fresh food and recover their health. While they were ashore fierce winds tore Anson's ship, the *Centurion*, from her anchorage, and the British seamen had an anxious time until she was recovered. But in the end Anson successfully completed his great voyage, reaching Portsmouth in 1744 with a rich haul of Spanish treasure.

Later visitors to the Marianas were two of the transports of the First Fleet, the *Scarborough* and *Charlotte*. Returning to England via China after unloading their cargo of convicts in Sydney Cove, they reached Tinian in August 1788, landed their sick there for a few days, and "loaded the boat with coconuts, oranges, and limes".

It is said that Palmer was buried in hallowed ground, but that Spanish missionaries later claimed he was a heretic, so his cadaver was dug up and reburied in unhallowed ground where bleach the bones of the blackbirders of the Coral Seas and the buccaneers of the Spanish Main. I cannot vouch for this as fact. Maybe some scholar will visit Seville and prowl through the Archives of the Indies to verify this unhappy incident.

Another statement about Palmer's burial comes from the Reverend L. Baker Short, a Unitarian Minister who once lived at Dundee, and became deeply interested in the doings of his distinguished predecessor. In a lengthy article in the *Unitarian* of October 1964, he writes: ". . . in 1804 an American captain received permission to remove Palmer's body to the United States, where it was re-interred in the cemetery of Boston, Mass. But subsequent research has not been able to discover any trace of his grave or memorial. So the storm-tossed Palmer at last found peace and rest in America, the land of liberty to which he had at one time thought of emigrating to join Joseph Priestley."

The Reverend L. Baker Short refers the reader to "an Article in *Christian Pioneer*, vol. ix (1835), page 254, for Reverend George Harris's account of Palmer's end. Harris gives no authority for his statement."

Another account of the last days of *El Plumier* has been found in the journal kept by William Haswell, first officer of the barque *Lydia*, on a voyage from Manila to Guam. John Earnshaw fortunately secured a copy of this journal.

The *Lydia* left Manila on 20th October 1801; she carried a crew of twelve, and twenty-four passengers, including the Governor of the Mariana Islands and his family. The crew, eleven in number were anxious while sailing through waters infested with pirates. But though pirates in dhows were sighted, the *Lydia* passed safely.

Days of anxiety ensued before "we on the *Lydia* saw the look-out of Sambongue, and at five the next morning, 3rd November, was abreast of the town. Here the Governor and lady and children went on shore, as we saluted with three guns which were answered with the same number from the fort." That night the Governor's sons brought dancing girls on the ship — not a success, as the deck was littered with lumber. In the morning the Governor returned, the anchor was hoisted, and the *Lydia* got under way.

"We had fine weather, light winds and easterly breezes so that it rendered our passage long and tedious; our passengers very anxious to arrive at the Island; the Friar praying day and night, but all would not bring a fair wind." After beating around in the doldrums, the lookout at last got sight of the Island of Guam on 4th January 1802, and the following day "we saw the town of Aquasia, and at one we entered the harbour de la Caldera. A gun was fired from the Island Fort on which we came to. A small boat came to enquire who we were, and as soon as they were informed that the new Governor was on board they set off in a great hurry to carry the news to Don Manuel Moore, the old Governor."

At midnight the Adjutant came out "with a letter from Don Manuel wishing our passenger Don Vincenty Blanco joy on his arrival and informing him that the boats should attend him in the morning". On 7th January 1802 the "three boats came on board, one of them a handsome Barge, the crew in uniform", to take His Excellency on shore, while the *Lydia* fired a nine-gun salute, followed by three cheers as the vice-regal party went ashore.

"That day," wrote William Haswell, "a ship came in sight. Not able to find the Passage over the Reef, I went out in a small boat and found her to be an English ship in distress; accordingly I piloted them in and brought them to anchor near the Hill Fort in 30 fathoms water. Their story is as follows: That the ship was taken from the Spaniards on the coast of Peru and carried to Port Jackson, New Holland, and condemned. The present owners bought her there and went with her to New Zealand to cut spars which they intended to carry to the Cape of Good Hope.

"But the ship getting on shore and bilging herself delayed them some time which caused a greater expenditure of provisions than what they expected. At length they got the ship repaired and loaded, and went to the Friendly Islands to get provisions. But they were disappointed as the natives were at war with one another and nothing to be got but yams, of which they got a slender stock. They set off again but the ship got aground on some rocks which made her leaky. They got her off and stopt the leak on the inside with clay as well as they could. The men then mutinied and insisted on carrying the ship to Macao but not being able to reach that place they put in here for Provisions."

Haswell then describes the efforts of the crew to repair the leak. This was impossible unless they got her keel out, a work of time. "I sent them some salt beef and the next morning went on board with an officer and 50 Indians and a Bower anchor and Cable with me to get her up in the Harbour which we were some time about. But plenty of men made light work and I warped her abaft of the *Lydia* and there moored her; I then returned with the anchor and cable to my ship again."

On 10th January, Haswell records ,"eight of the English ship's men took a Boat and went to Town to the Governor to Enquire how much he would give them to carry the Ship to Manila but he ordered them to be put into Irons for Mutiny".

While the crew unloaded cargo, Haswell wrote: "I used to take my gun ashore with two or three Indians and wander into the woods, but in all my stay I only shot one small Deer, with small Hogs and a few Birds among which was a large Bat near three feet from tip of wing to wing." The woods were thick with undergrowth except for villages carved from the scrub, in which "we always found the Indians hard at work with the Tobacco which all belongs to the King. As soon as it is dried it must be carried to the Governor, and he sells it at an enormous price as is everything. Even the Cattle they have is the King's."

Haswell found the huts of the Indians small and clean, made of basket-work and thatched with coconut leaves. "They are about twelve feet from the ground. Their furniture consists of two or three hammocks of Network and the same number of Mats, a Chest and one frying pan and a Large Copper Pan and a few earthen jars. . . . Their food is chiefly shell fish and Plantains, coconuts, and a kind of sweet potatoes which they fry and make flour of, and it makes good bread when new. I also found some Bullock's Hide in a wooden trough tanning. They wear sandals like the ancients."

The *Lydia* was "plentifully supplied with fresh provisions, such as Beef, Pork, and Fowls, all at the King's Expense; and in the greatest Plenty. We gave three-quarters of it to the English ship who had nothing allowed them but jerked Beef and Rice. As our crew was small and a great deal of duty a-going on I often got assistance from them and with this supply of men, the work went on, and I kept the Long boat constantly Employed bringing wood and water on board. Four men worked on shore cutting wood, and some hands repaired the rigging, painting ship, and getting ready for sea."

About this time the officers of the *Lydia* made a survey of the English ship and found her not fit to perform a passage to Manila, as the seams were open and required caulking. "I was sent to town with our Report. The Governor hinted it was impossible to get what was required but yet wished to send the ship to Manila. The poor owners hung their heads in expectation of the condemning of the Ship."

The *Lydia* was now "loaded with oxen, hogs, fowls, pigeons, two live deer and a boat load of yams, potatoes, water melons, oranges, limes, coconuts, etc. All the English gentlemen and some of the Spaniards came to the waterside to see us embark. I then went with Captain Barnard and bid the kind Governor farewell, and found scarcely a dry eye in the house."

All aboard as "the *Lydia* left the harbour of De Caldera with a fine Breeze Nor-east, and as soon as we were at sea a man belonging to the English ship that had secreted himself on board came on deck. We had also on board an Otaheite Indian that was under the care of Captain Barnard as his servant." Haswell now launches into a description of the isle of Guam, the forts, the people (11,000, of whom only 12 were white) but fails to state the date of their departure.

"We had a pleasant passage to Manila of 18 days and in about two months the former Governor, Don Manuel, arrived in a Galleon and brought with him Mr and Mrs Boston, the owner of the English Ship that we left at Guam, and part of her crew. From Mr Boston I heard that the ship was condemned as not seaworthy and that the remainder of the crew were building a small schooner to carry them to Macao out of the materials of the ship. They are assisting the Indians to build three Mills. There was none on the Island at the time of our being there; one is to be a Saw Mill, and another a Corn Mill, and the third a Sugar Mill, the cultivation of which the Governor is going to encourage."

Haswell's journal ends with a list of latitudes and longitudes of points of interest between Manila and Guam. No further mention of the "English ship", which was *El Plumier*, owned by the Reverend Thomas Palmer, John Boston, James Ellis, and Captain William Reid.

What about the Reverend George Harris's story that an American captain removed Palmer's remains from Guam to Boston and gave him burial there? Who was the captain, if he existed? My friend John Earnshaw has a clue. Twenty years ago, when researching into the life of Thomas Muir after his escape from Sydney Cove in 1796, John read somewhere a statement that Captain Balch of Boston disinterred the remains of Palmer and took them to Boston.

At that time John was not interested in the travels of Palmer, and neglected to make a record of this statement. But with the name Balch as a guide, I fossicked through the pages of the *Sydney Gazette* and came across the following item in the issue dated 29th January 1804: "On Tuesday came the ship *Mary*, Captain Balch, to and from Boston, bound for Manila." The *Mary* was lying in Botany Bay, with a cargo of goods for sale, and permission was granted by the Governor to sell rum, gin and brandy. Her arrival is confirmed by the *Historical Records of New South Wales*: "Arrived, 24th January 1804, Samuel Balch, ship *Mary*, 211 tons, 4 guns, 14 men, from Boston." The ship's departure is recorded in the *Sydney Gazette*, 19th February 1804. "On Sunday last, sailed the American ship *Mary*, Captain Balch, for Boston. The evening before she sailed a strict search was made of the vessel and six persons who had concealed themselves secured. They were sent on shore and lodged in custody of the Gaoler."

John Earnshaw told me that, in an endeavour to solve the problem of Palmer's burial, he had written to the trustees of the Boston Cemetery. But because Palmer had not died in Boston, his name was not listed in the Burials Register.

Question: Was Samuel Balch of the ship *May* the American captain who had removed Palmer's remains from a nameless grave in Guam, and gave them Christian burial in Boston?

Wherever his bones rest, Thomas Fyshe Palmer was a crusader, who died a martyr to the cause of reform and universal suffrage. His inspiration steeled others to fight on, and his cause triumphed in the end.

Before proceeding with the story of John Boston, we return to London where John Harris, a survivor of *El Plumier* in Guam, was begging aid from the Government. In November 1803 Harris submitted a memorial to Lord Hobart, Secretary of State, saying that in the year 1787 he was transported from England to Port Jackson. Two years later he was sent to Norfolk Island, where he was employed by Lieutenant-Governor King "as an officer of the police". King was in charge of Norfolk Island from 1788 to 1796, except when carrying dispatches to England.

His Lordship's Memorialist stated that he "discharged the duties of that office with zeal and fidelity for eight years, and that he then received an absolute and conditional emancipation, bearing date the 13th of September, 1796".

To check the above statements by John Harris, I got the expert staff of the Archives in the Public Library on the job. They found that John Harris was convicted at Middlesex County Quarter Sessions on 23rd February 1783 and sentenced to transportation for life, for "feloniously stealing on 30th December 1782, eight silver table spoons, value 3s. 1d., the goods of Peter Livies".

Harris, with two hundred and eight other convicts, arrived on the ship *Scarborough* with the First Fleet in January 1788. In 1789 Harris was sent to Norfolk Island, and served as "Principal of the night-watch".

On 6th November 1794 Lieutenant P. G. King wrote to Lieutenant-Governor Grose requesting a free pardon for Harris. After a further request on 14th July 1795, Captain David Collins, Judge-Advocate, informed King that Grose, previous to his departure, had "emancipated Harris absolutely".

Captain Collins, who appears to have had a soft spot for Harris, noted in his *Account of the English Colony in New South Wales*, that "a convict of the name of Harris presented to the Judge-Advocate a proposal for establishing a night-watch, to be selected from among the convicts with authority to secure all persons of that description who should be found straggling from the huts at improper hours". Governor Phillip approved of the proposal, and the first attempt towards a police force in the settlement commenced on 8th August 1789.

Good on John Harris, our first policeman!

In his memorial to Lord Hobart, Harris stated that he returned to Port Jackson from Norfolk Island and became a licensed victualler for five years, until September 1800, when Captain King arrived as Governor of the Colony, replacing Captain Hunter. Soon after King's arrival he sent for Harris and told him he should be employed at the head of the police, but "your Lordship's Memorialist, having a large family to support, was unwilling to abandon a trade, the profits of which afforded him and his children a decent subsistence, and humbly requested that he might be exused from accepting the office".

Enraged, the Governor ordered Harris into custody, charging him with "purchasing the rations of the convicts for spirituous liquors". Harris protested his innocence, and demanded a fair trial. Instead, he claimed, the Governor "directed that one end of his house be torn down; that all the spirits belonging to your Memorialist were then brought into the streets, where every cask was staved and every bottle emptied; that the value of what was then destroyed was more at prime cost than £400, and comprised the whole of the hard-earned reward of many years care and industry".

After release from prison, his wine and spirit licence was revoked. "Dreading worse persecutions, your Memorialist fled in terror from the colony, taking with him his eldest child, and leaving two young ones behind, That your Memorialist has since been shipwrecked and made a prisoner at the Spanish island of Guam from whence he reached this country only a few days ago, in great penury and distress."

The *Historical Records of New South Wales* carry Governor King's version of this cask-staving episode in a Government and General Order dated 31st December 1800. The irascible Governor stated: "John Harris, a licensed victualler . . . having given spirits to two convicts for their week's rations of salt meat from the public stores, is deprived of his licence, and the Government has directed all his liquors to be staved."

Governor King then gives a reason for his drastic action: "This transaction has long been carried on, in direct disobedience to every regulation, not only by the above delinquent, but also by several other persons. If the convicts, who have no means of maintenance but by the ration they receive from the store, are invited to part with it for a taste of spirits, they must consequently rob those who are nearest to them for support during the remainder of the week, which leads to a train of other evils that must be put a stop to."

A footnote to the above says that "the records contain no information as to the fate of this petition".

Thanks to diligent research by Dr George F. Bergman, the records of Harris during his stay in Sydney are pretty well covered. Dr Bergman, in an article, "John Harris, The First Australian Policeman", published in the *Journal of the Australian Jewish Historical Society* (vol. v), verified the story of the wreckage of Harris's inn by Governor King's orders and the ruin of his business. The informant who caused the trouble was the Reverend Samuel Marsden, who reported: "John Harris being sent for, admits that he purchased from two men, two pounds of pork from each." It was also stated in a police report that Harris had sent a cask of spirits to a convict. I gather that because of Governor King's attitude to him, Harris had decided to join the *Plumier* expedition.

I have only been able to trace one more survivor from the wreck of *El Plumier*. That was John Boston. John got a passage to Manila in a Spanish vessel, where he began a brewery, as stated earlier in this chapter.

Next news of John Boston was told in the *Sydney Gazette* of 28th October 1804. "On Tuesday (23rd) arrived the *Union*, which left this port for China the 29th August; came last from Tongataboo, one of the Friendly Islands, which she left on the 5th October." This news is followed by the depositions of witnesses sworn before Captain George Johnston and Surgeon John Harris. First witness was Elizabeth Morey, who said that she left the Cape of Good Hope with Mr Lovat Mellon, Captain of the American ship *Duke of Portland*, bound to Lima; that about 1st June 1802 the ship touched at an island on the Pacific Ocean called Tongataboo.

Captain Mellon, who seems to have been something of a pirate, had sailed from Manila about the end of April 1800 in a brig belonging to John Stewart Kerr, American Consul at Manila, according to the *Sydney Gazette* of 4th November 1804. His instructions were to dispose of the cargo, and purchase commodities adapted to the Manila market; but at Batavia he sold his cargo and the brig as well, and purchased the *Duke of Portland*. He had also used Mr Kerr's letter of credit for twenty thousand dollars, and had taken on a cargo of rice for a Dutch company, selling it at Mauritius and vanishing with the profits. He next turned up at the Cape of Good Hope, where he collected Elizabeth Morey, and sailed to Tongataboo.

According to Elizabeth Morey's evidence before the Court in Sydney, a white man named Doyle, lone survivor from a wreck, who was living with the natives on Tongataboo, persuaded Captain Mellon to send a ship's boat manned with sailors to help the native chief repel invaders from another island. This was done, and later Chief Ducava came on board to thank the Captain and stayed the night. At his invitation, a number of the crew went ashore for refreshments. Doyle then came aboard with natives and treacherously surrounded "the Captain, Chief Mate and sailors on board, seven in number, and killed them all except two boys, this deponent (Elizabeth Morey) and a black woman, her servant; and threw the bodies overboard".

Elizabeth Morey, seeing the massacre, tried to jump into the sea, but was prevented by Doyle. "Don't be frightened," he told her, "You won't get hurt." Elizabeth was taken ashore and given to the Chief's wife, where she "learned from the white boys, five in number, that all the ship's company that were on shore had been killed except themselves".

Elizabeth also deposed that Doyle ordered the five white boys to come on board the *Duke of Portland* to help in landing her cargo. After this was done, "the five whites drove the natives overboard, killing Doyle, cutting the cables and sailing away". I have found no record of the white boys' fate.

Commented the editor of the *Sydney Gazette*: "Doyle is supposed to be a survivor of the brig's crew that was wrecked about three or four years ago, whose people were murdered by the natives. The brig had sailed from Canton for Sydney, and belonged to Mr Berry at Canton. Another of the survivors had the good fortune to be brought away by Captain Read in the ship *Plomer* after a residence among the savages of two and twenty months."

Readers will recall that *El Plumier*, according to Captain Wilson's letter, had called at Tongataboo after leaving New Zealand, while Haswell's account mentions their attempt to get provisions at the Friendly Islands.

Back to the Court of Inquiry in Sydney, where the next witness was Daniel Wright, chief mate of the ship *Union* of New York. Being sworn, he stated that on 29th August 1804 he sailed the said ship from the harbour of Port Jackson, under the command of Captain Pendleton, having taken on board Mr John Boston, supercargo. Apparently Boston had returned to Sydney. "They touched at Norfolk Island, thence proceeded to Tongataboo, where they arrived about the 30th of September. As they came to anchor a number of canoes visited them, but left at sunset." Next morning the natives came in great numbers, "among whom was a Malay who spoke broken English, who told them that they could get plenty of wood, water and refreshments. He was very urgent for the ship's boats to be sent on shore; one of the boats was hoisted out, mann'd with six men, four muskets, and two cutlasses, in which boat Captain Pendleton and Mr John Boston went."

Afterwards the natives became troublesome, so the deponent, Daniel Wright, "stationed his men around the ship to prevent them coming on board. But they succeeded in getting up, contrary to his wish, to the number of thirty. The deponent observed that the natives had passed up a number of clubs, and from his observations he had no doubt but they meant to take the ship." Wright said "the chief urged him to let more men come on board, which he refused. After some refreshment the chief and his men went ashore. The deponent then hoisted the ship's colours, and fired a gun, to put those on shore (Captain Pendleton, John Boston and the six crew men) upon guard. Soon after, taking up the spy glass and looking towards the shore, he perceived the ship's boat lying broadside on, in the hands of the natives."

That night Daniel Wright kept an armed guard patrolling the *Union*, expecting an attack, but all was quiet. Next morning two canoes came within hail, but refused to come close. The crew, suspecting the worst, wanted Wright to fire on them in revenge. Another day and night passed, "when several canoes came within hail; in one of them was the Malay, who asked Wright to come on shore, for that the Captain and Boston wished him". Wright tried to get the Malay alongside, but he was cunning, and returned to shore.

A few hours later Wright observed the Malay approaching in a canoe, accompanied by others. "A European woman in another canoe spoke to Wright in English, inviting him on shore; but by signs from her when unnoticed by the natives, forbade them to comply with the request." Finding that the white men would not come ashore, the natives departed.

"On the third day after Captain Pendleton and John Boston had gone ashore, several canoes came off, in one of which was the white woman and the Malay, repeating the request to come ashore."

Wright, without effect, tried to get the Malay alongside by offering presents for the chief. "Then the white woman stood up in the canoe, cried out that those on shore were murdered, and leaping into the water swam towards the ship. The men on board presenting their muskets, thereby deterred the natives from picking her up, by which means she reached the vessel and was taken on board. She then told Daniel Wright that the Captain and crew had been murdered, upon which information Wright ordered the natives to be fired upon, and saw two fall; that he directed the cables to be cut, and putting to sea, shaped his course for Port Jackson, where he arrived in nineteen days without incident." Wright also stated that when getting under way and sheeting home his top-gallant sails he heard two muskets fired on shore.

The gallant white woman who had risked her life by warning the crew of the *Union*, Elizabeth Morey, again gave evidence.

Elizabeth stated that she was living on the opposite side of the island, when a native arrived "for the purpose of bringing Charley the Malay to go on board the ship. Three days later she was ordered by the Chief, to converse with one of the white boys who had come ashore, from whom she learnt the ship's name, *Union*. She later found that all the whites on shore had been murdered. She was then taken out to the *Union* and told to inform the whites that they were wanted ashore. At the same time she tried to warn them that all was not well."

Next day she was ordered to accompany four canoes, in one of which was Charley the Malay, and to repeat the message. Nearing the ship, she leapt into the water, shouting a warning to the whites and, furiously swimming, was taken on board the *Union*, safe from the foiled savages.

After reporting the massacre, as told before the court, the *Sydney Gazette* printed "A short Description of the Customs of Tongataboo, Collected from

157

a Person Three Years Resident among them". This unnamed person (presumably Elizabeth Morey) describes the islanders as "having a plurality of wives, as the number of females exceeds that of the opposite sex in a two-fold proportion, owing to an unrelaxed depopulation consequent on destructive usages and perpetual warfare; upon their prisoners of war they exercise very inhuman torture, and afterwards greedily solace upon the wretched victim; and frequently even boasted that those of the *Portland*'s unfortunate crew whom they treacherously inveigled and murdered on their shore served to assuage their inordinate and cursed appetites."

Their war weapons consist of the bow, arrow, spear and club. Canoes were numerous and war boats large and commodious. One of these "was launched during the *Union*'s stay, and was reported capable of containing 300 men. The black woman mentioned in Mrs Morey's deposition to have escaped the massacre with herself, was afterwards carried off by the natives of Anomoie."

The *Union* sailed from Sydney on 12th November 1804. Last news of her is told in the *Sydney Gazette* of 28th April 1805, when reporting the arrival of the *Marcia* (Captain Aikin) from the northward. "It was generally reported, that the American ship *Union*, formerly commanded by Captain Pendleton whose fate it was, in company with Mr Boston, to fall a sacrifice to the treachery of the natives at Tongataboo, has since been lost on the islands."

So ended John Boston, who left England on the *Surprize* in 1793 with the Reverend Mr Palmer and his fellow-prisoners. Boston stuck to Palmer through thick and thin, and his name will for ever be linked with the Scottish Martyrs. Another claim to fame is that he is said to have been the first man to brew beer in Sydney.

The end of James Ellis is obscure, but it is briefly mentioned in *Dundee Celebrities*, published at Dundee in 1873. "It may be remarked that Palmer and Ellis during the period they were together amassed a considerable sum of money. Ellis was appointed Palmer's executor, but dying soon after, the relatives of Ellis — three sisters who resided in Dundee — succeeded to the money, and with it bought a property behind the seminaries in the Chapelshade."

CHAPTER TWENTY

General Joseph Holt Arrives — Holt Meets Margarot — "Most Seditious House in the Colony" — Governor King Arrives — Margarot Writes to Him — Mrs Margarot Meets the Governor — Margarot Infuriates the Governor — George Mealmaker Arrives — Petitions Governor King — Arrested for Plotting — Freed — Appointed Weaver, Parramatta Factory — Welcomes Bligh — Dies at Parramatta — Inquiry by his Widow — Liverpool Writes to Macquarie — Isaac Nichols Reports — No Record of Mealmaker's Birth — Record of Marriage — Margarot, Mischief-maker — Irishitis — Margarot's Journals — G. W. Rusden — "Curiosities of Colonization" — Monument to the Martyrs — R. L. Stevenson's Poem to S. R. Crockett — Did it Refer to Covenanters or Political Martyrs?

DURING Palmer's last year in the Colony Margarot, the only other member of the original group of Martyrs left, had managed to embroil himself in fresh trouble.

On 11th January 1800 the transport *Minerva* from Cork sailed into Sydney with a cargo of convicts who had been sentenced to transportation for terms ranging from seven years to twenty-one years. Most of these were political prisoners, survivors of the Rising of 1798.

One of the new-comers was the self-styled General, Joseph Holt, who had valiantly led a band of insurgents against the British for many months, and later was tricked into surrendering, after a false promise of freedom. Many years later, after his return to Ireland, his friend T. Crofton Croker edited the *Memoirs of General Joseph Holt*, based on a journal kept by the fighting Irishman. Here is an extract: "I had received an invitation from Mr Maurice Margarot to go to his house when I should land. He received me with kindness and hospitality, shaking me by the hand; he was a man of great conversational powers, and of literary acquirements, being well educated. His wife was of the same rank and character, a lady of elegant manner. They were both of hasty tempers, and very irritable. He told me his history briefly, and why he was sent away from his own country. For lunch we ate an animal somewhat like a rabbit, called a bandy-coot, which I found of good flavour. We ate some beautiful peaches and nectarines."

General Holt stayed overnight with Mr Margarot, and the Irish Exile and the Scottish Martyr "had an enjoyable evening over the rum punch, chatting over our adventures". The next morning General Holt received directions to attend a muster of the ship's company, and the following dialogue took place:

"Captain Johnson asked me if I knew where I had lodged last night?

" 'Not very well,' I replied, 'as it was the first I had passed in the Colony.

All I knew was that Mr Margarot received me kindly and hospitably, and I was much obliged to him.'

" 'Well, sir,' said Captain Johnston, "you lodged in the most seditious house in the Colony.'

" 'Indeed!' said I, 'I heard no sedition there. Mr Margarot appears to me a gentleman of great learning and polished manners, one whose society I should covet much, as I felt I should receive information and instruction from him. I hope, sir, you do not wish me to associate with thieves and robbers! I am not disposed to meet such characters, except at arm's length.' We were then dismissed."

General Holt became a successful farmer, working for Captain William Cox, also managing his own farm, until in 1812 the British Government allowed him to return to the land of his birth, where he died in May 1826.

On 15th April 1800 Philip Gidley King, Governor designate, arrived in the transport *Speedy* from England, with instructions to await the departure of Governor Hunter, which took place on 28th September 1800.

King had been in the country only a few weeks when he received a letter from Margarot, dated 13th May 1800, saying, "Hazardous as is this step, my duty to society urges me to take it, and to confide in your discretion; otherways delicacy towards Governor Hunter, whose most sincere well-wisher I am, would prevent my paying my respects to his successor until his departure, when, by the introduction of Mr Commissary Palmer, I could do so more conformably to rules and forms. As I am much confined by sickness, unless you are possessed of any private orders of Ministry relating to me, and require my attendance to impart them, there is little chance of my having the good fortune to converse with you. Yet, if you feel yourself inclined to give birth to any *accident* which may occasion to enter my habitation, you shall find that an hour will not be spent unprofitably, and that I can throw light on several of the transactions of this Colony which may not perhaps have reached you in the shape they will then assume. I, moreover, will then submit to your perusal several papers, the contents of which it is important you should be early acquainted with."

Of course, the Governor-in-expectancy did not answer this offer to supply incriminating papers. He ignored Margarot and naturally became a target for his barbed penmanship.

On 1st October 1800 Margarot wrote to Under-secretary John King in London — no relation of Governor King — saying: "Long before the arrival of Governor King, the officers who had the most abused Governor Hunter's facility and faith, and who consequently had the most plundered the nation and the colony, to save their own necks, had laid heavy charges against their upholder, had entered into a conspiracy to effect his disgrace and ruin, and on Governor King's arrival contrived to win him over to their side."

Margarot now admits that he had been acting as a spy and informer, when he wrote: "Having kept an account of all or most of the colonial abuses, having ever set my face against the perpetrator of them, and having given Ministry and others at home constant intelligence of the Colonial malpractices, I thought as Governor King had been sent out purposely to detect and check those abuses, I say I thought he was misled, and that unwittingly, I imagined

George Mealmaker

Governor King

Maurice Margarot

I could serve my country no better than by offering him the perusal of my notes and other papers, together with such explanations as might be requisite, little suspecting Government had pitched upon a Governor ready to take umbrage at any persons knowing anything so well after six years' residence as he himself could at first landing."

Margarot then added that he was tipped off by a friend that because of his letter to Governor King of 13th May "much michief was intended" to him. Soon after Governor King called a General Muster of men and women, including Mrs Margarot. "No man of but even decent education and behaviour," Margarot continued, "could have expected her to attend his levee of female prostitutes and thieves."

Mrs Margarot, however, had to attend, and, according to her husband, the following dialogue took place:

"*G. King* — Who are you (in surly tone)?

"*Answer* — Mrs Margarot.

"*G. King* — Oh very well; go along, go along, go along; get out."

The next day Margarot attended. When the Acting-Commissary told the Governor his name, King said, according to Margarot: "Mr Margarot, I would advise you to be quiet, very quiet, and deserve the indulgence Governor Hunter has shown you; be very cautious not to give us any suspicions."

Margarot said that he hoped his behaviour had not given rise to any suspicion.

"No, sir, no, to be sure, we have not found you out yet, but take care, sir. Mind you do not give any reason for complaint; sir, go along."

"Sir, I know my duty," Margarot replied, "and you may depend upon my fulfilling it."

"Now for that insolence, sir, get out of my house. Commissary, strike him off the store, and send his man to the camp-gang." Then the Governor, "uprising from his chair in a maniacal rage", shouted at the retreating Margarot, "Get along out of the house! What do you mean by insulting me thus? . . . None of your wry faces. I'll take your house from you and send you to Toongabbie with an hoe in your hand."

After describing this stormy scene, Margarot ended his letter to Under-Secretary John King in London with a statement that under Governor King's maladministration the hitherto flourishing colony would have ruin staring it in the face.

We leave Margarot awhile and welcome George Mealmaker from Dundee, who, as we have seen, arrived at Port Jackson aboard the *Royal Admiral* on 21st November 1800. News of him is scarce. The first that I can trace is a petition dated 31st March 1802 by Mealmaker to Governor King. The petitioner claimed that he "was taken out of bed on the night of the 26th, and carried to the guard-house, Parramatta, from which brought down to Sydney jail, where he now is, on a charge of being concerned in some plot against the state; what the plot is or who is the maker of it he knows not, or whether there is one at all; though sent to this country as convicted of sedition, he ever would have spurned with indignation the man who would mention a plot or Rebellious movement to him; that your petitioner hath never been actuated by any principles but the love of his country and of mankind in General; if he hath been mistaken his Mistake hath been that of many Good and Great both in this and the last age."

Mealmaker added "that he was aggrieved by his present situation, as he never hath Given any cause in word, write, or act to bring his name in Question, but hath lived in the retiredest manner possible, having no correspondence nor no connection with nobody but as your Business led him. . . . That if the life, liberty, and happiness of your petitioner may be taken or destroyed by the villainy or perfidy of any one, then is your petitioner Miserable indeed, for never can he Give less occasion than at present he hath done. . . . May it therefore please your Excellency to take the above into your consideration, and Grant that Justice which his extraordinary case requires, and your petitioner will ever pray."

Mealmaker had been arrested on suspicion of being connected with the Irishmen of Castle Hill, who were accused of fomenting rebellion. But he was soon freed and, since he was a weaver by trade and could be of use to the community, we find in the *Sydney Gazette* of 19th June 1803 that "George Mealmaker was given a Conditional Emancipation". Many other convicts were also freed, including Dr William Redfern, who received a free pardon.

A few months later, on 31st August, an agreement was drawn up between Governor King and Mealmaker, who is described as "Emancipated Woollen and Linen Manufacturer now resident at Parramatta". By this agreement, which is preserved in the *Historical Records of Australia*, Mealmaker was appointed "Superintending Grower, Manufacturer, and Weaver of the Flax now growing and as much as he can grow with proper assistance from Government". He was also to "manufacture all the wool that can be obtained", and was to be given a house and garden, clothing, rations, and the labour of a convict for domestic purposes, as well as a salary of £50 a year. In addition, he was to be granted a free pardon if he gave satisfaction in his new position. The *Historical Records of New South Wales* lists, at 30th April 1805, numerous Government servants, including "George Mealmaker, Superintendent, conducts the manufactory of Linen and Woollens at Parramatta".

On 29th June 1806 the *Sydney Gazette* noted: "George Mealmaker applies for position of overseer." Since he had been appointed Superintendent for four years, the two positions would presumably have been held concurrently. On 12th August 1806 Governor King reported that: "George Mealmaker, Superintendent, etc., superintends the manufactories of linen and wool at Parramatta, and has charge of the convicts (male and female) employed on that object, under the inspection of the Governor and Magistrate in command at Parramatta to whom he reports progress, the quantity linen and woollen which is delivered into the stores, and either issued to those at public labour or disposed of in barter for grain or animal food."

Under Mealmaker's supervision, the number of looms and the variety of manufactures increased, but in 1807, just before Christmas, the factory was destroyed by fire. On 1st January 1808 George Mealmaker was one of 850 signatories in an Address to Governor William Bligh, soon to be deposed, on 26th January 1808, by Major George Johnston of the New South Wales Corps. But he took little further part in the affairs of the Colony. The next news of him is on 1st April 1808, when "George Mealmaker, age 40, was buried at

Parramatta". His death was registered at St. John's Church of England there.

Back in Scotland, his worried wife saw a minister of the Kirk, James Thomas, who, on 27th March 1810 wrote on her behalf to Lord Liverpool, Secretary of State for the Colonies. He stated that Mrs Mealmaker was anxious about her husband, who had not written to her for five years. As it was rumoured that he was drowned, she would like His Lordship to advise her if this rumour was true.

Lord Liverpool wrote to Lachlan Macquarie, who had been Governor of New South Wales since 1st January 1811, for information. The worst fears of the widow were confirmed in a letter written on 15th October 1811 by Isaac Nichols, newly appointed Postmaster of New South Wales, who replied to an inquiry from the Governor as follows: "Sir, In obedience to your Excellency's command I beg leave to inform you as far as comes within my knowledge respecting how and what time George Mealmaker a native of Scotland who was transported some years since came by his death. The above-named George Mealmaker died at Parramatta in March 1808. Supposed to have been suffocated by drinking spirits; at the time of his death he possessed no property not even as much as defrayed his Funeral expenses."

When I visited Edinburgh in May 1967 I made a search in the Registrar's office for the birth of George Mealmaker, without luck. Then I put my Scottish pal Dougal McCallum Hay on the job. Dougal wrote to the Chief Librarian in Dundee, where Mealmaker was reared, married, and arrested, and the Librarian replied: "I regret that a search of our records has been fruitless in tracing the date and place of birth of George Mealmaker. A biography of him in published form does not appear to be available, but we do know that his widow died in Dundee on the 13th November 1843."

But Dougal McCallum Hay was undaunted. After my return to Sydney, I received a letter from him enclosing an extract of an entry in a Register kept at the General Register Office, Edinburgh. The extract stated that "George Meal-maker, Weaver, and Marjory Thoms, Daughter of John Thoms, both in the parish of Dundee, in the county of Forfar, were married on 23rd November 1795".

Thanks, Dougal, for your tenacity. Here's hoping that some historians will locate the date and place of his birth.

We return to Maurice Margarot, martyr and mischief-maker, who had been stirring the Irish stew, the result being an attack of "Irishitis" by Governor King.

As a result, the irate Governor wrote to Under-Secretary King in London on 14th August 1804: "Our Irish insurgents are now quiet, perhaps only for a short time, as they do not want very active but concealed Councillors in Muir, Margarot, Henry Browne Hayes, and often other Incendiaries. From some very good information I received since the Insurrection, I caused Margarot's house to be searched for seditious papers, which brought to light some very elegant Republican Sentiments, and general infamous abuse of every person in the Colony from the period he landed. . . . And what is a convincing proof of his villainy is his abuse of the very people who have supported him. By some of his papers I find he carries on a correspondence with Hardy and some other violent Republicans."

The Governor's reference to Muir must have been a slip of the pen, since Muir had long since left the Colony.

Seeking to find the seditious papers and letters the Governor seized from the home of Margarot, I sought in the Mitchell Library, treasure house of Australiana, but no luck. Chance prompted me to write to my old pal Jack Feely, Chief Librarian in the State Library at Melbourne. He replied: "The papers of Maurice Margarot were seized by Governor King in 1804, and are believed to have remained in the King family until 1870. About that time G. W. Rusden had access to them and used them in his *Curiosites of Colonization*. The present location of the papers is unknown, but extracts from them are among the Rusden Papers in the Library of Trinity College, University of Melbourne."

Next job was to write to Trinity College. In reply, the Warden, R. W. T. Cowan, informed me that the Rusden Papers included some thirty pages of notes and extracts from Margarot's diaries, beginning in 1801 and ending in 1804, with one year missing. Mr Cowan generously sent me these pages, which appear to have been scribbled on in the margin by someone else, probably Rusden, in scorn for what Margarot had written. A typical comment reads: "Macaulay would not take part in the glorification of these fellows, three of whom were crazy enthusiasts, and two of whom were specially bad."

George William Rusden was born in 1819, the son of a clergyman living in Surrey, England. Thirty years later, in 1849, the Rusden family migrated to New South Wales where the Reverend Mr Rusden had been appointed chaplain at Maitland. George became a jackeroo, then a civil servant, and finally an author. In 1874 Rusden wrote *Curiosities of Colonization*, in which he made many references to Maurice Margarot. Early in the book Rusden states: "Chance has thrown my way a number of original MS. journals kept by Margarot, which makes it a curiosity of colonization that such a man should ever have been worshipped, and honoured with a share in a monument in Scotland."

After reading this statement I wrote to my friend Dougal McCallum Hay in Edinburgh for information about the monument. From Dougal by return came a photograph of an obelisk ninety feet high in the Old Calton Burying Ground in Waterloo Place, in the heart of Edinburgh. It is inscribed as follows: "To the memory of Thomas Muir, Thomas Fyshe Palmer, William Skirving, Maurice Margarot, and Joseph Gerrald. Erected by the Friends of Parliamentary Reform in England and Scotland. 1844."

On the other side is inscribed: "I have devoted myself to the cause of the people. It is a good cause — it shall ultimately prevail — it shall finally triumph. Speech of Thomas Muir in the Court of Justiciary on 30th August 1793."

An article in the *Scotsman* of 1st October 1845 states: "Last Friday the monument erected in the Old Calton Churchyard to perpetuate the memory of Muir, Palmer, Gerrald, Skirving and Margarot, the Political Martyrs of 1793-95, was completed. A flag was hoisted in honour of the event, and several gentlemen ascended the structure to witness the laying of the Cope Stone. The monument, which is 90 feet high was designed by Mr Hamilton,

164

architect, after the model of Cleopatra's Needle in London."

A Scottish friend of mine, interested in my researches, has suggested that the "martyrs" mentioned in Robert Louis Stevenson's poem, "To S. R. Crockett", might be the political martyrs. These are the words of R.L.S., written in his island home at Vailima, Samoa:

> *Blows the wind to-day, and the sun and the rain are flying,*
> *Blows the wind on the moors to-day and now,*
> *Where about the graves of the martyrs the whaups are crying,*
> *My heart remembers how!*

But another Scot in Sydney, Andrew Hope, of McCallum's Whisky fame, says the reference is to the religious martyrs of the seventeenth century, the Covenanters. To prove this point he quotes the second verse:

> *Grey recumbent tombs of the dead in desert places,*
> *Standing stones on the vacant wine-red moor,*
> *Hills of sheep, and the homes of the silent vanished races,*
> *And winds, austere and pure:*

The description is obviously of the Scottish countryside, but the graves of the political martyrs are scattered about the world, none of them being in Scotland, and their memorial is in a crowded city. Another thing that makes the reference to religious martyrs more likely is that Samuel Rutherford Crockett, to whom Stevenson dedicated this poem, wrote about them in his novels. Rutherford was a minister of the Free Church of Scotland, but resigned his charge to devote all his time to novel-writing. He dedicated one of his novels to R.L.S., who reciprocated with this poem, full of longing for the homeland that both writers shared.

CHAPTER TWENTY-ONE

Now THAT we've solved the location of the remains of Margarot's missing diaries, I propose to print a few extracts from them. Some were written in French, evidently to baffle Captain King, an old sea-dog who presumably could not read that language. My secretary, Mrs Chiquita Cullip, has translated some of Margarot's remarks, as follows:

1st March 1801. "Mr Barnes dined with us and reported a conversation he heard in church. This gives us reason to believe that the Revolution has succeeded in England."

This was obviously wishful thinking by the republican Margarot.

9th May. "Short rations commence."

19th May. "John Palmer, Commissariat Office, sent me seven pounds of butter and four and a half gallons of rum; Smith sent to ask me for a B of rum!!!"

23rd May. "Governor King strikes my wife from the ration!!"

27th May. "The ship *Greenwich* enters port. Brings news that the Russians have exterminated the British Navy."

4th June. "Great rejoicings. Union with Ireland proclaimed."

24th July. "Today I complete my 51st year. Protected by the Deity what have I to fear for the future? Nothing, but all to hope for."

If Margarot completed his fifty-first year on 24th July 1801, he must have been born in 1750, which means that when he died in November 1815 he was sixty-five years of age, not sixty-seven years as stated on his death certificate.

8th November. "Barnes told me some news in confidence about England. It appears that an attempt is being made to expunge all traces of the old tyranny."

14th November. "We have been sent rotten meat. I am keeping it and will make the scoundrel who is cheating the prisoners eat it."

31st December. "This ends the year 1801. Divine protection is too powerful for me to fear anything. On the contrary Providence appears to have destined me for an unusual part and guides me over all obstacles."

26th March 1802. "Great alarm tonight. Governor King ready to flee."

27th March. "Several prisoners came from Parramatta. The great alarm was caused by Irish prisoners in revolt."

1st May. "The play commences. The atrocities practised in Ireland started here today. All the Irish rounded up, imprisoned, etc."

4th May. "Madame Rose passed, and poor Jenny. All the Irish are being put in chains."

10th May. "Smith brought me a letter from Paine."

This would be Thomas Paine, whose works played a part in causing many of the troubles told of in this book.

19th July. "Sent a permit for the Governor to sign. He tore it up without saying a word."

This was a request to house twenty gallons of rum, which Governor King refused.

Mr Rusden states that Margarot's diary for 1803 had disappeared, and there are no more entries until the new diary began in January 1804.

21st January 1804. "The natives having reported a ship in Botany Bay, our warriors took alarm. The Governor mounted horses with some officers. The troops took up arms; the ladies wailed and fainted."

22nd January. "A ship has entered — reports that all men are mobilized in England."

23rd January. "Sir Henry Hayes passed three times to tell me about the massacre of the first judge of Ireland and others."

31st January. "St Leger escaped in the American *The Rose*, which set sail today with the *Ferret*. I count on having good news today."

4th March. "At midnight the cannons were fired, general alarm sounded, and Governor King raced to Parramatta with one hundred soldiers against the insurgent Irishmen."

5th March. "Martial law proclaimed."

10th March. "Governor King returns from Parramatta. Two Irishmen were hanged at Sydney, and I suppose that this finished the tragedy."

28th March. "The *Lady Nelson* and the *Resource*, with the unfortunates aboard, set sail for the Coal River."

These "unforunates" were the survivors of the Irish insurgents who rose in rebellion on 4th March 1804 at Castle Hill, eight miles beyond Parramatta and about twenty miles west of Sydney, and fought a battle with soldiers and settlers the next day. Twelve rebels were killed, six were wounded, and twenty-six were taken prisoner. After a hasty court martial, ten men were sentenced to death and three hanged at Parramatta soon after. Three more were executed at Castle Hill, and two at Sydney. Two men, Burke and McCormick, were "respited during the Governor's pleasure." Others were severely flogged.

Back to Margarot's diary.

29th March. "An American ship, the *Union*, has received orders to leave port for not having dipped her flag to the *Lady Nelson*."

In 1670, when Samuel Pepys ran the Royal Navy, it was the custom to fire a shot at a merchant ship which failed to lower her top-gallant sail when passing a warship — in other words, to salute the King. After this, the master gunner of the warship went aboard the merchantman and fined the captain a few shillings for contempt.

The *Union* was the American ship mentioned earlier, which left Sydney for the South Seas five months later, in August 1804, with Palmer's old mate, John Boston, on board on his last voyage.

Governor King's letter of 14th August 1804, in which he referred to Margarot and other "incendiaries" as being "very active but concealed councillors" of "our Irish insurgents", has already been quoted.

Writing to Under-secretary Sullivan on 21st August 1804, Governor King said that Margarot was "well known in England and Scotland as a violent unprincipled Republican". The Governor was convinced that Margarot "was deeply concerned in the late insurrection of the 4th March". Margarot's papers seized on that occasion, he said, "contained many republic sentiments, and the grossest scurrility against my predecessor and myself and many others, as well as against the executive authority in England. Every officer's and many others' decided wish was that he might be sent to the coal works [Newcastle]. However, contrary to the merited resentment of every person here, I was induced to forego that punishment from his being infirm, exclusive of which I had a more powerful reason, arising from his having declared in writing to me, that he was employed by those for whose character and known honour I have the highest veneration as a reporter of my and every other person's conduct in this colony. To enable him to continue that imaginary office I have directed him to be supplied with pens, ink, and paper. But this will not prevent him and his colleagues being narrowly watched."

One of Margarot's associates was a convict named John Grant, another penner of irritating letters, who was serving a sentence for forgery. Grant, a Scottish attorney, was deported on the *Surprize* with the Scottish Martyrs. Grant wrote to Governor King on 8th May 1805 as follows: "Now Sir, I ask you, as an independent Englishman, viewing with astonishment the miserable state to which thousands of unfortunate men are reduced in this Colony, by what authority do those in power at Home — by what right do you — make slaves of Britons in this distant quarter of the Globe?"

I have no record of King's reply, if any, but King awaited his chance and fixed Grant up, as will be told later.

On 13th July 1805 Governor King called a meeting of magistrates to discuss the subject of "Malcontents". They decided that "Michael Massey Robinson, Sir Henry Browne Hayes and Maurice Margarot, were dangerous characters to the tranquility of the Colony, and it is deemed advisable to separate them. As they are convicts and their conduct is highly reprehensible, it would conduce to the peace and happiness of this Colony to send them to such different settlements as His Excellency may direct."

This document was signed by five magistrates, including the zealous Samuel Marsden. Evidently Governor King got tired of breathing the same air as Margarot, because the next we hear about him is in a letter dated 14th

December 1805, from Lieutenant-Governor David Collins in Hobart to Governor King in Sydney. Says Collins: "I conceived it my duty to lay before you the particulars of Maurice Margarot, a person aboard H.M.S. *Buffalo*, which touched here on its way to Port Dalrymple, of exercising that incorrigible propensity in his disposition, which led him to condemn the constituted authorities of whatever government he might be placed under. Margarot's conduct incensed me so much that I determined to state the whole of it to you. He is a dangerous scoundrel — worse a thousand times than Stuart, *vaurien* [worthless fellow] as he is. Upon his arrival I received a letter from him, of which the enclosed is a copy, which I had scarcely perused, before his being at my door was announced. He was of course denied admittance."

The letter Collins enclosed was headed "H.M.S. *Buffalo*, 6th November 1805", and began: "Sir, *Linquenda tellus et domus, et placens uxor*", meaning "Earth we must leave, and home and darling wife".

Having shown his knowledge of the classics with this quotation from Horace, Margarot continued: "Chance has blunted the asperity of the shafts of malice by sending me to a place where you command. Sir Henry Browne Hayes and myself anxiously wish to receive your orders to repair on shore, and pay you our respects; much we are in hopes of hearing from your mouth and we may also be able to throw in our mite of information." The letter rambled on with several libellous statements about Governor King.

Collins's reply was prompt and crushing: "Lieutenant-Governor Collins was surprised at the presumption and audacity of the letter, being an infamous libel on the character of the Governor-in-chief of these settlements."

His letter to Governor King went on to relate that when his servant Hopkins went on board the *Buffalo* "with a present to a New Zealand Chief" Margarot called Hopkins aside, saying, "I did not think Governor Collins would have served me in the manner he did. I could tell him more than he knows, or ever will know. They have tight hold of him in Sydney, and he is obliged to humble himself to Governor King. Your Master ought to have taken us both in his arms" — meaning Hayes and himself — "and treated us as bosom friends. I am Governor King's prosecutor, and that he knows well; he sent me about in this manner that I may be drowned or lose my life, but I am a bit of good stuff. When the Commissioners come I shall be sent for; they will hear me, and soon see into the conduct of the Governor. I have written home to England, laying everything before them, saying the salary is too little, as the Governor cannot live without selling spirits. Though I am sent away, my wife is left behind. Governor King will be hanged as ever Governor Wall was."

Joseph Wall was appointed Lieutenant-Governor of Senegal in 1779. On 10th July 1782, while drunk, he charged Sergeant Benjamin Armstrong with mutiny and, without calling a court martial, ordered him to be flogged by black slaves. After eight hundred lashes Armstrong collapsed and died. Wall returned to England and was summoned to appear before a court martial, but evaded trial. Nearly twenty years elapsed, until on 20th January 1802 Wall was charged at the Old Bailey, London, with the murder of Armstrong, before a special commission presided over by Chief Baron Sir Archibald

Macdonald. The jury returned a verdict of guilty. Wall was sentenced to death, and was executed on 28th January 1802. The story is told in the *Dictionary of National Biography*, and also in Howell's *State Trials*. Wall was a brutal monster with a history of inflicting cruel punishments. He certainly deserved his fate.

Back to Lieutenant-Governor Collins in Hobart Town. His letters reached Governor King on 23rd January 1806. His Excellency saw red, and asked Judge-Advocate Atkins and the magistrates for advice on the documents he had received. "The incendiary character of the writer is too well known to require notice being taken of such libellous papers, but as they have been transmitted officially to me, it becomes my duty to request your opinion from the infamous statement that the *Governor cannot live without selling spirits*. No transaction of that kind has ever taken place under this roof, except on exchanging a portion of spirits I have drawn with other officers for domestic uses, with settlers for fowls and produce from their farms."

On 23rd January 1806, says Rusden, "The Judge-Advocate and Major Johnston, Reverend S. Marsden, Thomas Jamison and Captain John Houston, Esquires, reported to the incensed Governor that they were of the opinion that a man of Margarot's infamous conduct and principles has forfeited every pretension to the smallest indulgence and beg leave to recommend to his Excellency that he should be put to hard labour."

There is no mention in the records of how Margarot returned to Sydney from Hobart Town, but I assume that Captain Houston, acting on instructions from Collins, brought him back to Sydney on H.M.S. *Buffalo*, since he was too hot to handle in Van Diemen's Land.

King wrote to Collins: "As his body cannot bear the punishment he has so often merited, and the contagious principles he professes and disseminates are of so destructive a tendency, I have sent him to the settlement at Coal River to ruminate on his infamous conduct, if he is capable of entertaining any thoughts excepting those of anarchy and assassination."

On 3rd February 1806 the Governor's Secretary wrote to Charles Throsby, Commandant of the Coal River Settlement, by the ship *Resource*. On board, he informed him, was Margarot, "well known as a troublesome character". Throsby was to keep a watchful eye over him, and prevent his having any conversation with the soldiers. "Should he continue peaceable, let him remain so, but if he should become refractory, His Excellency desires you will check it, and if he deserves punishment, you will cause it to be inflicted as far as twenty-five lashes, and work him at public labour, the same as the other convicts."

Margarot, stewing in his own juice at Newcastle, must have been happy when in August 1806 Governor King retired because of ill health. He sailed for England aboard H.M.S. *Buffalo* on 10th February 1807, with his wife and family, nineteen years after his arrival with the First Fleet as Second Lieutenant on the *Sirius*.

King had played an active part in the Colony's fortunes from the beginning. A few weeks after reaching Sydney, on 15th February 1788, he had been sent to Norfolk Island, with twenty-three volunteers, to establish a new settlement, which was to provide food for Sydney Town. Their efforts were successful, gardens prospered, stock increased. The Commandant took into his house Ann Inett, a convict lass, and their son, Norfolk, was the first white child born on the island. A second son of the union was named Sydney; both sons became officers in the Royal Navy.

In 1790 Lieutenant King sailed for England with dispatches to Lord Greville from Governor Phillip, and the next year married Anna Josepha Coombes. The happy couple returned to Norfolk Island in November 1791, King with the rank of Lieutenant-Governor, and there a son, Phillip Parker King, was born to them. Later he won distinction as a navigator, and was the first native-born Australian to hold the rank of Rear-Admiral.

As we have seen, Philip Gidley King became Governor of New South Wales in 1800, with all the responsibilities of Scottish Martyrs, Irish Exiles, and confidence tricksters from Great Britain, plus officers of the New South Wales Corps and emancipated convicts. Whatever his failings as a Governor, he and his wife deserve credit for their work for the waifs of Sydney Town, for whom they established an orphanage.

King died on 3rd September 1808, aged fifty years, mostly spent in the service of an ungrateful country which refused him a pension. Mrs King returned to Sydney in 1832, and lived near Parramatta, where she devoted her life to helping the sick and needy, until her death at the age of eighty.

Things appear to have been all quiet on the Margarot front for several years, since the records are hazy about his doings. Next news is an item in the *Sydney Gazette* of 7th April 1810: "Mr Margarot, being about to quit the Colony, requests that those citizens who have claims upon him will present them."

A further notice appeared in the *Sydney Gazette* of 16th June 1810: "Freedom granted to Maurice Margarot, who arrived in the *Surprize* in 1794. The Governor has granted Certificate restoring all rights of free subjects in consequence of their terms of transportation having expired."

Margarot was sentenced in 1794 for fourteen years; this means that he had served over sixteen years, probably extra penalties for "malcontency".

Back in England, Margarot's name appeared as one of the "evidences" summoned by "The Committee to inquire into the manner in which Sentences of Transportation were executed and the Effects which have been produced by that mode of Punishment". At this inquiry, held in 1812, Margarot had an open go to air his grievances about the Colony from 1794 to 1810. As the following extract shows, he blamed the Army and the Government for causing the troubles of the Colony by monopolizing trade and charging exorbitant prices, up to five hundred per cent profit.

Margarot: "I believe I am not out when I say that a sieve to sift meal which costs 5s. 9d. has been sold for three guineas, and rum I have known sold at £8 a gallon, which cost 7s. 6d. a gallon."

The Commission: "Do you mean that civil officers, or military, or both, are engaged in this trade?"

Margarot: "All of them to a man. In the year 1797 a combination-bond was entered into by them, by which they were neither to underbuy or undersell one from the other. It was offered me to sign, and I refused it, and from thence began my persecution."

The Commission: "By what means did you procure a passage to return to Europe?"

Margarot: "At my own expense. To reach London it cost me £450 for myself, my wife and a servant."

The Commission: "What means had women convicts of procuring a passage to Europe?"

Margarot: "By prostitution. Hundreds of women whose period of transportation was expired had generally cohabited with some man, and they continue in the same way."

Margarot's last days in England are hard to catalogue. In Dr W. H. Drummond's *Biography of Archibald Hamilton Rowan*, printed in 1840, the author states: "In 1813, Mr Rowan received a letter from Maurice Margarot, the *Scottish Martyr*, who, after a tedious exile, had returned to England with his wife, this faithful companion in all his misfortunes, who *after numberless fatigues and dangers, dared yet to hope for better days*. He reminds Rowan of their having met nearly twenty years ago, after a short intercourse, to part, each to encounter a long series of tribulation and persecution. He had returned to England with *principles unchanged*, a ministerial victim, pinned down to penury in a place where he can do no good."

Margarot asked "the temporary assistance of £400; as a chrysalis, warmed by the general heat of the sun, receives thereform animation, so that will afford new life, and without producing a butterfly, will, notwithstanding, give me wings".

Continues Dr Drummond: "Though Mr Rowan's intercourse with Margarot had been very brief, and there could be no claim on the ground of past intimacy, such an appeal from an old sufferer in the same cause was not to be treated with neglect; he wrote to him kindly, and sent him a draft for £100, which was as large a sum as, at that time, could with prudence or justice afford."

Margarot, replying to Rowan, said that the sum would "enable him, if not to soar, at least to make his way in a more humble manner, somewhat like an ostrich". After his return to England, he went on, he had "endeavoured to collect the scattered fragments of a small fortune broken to atoms in the public service". He had also "projected a history of New South Wales, from which with the sanguine hopes of an inexperienced author, he anticipated a mine of riches".

Rowan had written of his own misfortunes, and Margarot answered encouragingly: "With regret, but without surprise, I hear you say your spirit is broken. Believe me, however, you are mistaken in this; it only sleepeth. The storm-beaten mariner does not therefore forsake the sea, but refreshed only awaits a favourable breeze to again unfurl his sails. Your trip to, and adventures in America, reached even New South Wales, embellished with a decent portion of scandal and calumny. Your ill-success in trade most likely originated in your being placed out of your sphere. My illustrious debtors, the B—s, in your place would have thriven from a contrary reason. It is much easier to assume the gentleman than to lay it aside."

Archibald Hamilton Rowan was born in County Down, Ireland, in 1751. Born with the name of Hamilton, at the age of sixteen he inherited considerable wealth from his maternal grandfather, William Rowan, on condition that he adopted the name of Rowan. Other provisions of this strange will required him to be educated at Oxford or Cambridge, and to refrain from visiting Ireland, under penalty of forfeiting his estates, until he reached the age of twenty-five.

Young Hamilton Rowan got in with a flash set at Queen's College, Cambridge, and became more famous for love of hunting and feats of strength than for love of learning. It is recorded that to demonstrate his prowess he threw his tutor into the Cam River; for this misdemeanour he was rusticated. Another of his crimes was to climb the signposts surrounding the college and turn them in different directions, with resultant loss of temper by lost travellers.

Years passed; Rowan married and gambled his wealth away, then in 1784 he returned to the land of his birth. There he became interested in politics, an interest he retained until his death in 1834. In the year 1790 Rowan became friends with Theobald Wolfe Tone, Irish patriot and firebrand, who persuaded him to become a member of the Society of United Irishmen.

Readers may recall that one of Thomas Muir's offences was to read an Address from the Society of United Irishmen in Dublin, to the Reformers in Scotland, signed by Rowan. In the same month, December 1792, Rowan was arrested and falsely charged with writing and circulating a seditious paper headed, "Citizen soldiers, to arms!" Out on bail, he evaded trial until 1st January 1794, when he was brought before the Irish Court. Found guilty, he was sentenced to a fine of £500 and imprisonment for two years, "and to find security himself in £2000, and two others in £1000 each, for his good behaviour for seven years". Loyal friends helped Rowan to escape from prison and to reach France, where he was arrested as an English spy. Freed, Rowan went to America in July 1795, where he met his United Irish friends, Wolfe Tone and Napper Tandy, both on the run from the British.

Rowan's opinions mellowed with age as his opponents of the 1790s died; the ban of outlawry on him was lifted, and in July 1803 he was allowed to return to England, after "publicly thanking the King for the clemency shown to him and his family during his exile". He died in 1834, and is buried in the vaults of St Mary's Church, Dublin.

Says the *Dictionary of National Biography*: "His friend, Dr Drummond, says Rowan in his youth was a singularly handsome man, of a tall and commanding person, in which agility, strength and grace were combined. His besetting fault was vanity, which rendered him an easy tool in the hands of clever men like Wolfe Tone. There can be little doubt that for the prominent place he holds in the history of the United Irish movement he was indebted rather to his position in society and to a readiness *to go out* than to any special qualification as a politician."

Maurice Margarot died on 11th November 1815, "in poor circumstances, while a subscription was being raised for his relief".

A burial certificate, in my possession, from the St Pancras Register, states that "Maurice Margarot, aged sixty-seven, died in Bull Place". A large poor hospital was situated there. The *Examiner* of 1st December 1815 has a lengthy obituary notice about Margarot, from which I quote extracts.

"This gentleman, who was one of the five persons condemned to fourteen years' transportation for connection with the London Correspondence Society, died on the 11th of last month at the advanced age of seventy. He was of a highly respectable, and we are informed, noble family, originally from Rome; and may be said to have had a love of liberty for a part of his patrimony; his father an eminent merchant, having been in the habit of entertaining at his home the most popular leaders of the day, during the very awkward contest into which the Court got with Wilkes."

John Wilkes, a radical agitator and a member of Parliament, founded the *North Briton* newspaper and, by way of attracting readers, attacked statements by King George III in his speech to Parliament as "false". A warrant was issued for the arrest of Wilkes on 3rd April 1763, and he was lodged in the Tower. Fortunately for him, Lord Chief Justice Pratt considered his arrest a breach of privilege, and he was released. This was evidently the "awkward contest" mentioned in the obituary of Margarot. No doubt when Mr Wilkes dined at the house of Margarot senior the youthful Maurice listened eagerly to the anti-royalist remarks of their distinguished guest.

Back to the *Examiner*: "Mr Margarot's passion for independence, however, seems to have been unpolluted with any of the equivocal feelings which must always attach to the character of one who is a mere man of the world in other respects, and which will hand down Wilkes to posterity as the rake, rather than the lover of liberty."

After "finishing his studies at Geneva, where Margarot was not likely to lose the spirit imbibed in his boyhood, he entered into his father's business, and pursued it for several years in various quarters of the world".

On the death of his father, the family business declined. Maurice, finding himself in Paris at the time of the French Revolution in 1789, returned to England, where many thinkers had turned their attention to reform in Parliament "because of abuses that had crept into the constitution. Mr Burke had made one of his elaborate efforts on the abuses in expenditure, and Mr Pitt, though he afterwards thought proper to suppress what he had excited, had actually been a member of a Society for obtaining a reform in the Representation. He was connected in fact with the very men who were subsequently the objects of the severest measures of his administrations, and among whom Mr Margarot became speedily enrolled. The latter remained firm to their reforming purposes, when the Burkes and the Pitts, alarmed by the appearances of the French Revolution, feeling themselves more connected with the aristocracy, declared against their old objects and associates, and resolved to use the most arbitrary weapons rather than not defeat them."

Margarot, "active, eloquent and intrepid, became one of the most important members of the Corresponding Society. He wrote some of the best of their reports and addresses; and was chosen one of the Delegates to go to Scotland for the purpose of animating the people there to a sense of the need for Parliamentary Reform, until a sudden stop was put to his career."

After his arrest and trial, Margarot "was banished to Botany Bay for fourteen years. He went there with his wife — truly a wife who never forsook him, and surviving the whole period. He was the only one out of five fellow-sufferers who returned. Age, a series of sensations which must have weakened his vigour of mind and body, and a total want of pecuniary resources, bent him at last to the earth, which took the undaunted but worn-out old man to its bosom, the beginning of the present winter."

Margarot was of middle stature, and "had been handsome in his youth, was well-proportioned, full of pleasantry and anecdote, with elegant manners — a scholar and a gentleman. Age and care had made havoc with his appearance, but the lively and intelligent spirit still shone through it; and we understand it was so unsubdued to the last, that on the verge of the grave, he was meditating a history of his life."

The article ended with a eulogy on Mrs Margarot, "the wife who went with him into exile, that had shared his prosperity and his adversity, who had admired his accomplishments, had loved him kind and generous, and had clung to him to the last, is now left poor and desolate. It is now necessary to make her wants known through a medium like this. They should be known, in order to be relieved."

The article concludes with "a list of persons who will receive donations on behalf of Mrs Margarot".

And so the bell tolled for Maurice Margarot.

Did he rubbish his fellow-martyrs on the *Surprize?*

Did he deserve to be sent to Coventry in Sydney Cove by Palmer, Muir, and Skirving?

Did he deserve to have his name etched with the others on the monument in Edinburgh?

I take no sides. I've only quoted statements made by those who knew him. Readers, consider your verdict.

So passed Maurice Margarot, the last of the Scottish Martyrs. He was the only one who returned from exile — in his case to England, home, and poverty.

CHAPTER TWENTY-TWO

The Reform Bill — Forty Years of Battling — Earl Grey — Curse of Rotten Boroughs — Events in Sixteen Years Leading to the Reform Bill — Gagging Bills — Suspension of Habeas Corpus — William Cobbett — Samuel Bamford — Corn Laws — Peterloo — Cobbett Brings Home Paine's Bones — Cato Street Conspiracy — Catholic Relief Bill — Brougham — The Duke of Wellington Fights a Duel — Death of George IV — William IV — Wellington Resigns — Whigs in Power — Lord John Russell — Fight for the Reform Bill — Sydney Smith's Story of Dame Partington — Reform Bill Passed — Blight of Rotten Boroughs Removed — Last Years of Reform Leaders — Scottish Martyrs Vindicated — Monument to their Memory.

ON 17th May 1832 William IV intimated that he had accepted the advice of Earl Grey, the Prime Minister, and his Chancellor, Lord Brougham, to create such a number of peers as would be sufficient to ensure the passing of the Reform Bill.

This was the death-sentence of the rotten boroughs and many other abuses against which the Scottish Martyrs had taken their stand. And the chosen instrument of destruction, Earl Grey, was a Whig politician, who on 30th April 1792 had given notice to Parliament that in 1793 he would introduce the question of parliamentary reform. It had taken him forty years to turn the tables on his Tory opponents, but, thanks to his tenacity of purpose, he had achieved victory for the cause in which Palmer, Muir and other members of the Friends of the People, had sacrificed their freedom and their lives.

Charles, second Earl Grey, was born at Fallodon, Northumberland, on 13th March 1764. A bright youth and a classical scholar, he went from Eton to Cambridge, and visited Europe. He settled down in 1786 and served in Parliament as the member for Northumberland until 1807, when he resigned for financial reasons. While a member of Parliament he became a member of the Whig Club, joined the "Friends of the People", and was chosen by them, together with Thomas Hardy, Joseph Gerrald, Maurice Margarot and others, to take charge of the principle of parliamentary reform.

We now return to the year 1815, when Maurice Margarot, last of the Scottish Martyrs died.

Though Muir, Palmer, Gerrald, Skirving, Mealmaker, and Margarot were dead, they had left a fervent group of gospellers to harass and agitate the Tories of Westminster by incessant demands for universal suffrage, annual parliaments, and the reformation of Parliament by the elimination of rotten boroughs.

England, Ireland, and Scotland, after the union of these three countries in

LEFT: Thomas Paine.

From the portrait by John Wesley Jarvis, National Gallery of Art, Washington.

BELOW: Thomas Paine's birthplace, Thetford, Norfolk

Frank Clune with Dougal McCallum Hay
at the Memorial to the Scottish Martyrs, Old Calton Burying Ground,
Edinburgh, May 1967

1801, all had bitter cause to complain about the lords who controlled the Government by the ownership of pocket boroughs, who always demanded a pledge from those whom they nominated to Parliament to vote whichever way their patron commanded. Whigs did this as well as Tories. W. L. Mathieson, author of *England in Transition*, wrote: "The majority of patrons gave their nominations to relatives and friends whom they could trust to further their political views. The Duke of Norfolk had eleven seats at his disposal; Lord Lonsdale nine; Lord Fitzwilliam eight; Lord Darlington seven. England and Wales were represented in the unreformed Parliament by 513 members; of these, according to a computation published in 1810, 371 owed their seats practically to nomination — 287 being returned by 87 peers, 137 by 90 commoners, and 16 by the Government."

The *Encyclopaedia Britannica* says of the rotten boroughs that fifty had fewer than fifty votes each, and Old Sarum only seven.

Now follows a brief summary of events from the death of Margarot in 1815 to the memorable moment in 1832 when King William IV gave Earl Grey the power to ram the Reform Bill down the throats of the recalcitrant Tory peers who controlled the destiny of not so Merrie England.

On 2nd December 1816 there were riots in Spa Fields, East London. A huge multitude gathered, but though there were many threats there was only one casualty. The next year an attack on the Prince Regent led the Chief Secretary, Lord Sidmouth, to fear a revolution, and he passed his Gagging Bill and procured the suspension of the Habeas Corpus Act on 4th March 1817. To evade arrest, William Cobbett escaped via Liverpool to America on 27th March 1817.

The war that had been thrust upon England by the French revolutionaries in February 1793 had ended with the crushing of Napoleon by Wellington in June 1815. War's end left the labouring class of England free from the call-up, and free from seizure by press-gangs seeking soldiers and sailors to fight for King and country. And it also left them plenty of time to worry over the woes of earning a crust, and staying one jump ahead of the poor-house. They also had heaps of time to listen to orators who harangued them from every corner stump on the need to reform the Poor Laws.

One such agitator was William Cobbett. His biographer, Samuel Bamford, in *Passages in the Life of a Radical* (1840), wrote that "the writings of William Cobbett suddenly became of great authority; they were read on nearly every cottage hearth . . . their influence was speedily visible". Bamford, born in 1788, was a weaver who became a crusader for parliamentary reform. More of Bamford later.

William Cobbett, a farmer's son, born in 1763, ran away from home at the age of fourteen and worked at many jobs before we find him in the British Army in Nova Scotia, at the age of nineteen, as a regimental sergeant-major. Because of arguments with his officers about their peculations, Cobbett deserted, and in March 1792 went to France seeking knowledge of the Revolution. He next took passage to Philadelphia, where he became a teacher of English to French *émigrés*. Here, in 1794, Cobbett met Dr Joseph Priestley, who had advocated the cause of the Scottish Martyrs one year earlier.

Cobbett now became a political writer, and soon the printing presses were turning out tirades such as *A Bone to Gnaw for the Democrats*, *A Kick for a Bite*, *The Cannibal's Progress*, and other pamphlets with catchy titles, denigrating the French Revolution. In 1800 we find Cobbett back in England, writing on radical subjects, equally attacking Whigs and Tories, calling for reform of Parliament, and Poor Law relief.

Then came his downfall in 1809, when soldiers in barracks at Ely mutinied over unfair pay deductions. The mutiny was suppressed, and the ringleaders were flogged. Cobbett denounced the floggings and was prosecuted for sedition, his sentence including a fine of £1000, two years in Newgate Jail, bail in £3000, and the finding of two sureties of £1000 each.

In jail and bankrupt, his farm and printing presses sold, Cobbett faced a grim future. But he doggedly began a new life at the age of forty-nine by starting a cheap twopenny periodical, the *Register*. This sold like hot cakes to the masses, and Cobbett became their leader until his flight to America in 1817. Alarmed by food riots, the Government began repressing the rioters, filling the jails with innocent and guilty alike, and, when the prisons became overcrowded, transporting them to Botany Bay. So England's loss became Australia's gain.

The year of Princess Victoria's birth, 1819, saw the renewal of industrial distress, with agitation against the Corn Laws and demands for annual Parliaments, universal suffrage, and vote by ballot. On 16th August a mob estimated at 60,000 held a meeting in St Peter's Fields, Manchester, to demand the reform of Parliament. Many unarmed women and children were present and their intentions were peaceable. The magistrates of Manchester foolishly ordered the 15th Hussars and the Cheshire Yeomanry to charge the unarmed crowd. They attacked ruthlessly, shouting, "Have at their legs", while slashing them down with the edge as well as the flat of their sabres. ". . . Soon the place was cleared except for bodies, some still groaning, others with staring eyes, gasping for breath; others will never breathe more, all silent save those low sounds and the snorting and pawing of steeds".

The site of the massacre was called Peterloo. The number of killed and wounded are disputed; several hundred authenticated cases are known. A Peterloo medal was struck, bearing the legend, "The wicked have drawn out the sword, they have cut down the needy and such as be of upright conversation" (Psalm 37.14).

The indignation caused by the behaviour of the Yeomanry and its endorsement by the Government contributed largely to the success of the reform movement.

Among the orators speaking at Peterloo in favour of parliamentary reform and the abolition of the Corn Laws was the Lancashire writer, Samuel Bamford. Despite his pleas of innocence, he was arrested, and sentenced to one year's imprisonment. Bamford's *Passages in the Life of a Radical* shows his intense interest in alleviating the woes of the working class. After his death on 13th April 1872, he was given a public funeral, which was attended by thousands of mourners.

Back to 1819. On 20th November of that year, the Act suspending the Habeas Corpus Act having lapsed, William Cobbett returned to England. One of Cobbet's last acts before leaving America was to disinter the bones of his friend Thomas Paine from Paine's farm at New Rochelle. Paine had left France to spend his last years in America, dying there in 1809. Because Paine was a Deist, the Christians of the county, even the Quakers, had refused to let him be buried in consecrated ground, hence the body was interred on his farm. Cobbett's final act of charity was to get permission to bring the body of Paine out of America for reburial at Thetford, his birthplace. But the church authorities of Thetford also refused permission to bury the bones in hallowed ground, and after the death of Cobbett his bones were lost and forgotten.

G. D. H. Cole, in his *Life of William Cobbett*, quotes a poem written by the Irish poet Thomas Moore:

> *In digging up your bones, Tom Paine,*
> *Will Cobbet has done well.*
> *You'll visit him on earth again,*
> *He'll visit you in hell.*

In 1820 William Cobbett published *Rural Rides* in his *Weekly Register*, a pot-pourri of his impressions while riding through the villages of England. Naturally, he attacked rotten boroughs — "Westbury, a nasty odious rotten borough, a really rotten place" — which gave him a chance to plead for reform of Parliament. The same year saw the death of George III and the accession of George IV. In May the Cato Street Conspiracy startled the country; five men were executed, and five transported to Botany Bay.

During the 1820s the movement for reform gathered momentum, though the opposition was still powerful. In 1821 the Catholic Relief Bill, designed to relieve the oppressive restrictions that Catholics had suffered for so long, was passed by the House of Commons. But the House of Lords rejected it, and the fight went on, providing one of the most controversial topics in public affairs for the next few years. In 1823 there were reforms in criminal law, and in 1824 the Acts that limited the free travelling of workmen were repealed.

Another outstanding advocate of reform in these years was Henry Brougham, later Lord Brougham, whom we find in 1828 making a six-hour speech in Parliament asking for an inquiry "into the defects occasioned by time and otherwise in the laws of this realm of England, as administered in the courts of common law".

Brougham, born in 1778 at Edinburgh of poor but honest parents, had clawed his way up and up and up. At the age of twenty-two he was called to the Bar in Scotland, but, briefs being scarce, he migrated to London in 1803. Like many young lawyers, he supported himself by writing articles for the newly published *Edinburgh Review*. In 1810 the Duke of Bedford, a Whig, appreciating Brougham's capabilities, had granted him the rotten borough of Camelford, in return for which he pledged his vote to the noble Duke. For nearly two decades Brougham had remarkable success at the English Bar, until we find him in Parliament on 7th February 1828, pleading eloquently for law reform. His peroration was lengthy, and I only have space for a few impressive words: "It was the boast of Augustus, it formed part of the glare in which the perfidies of his earlier years were lost — that he found Rome of brick, and left it of marble; a praise not unworthy a great prince, and one to which the present reign has its claims. But how much nobler will be the sovereign's boast when he shall have it to say, that he found law dear, and left it cheap; found it a sealed book — left it a living letter; found it the patrimony of the rich — left it the inheritance of the poor; found it the two-edged sword of craft and oppression — left it the staff of honesty and the shield of innocence!"

By the next year the Catholic Relief Bill was again the burning topic, and for several months there was intense strife in both Houses of Parliament. While the tumult was at its height the Earl of Winchelsea published a letter in which he insinuated that the Duke of Wellington, then Prime Minister, had supported the establishment of King's College, that he "might the more effectually under the cloak of some outward show of zeal for the Protestant religion, carry on his insidious designs for the introduction of Popery into every department of the state".

Wellington demanded that the letter should be withdrawn; the Earl refused, and on 21st March the two peers met in Battersea Fields, to avenge their honour in a duel. The Duke fired and missed; the Earl fired his pistol at the sky, after which he tendered a written apology. Three weeks later, on 13th April 1829, the Catholic Relief Bill received the royal assent, and, for the first time in centuries of oppression, the laws relating to the civil disabilities of Catholics were made more flexible. The Bill would admit a Roman Catholic to Parliament upon taking an oath, in place of the old Oath of Supremacy, that he would support the existing institutions of the State, and not injure those of the Church. This was only one of many advantages that Roman Catholics received.

The year 1829 ended after months of misery during a most severe winter, followed by a trade depression, mainly felt by the working class. Relief was granted on 15th March 1830 by the remission of the excise duties on beer, cider and leather.

On 26th June 1830 King George IV, who had suffered a slight stroke, expired at Windsor Castle. Commented the Duke of Wellington, "He was indeed, the most extraordinary compound of talent, wit, buffoonery, obstinacy, and good feeling — in short, a medley of the most opposite qualities, with a great preponderance of good — that I ever saw in any character in my life."

The coronation of King William IV took place on 8th September, and on 26th October Parliament assembled. The rallying cry from opposition Whigs, led by Earl Grey, was parliamentary reform. The Duke of Wellington was adamant — no reform. Brougham, in the House of Commons, demanded reform. The battle raged, until on 15th November, after a short debate in the House of Lords over a minor issue, which the Government had lost, the Duke of Wellington in the Lords, and Sir Robert Peel in the Commons, announced that in consequence of the vote of the preceding evening they had tendered their resignation.

At long last the Whigs had their chance. The King authorized Earl Grey to form a new administration, and on 3rd February 1831 Parliament met, and the Reform Bill was announced.

Most of the Cabinet Ministers were ardent reformers; Brougham, now Lord Chancellor, and Lord John Russell had been advocating these measures nearly all their lives. Says the *Historians' History of the World*: "The demand for parliamentary reform had assumed a new character and aspect. It was no longer the mere war-cry of a political party. .... It was to be upon a scale so ample that instead of being a political step in advance, which the contention of parties might favour or retard, it was to be a national revolution; and not only was it to be granted by wholesale, instead of instalments, but granted immediately — upon the instant. Never indeed was the *omnipotence* of parliament so devoutly believed in as now for the cure of every evil, and in proportion to the extravagance of such a hope, was the loudness and universality of the outcry."

From the above sentence dear reader, you can gather that the attack was as carefully planned as the invasion of France by the Allied armies over a century later.

The leader chosen by Earl Grey to promote the attack was Lord John Russell, son of the sixth Duke of Bedford. He had been a delicate boy, according to the *Dictionary of National Biography*, and was removed from school at the age of twelve, and educated by a tutor. He wrote verses and plays, and at the age of fourteen noted in his diary: "What a pity that he who steals a penny loaf should be hanged, while he who steals thousands of the public money should be acquitted!"

In the next few years Russell travelled and studied, and in 1813 was elected a member of Parliament for the family constituency of Tavistock, in the Whig interest. He opposed the suspension of the Habeas Corpus Act in 1817, and in 1819 delivered the first of many speeches on parliamentary reform. He also dabbled in literature, and supported the Catholic Relief Bill, which became law in 1829.

In the election following the death of King George IV in June 1830, Lord John was a candidate for Bedford. Alas, "he lost the election by one vote, his defeat was due to the Wesleyans it is said, who had taken exception to some of his remarks on prayer". His father's influence caused a vacancy to be made for him at Tavistock, and he was returned to Parliament on 27th November 1830. Then came his chance when Early Grey appointed him to a committee to prepare a draft Bill on parliamentary reform.

On 1st March 1831 Lord John Russell explained the Bill with great vigour, to be loudly applauded by his supporters in the Commons. The first reading of the Bill led to fiery debate by opposition Tories, who claimed "that the essence of the scheme was not reform but revolution; that the measure proposed nothing less than to remove from the House of Commons every alloy of monarchical or aristocractical principle, and convert it into a pure and resistless democracy, which it never had been, and which, consistently with the British Constitution, it never should be."

Opponents staunchly rallied for the second reading of the Bill in the House of Commons, the debate lasting two days. At the division there were, including the Speaker and the four tellers, 603 members present, the largest number that had ever divided in the House. This Reform Bill proposed to disfranchise sixty boroughs, and deprive forty-one boroughs of one member each. It also proposed allocating members to counties which never had a representative in Parliament.

Because the division resulted in a win of only one vote for the Bill, Earl

Grey, the Prime Minister, delivered his resignation to the King.

Much argument in both Houses ensued without getting anywhere. Lord Mansfield, according to the *Historians' History of the World,* said that he had never before witnessed such a scene in the House, and he hoped never to see anything like it again. "He would use no intemperate language, but he would nevertheless assert, as far as God Almighty gave him the means of under-standing, that the Crown and the country were now about to be placed in a most awful predicament."

The King then entered Parliament and put an end to all discussion by proroguing Parliament, "with a view to immediate dissolution". He had been induced to resort to this measure, he said, for the purpose of ascertaining the will of the people. Next day a proclamation announced the dissolution and directed that a new election should be held.

At this election Earl Grey's Whigs were returned by a majority of one hundred, and the Reform Bill, with little alteration, was introduced to the House of Commons for the second time on 22nd September 1831. On 7th October 1831 the troublesome Bill was again placed before the House of Lords, and once more they rejected it by 329 votes to 198.

While this debate was going on the Reverend Sydney Smith made a whimsical forecast at Taunton on 11th October 1831. "As for the possibility of the House of Lords preventing ere long a reform of parliament, I hold it to be the most absurd notion that ever entered into human imagination. I do not mean to be disrespectful, but the attempt of the lords to stop the progress of reform reminds me very forcibly of the great storm at Sidmouth, and of the conduct of the excellent Mrs Partington on that occasion.

"In the winter of 1824 there set in a great flood upon that town — the tide rose to an incredible height — the waves rushed upon the houses, and all were threatened with destruction. In the midst of this sublime and terrible storm, Dame Partington, who lived on the beach, was seen at the door of her house with mop and pattens, trundling her mop, squeezing out the sea-water, and vigorously pushing away the Atlantic Ocean. The Atlantic was roused. Mrs Partington's spirit was up; but I need not tell you that the contest was unequal. The Atlantic Ocean beat Mrs Partington. She was excellent at a slop, or a puddle, but she should not have meddled with a tempest. Gentlemen, be at your ease — be quiet and steady, you will beat Mrs Partington."

This story is one of many told in *The Wit and Wisdom of the Reverend Sydney Smith,* published in 1860, after he had been dead fifteen years.

Smith's attitude of calm confidence was not shared by everyone. Green, in his *Short History of the English People,* describes the demonstrations of protest that followed the rejection of the Bill. "At Birmingham a meeting, said to have been attended by 150,000 persons, was held and resolutions were carried affirming that no taxes should be paid until the Bill was passed. At Nottingham the Castle was burnt down; at Bristol the Mansion House and Bishop's Palace were set on fire."

On 12th December 1831 Russell introduced the Reform Bill into the Commons for the third time. Again it was rejected by the Lords on 7th May 1832, and this rejection created a climax.

Next morning Cabinet asked the King to sanction a large creation of peers.

The King, without hesitation, refused, and the Ministers resigned. The Duke of Wellington was then granted permission by the King to form a government, but on 17th May he informed the House of Lords of his failure to form a Ministry.

Says the *Historians' History of the World*: "The Duke of Wellington withdrew after his statement on the 17th May, and did not return to the House of Lords till the night after the passing of the Reform Bill. His wise and patriotic example was followed by a sufficient number of peers to afford a decided majority."

After ten days of pleadings by Grey and Brougham, the King gave them the assurance they sought, agreeing to the creation of enough peers to ensure the passing of the Reform Bill, first calling up peers' eldest sons.

This threat to swamp the House of Lords was never exercised. The King, though it was unconstitutional, used pressure on the recalcitrant peers, and this royal blackmail made any such move unnecessary.

At last, on 4th June 1832, occurred on of the most memorable events in the long history of parliaments. On that day the Bill was passed in the House of Lords by a majority of eighty-four, and on 7th June the English Reform Bill received the royal assent, followed by the Reform Bill for Scotland on 13th July, and the Irish Reform Bill on 18th July.

So, after forty years of in-fighting since the Scottish Martyrs were tried in 1793, sanity prevailed, and the follies and crimes of 1793 became the virtues and laws of 1832. The dismal forebodings by die-hard Tories that the sun of England had set for ever with the passage of the Reform Bill proved to be unfounded.

The principal design of the Act was to remove the evil blight of rotten boroughs, and 56 with less than 2000 inhabitants and returning 111 members were wiped out. Thirty boroughs having less than 4000 inhabitants each lost a member, and 22 large towns, previously voteless, were given two members each, which rectified their complaints. And so on, all down the line, in England, Scotland, and Ireland, this measure lopped the heads off landed interests which had influence beyond their capacity to give service in return.

It is said that amidst the shouting and turmoil in the Commons during the debates someone complimented Lord John Russell on his tenacity in campaigning for the Reform Bill, to which His Lordship made his famous reply, "It is impossibe that the whisper of a faction should prevail against the voice of a nation."

Now that the Reform Bill has been made law, our story is coming to an end.

Earl Grey remained in Parliament until 1834, when he resigned. He lived in retirement until his death at Horwick on 17th July 1845, in the eighty-second year of his age, "a great orator, a great debater, exceedingly ready in apprehending complicated statements of fact, and in bringing them home to his hearers".

Another of these fighters who helped to mould the minds of people for reform in Parliament was our old friend William Cobbett. When Grey became Prime Minister he attributed revolts among the labouring classes to Cobbett, and, since he was anxious to prove his party's respect for the landed interests, he ordered Cobbett's arrest. But wily William cleverly out-harangued the prosecutor, and he was discharged.

After the Reform Act became law in 1832, Cobbett stood for the Oldham district, and was elected. In 1834 he campaigned against the Poor Law Bill, which became law, despite his opposition. A year later, on 18th June 1835, he died from an attack of influenza, survived by his wife and seven children.

Cobbett, it has been said, "was always extremely pugnacious, and made many enemies. But he made also many firm friends." And that's where we'll leave him — a friend to his many friends, rich and poor alike. Cobbett had the capacity to depict the sufferings of the working class, and to make others realize the need for reform. Wrote Thomas Carlyle: "William Cobbett was the pattern John Bull of his century." To which I add, of many centuries. His head was often bloody, but always unbowed. Wherever the fray was thickest Cobbett was there with his pen and voice, ready to champion the cause of the underdog.

Another campaigner for parliamentary reform was Henry Brougham, whom Earl Grey had made Lord Chancellor, also causing him to be raised to the peerage as Baron Brougham and Vaux. Because of his activities in promoting law reform, he incurred the dislike of many of his legal colleagues. Says the *Encyclopaedia Britannica*: "Brougham's was the unhappy role of the political liberal, unable to subordinate either himself or his principles to the demand of party. . . . Whatever burdens he placed on his contemporaries, history must acknowledge that he was a man who made England a better place to live for all those who followed him." A beautiful park named after him honours his memory at Cannes, where he died on 7th May 1868 in his ninetieth year.

Last, but not least, of the great cast of characters who took part in the drama was Lord John Russell, architect of the Reform Bill. In April 1835, when Lord Melbourne was Prime Minister, Russell became Home Secretary and leader of the House of Commons. He was in and out of power in many Ministries, and in 1846, aged fifty-four, he became Prime Minister. In 1861 Russell became an Earl, and four years later, in October 1865, became Prime Minister for the second time, after the death of Lord Palmerston.

He retired from politics to Pembroke Lodge, Richmond, which Queen Victoria presented to him in 1847. There he died on 28th May 1878, in his eighty-sixth year. Lord John Russell was a man of many parts. His friend and contemporary the Reverend Sydney Smith, regarded "self-reliance" as his worst fault. "I believe Lord John Russell would perform the operation for the stone, build St Peter's, or assume — with or without ten minutes' notice — the command of the Channel Fleet; and no one would discover by his manner that the patient had died, the church tumbled down, and the Channel Fleet been blown to atoms."

And so the leaders passed on, to be followed by more enthusiasts, and more Reform Bills, extending the franchise still further and advancing the cause of democracy.

The Scottish Martyrs did not live to see the triumph of their cause, but they were not forgotten. On 21st August 1844 over three thousand people assembled in the Old Calton burial ground, on the hilly slopes of Edinburgh, only a few hundred yards from Holyroodhouse, the ancestral home of Scottish Kings and Queens, where Bonnie Prince Charlie held court in 1745.

The story of this memorable day was told in the *Scotsman* of 24th August 1844, which described how "the foundation stone of the monument intended to be erected to the memories of Muir, Palmer, Gerrald, Skirving and Margarot (the political martyrs of 1793–94) was laid by Joseph Hume, M.P., in the Old Calton burying-ground, where a site had been obtained for the purpose, in the most elevated position in the churchyard, and about twenty feet from David Hume's funeral vault."

Four hundred members of the Complete Suffrage Association, dressed in black, gave éclat to the ceremony by marching four abreast through the Parliament Square, passing the law courts where the patriots had received their unmerited sentences, down the High Street and along the North and Waterloo bridges to the burial ground. They were welcomed by Mr Hume, also "Mr Skirving, manufacturer in Kircaldy, son of one of the Martyrs, and Mr William Moffat, who acted as agent for Mr Muir at the trial".

Mr Hume addressed the meeting by saying he was happy to see so many reformers present to perform an act of justice to the pioneers sentenced fifty years earlier. Said Hume: "I am one of those, who in 1792–93, while attending the University, was witness to the proceedings that then took place. . . . I have never forgotten the enormities which were perpetrated at this time, and I am happy to think that reparation to these men is now about to be made."

The eloquent speaker then narrated how William Pitt, with the Duke of Richmond, proposed to Parliament in 1782 the very laws that Muir and others had proposed in 1793, for which they were condemned and transported to Botany Bay. During a lengthy address Hume described most of the exiles' misfortunes, but wrongly outlined Muir's journey down the Californian coast, which he had evidently secured from Mackenzie's *Life of Muir*, since he had Muir crossing the isthmus at Panama.

After Hume ended his oration, "he descended to the foundation stone, placed under it a sealed jar containing copies of the newspapers of the day; Oliver and Boyd's *Almanac*; a report of the trial of the Martyrs; a list of the Scots subscribing to the monument, and a few coins of the present reign." Hume then asked permission to read "the remarkable prayer which Joseph Gerrald had offered when he was arrested at the last meeting of the Convention".

Readers will recall what Gerrald said: "O Thou Governor of the Universe! We rejoice that, at all times and in all circumstances, we have liberty to approach Thy Throne; and that we are assured that no sacrifice is more acceptable to Thee, than that which is made for the relief of the oppressed. In this moment of trial and persecution, we pray that Thou wouldst be our defender, our consellor, and our guide. O be Thou a pillar of fire to us, as Thou wast to our fathers of old, to enlighten and to direct us; and to our enemies a pillar of cloud, and darkness, and confusion."

The Chairman then announced that "a relative of Mr Skirving, one of the Martyrs, was on the platform, which produced a thrilling cheer from the multitude". After which the committee adjourned to Gibb's Royal Hotel in

Princes Street to give Mr Hume a dinner, and drink several toasts to patriots like Earl Grey and other illustrious espousers of the Reform Bill of 1832.

At the dinner Mr Skirving of Kircaldy thanked the meeting for the interest they had shown in the reform struggle of 1793. "At this period I was a young man, indeed a boy, but I have a vivid recollection of those who distinguished themselves in the cause of reform. And it has often struck me, in taking a view of the characters of the leaders of that movement, that on no occasion was there ever such a number of men eminent alike for their moral and religious worth, united for the attainment of a popular right, all of them, with few exceptions, being men who enjoyed the confidence of their fellow citizens, being selected by them to manage their affairs both of a religious and civil description."

Mr Skirving then added, "that of those whom you have this day pronounced worthy to have their deeds commemorated by a public monument, I would just remark, that their political career affords proof of the purity of their motives, disinterested patriotism, and unfeigned love of liberty. May the generous efforts of the Reformers of the present day to perpetuate their sense of their worth, prove a stimulant to the patriot and a terror to the oppressor." (Cheers.)

Mr Skirving sat down, to be followed by more speakers, until, said the *Scotsman*, "Thanks having been voted to the Chairman, the meeting then separated, it being close upon twelve o'clock".

And it's nigh on twelve o'clock as I bring the story of the Martyrs to a close. From my library high over Sydney Cove, shimmering silvery under the autumn moon, I view the roadstead where the *Surprize* dropped anchor in 1794, after her dreadful voyage from London Town. Imprisoned on this transport were the shackled fighters for liberty, banished from the British Isles, a journey from which only one of the exiles returned.

They were not silenced. They had the courage of their convictions. They died for them.

EPILOGUE

In the merry month of May 1967 I flew by Qantas from Sydney Town on a pilgrimage to the Old Country in the tracks of the Scottish Martyrs.

On the way I landed at Monterey, and in the suburb of Carmel I yarned with Harry Downie, historian of the Mission of San Carlos, completed in 1796 when Thomas Muir was granted sanctuary by the Governor of Alta California.

By car to Los Angeles with my Sydney friend, Dr John Vyden, by plane to Mexico City, and a hearty welcome by an old New Guinea friend, His Excellency Desmond McCarthy, Australian Ambassador to the Republic of Mexico. At the Embassy I met a friend from Sydney, Cavan Hogue, now First Secretary. Cavan, a Spanish scholar, has spent many hours in the Archives of Mexico City seeking fresh light on Muir's journey through New Spain in 1796–7. Cavan also found documents about the convicts who escaped with Muir from Sydney on the whaler *Otter* in February 1796.

Thanks to the Sydney historian John Earnshaw, who supplied index numbers, we found in the Archives over two hundred pages of documents, tracing the arrival of the Sydney-siders in New Spain, their route across the isthmus from San Blas through Mexico City to Vera Cruz, and their departure from Spanish territory in 1796 and 1797.

By air to London for a brief spell in the Archives, before flying to journey's end at Edinburgh, where I dallied for days in the Public Library and Archives, seeking original records of the trials of the Martyrs.

One day, with some Scottish friends, Dougal McCallum Hay, Dr Alex Dunbar, and Wing Commander Arthur Hill, enthusiasts who had assisted me in my researches, we walked from Princes Street to the Old Calton Burying Ground. There stands a tall obelisk, weathered by bleak winds from the Highlands for a century or more, and inscribed with the names of Palmer, Muir, Skirving, Gerrald, and Margarot.

Alas for history! A well-known guide-book of Scotland says this obelisk is "In memory of five Chartist Martyrs, sentenced 1793–94 to transportation". Evidently the author was unaware that the Chartists as a political group did not come into being until forty years after Muir and his comrades were banished to Botany Bay.

As I read the names of the unlucky men, I thought of Muir's last words to the judges who exiled him to Botany Bay because he battled for a cause.

"I have engaged in a good, a just, and a glorious cause," said Muir, "a cause which, sooner or later, must and will prevail."

Then I placed a wreath of fresh flowers on the Memorial, happy in the knowledge that truth *did* prevail, and the cause *did* triumph.

187

BIBLIOGRAPHY

ASPINALL, A., and SMITH, E. A., *English Historical Documents 1783–1832*.
Australian Dictionary of Biography. Melbourne, 1966–.
Australian Encyclopaedia. Sydney, 1958.

BAMFORD, S., *Passages in the Life of a Radical*. 1840.
BEAGLEHOLE, J. C., *Exploration of the Pacific*. 1934.
BELSHAM, T., *The Memoirs of the Reverend T. Lindsey*. 1812.
BLACKSTONE, W., *Commentaries on the Laws of England*. 1758.
BLANCHARD, C., *Life of Thomas Paine*.
BROUGHTON, W. R., *A Voyage of Discovery to the North Pacific Ocean*. London, 1804.
BURKE, E., *Appeal from the New to the Old Whigs*. 1791.
——, *Reflections on the Revolution in France*. 1790.

CHAMBERS, R., *Life and Works of Robert Burns*.
COBBETT, W., *Rural Rides*. 1820.
COCKBURN, H. T., *Examination of the Trials for Sedition in Scotland*. Edinburgh, 1888.
COLE, G. D. H., *Life of William Cobbett*.
COLLINS, D., *An Account of the English Colony in New South Wales*. London, 1798.
CONWAY, M. D., *Life of Thomas Paine*. 1892.
COOK, J., and KING, J., *A Voyage to the Pacific Ocean . . . in the Resolution and Discovery*. 1758.
CUMPSTON, JOHN, *Shipping Arrivals and Departures 1788–1825*. Sydney, 1963.
CUTTER, D. C., *Malaspina in California*.

DAMPIER, W., *A New Voyage Round the World*. 1697.
Dictionary of National Biography. 1885 Edition.

EARNSHAW, J., *A Letter from the South Seas: The Story of the Daedalus*. Cremorne, N.S.W., 1957.
——, *Thomas Muir, Scottish Martyr*. Cremorne, N.S.W., 1959.
Encyclopaedia Britannica. 1796 and 1961 Editions.

FIELD, W., *Memoirs of the Life, Writings, and Opinions of the Rev. Samuel Parr, LL.D.* 1828.
FINDLAY, A. G., *The North Pacific Ocean*.

GALBRAITH, E. C., "Malaspina", *California Historical Society Quarterly*, October 1924.
GEIGER, Father, *The Life and Times of Junipero Serra*.
GERRALD, J., *The Trial of Joseph Gerrald*.
GLEASON, D., *The Islands and Ports of California*.
GODWIN, G., *Vancouver — A Life*.

HARDY, T., *Memoirs of Thomas Hardy* (ed. McPherson). London, 1832.
HASWELL, W., *Remarks on a Voyage to the Marianna Islands,* 1801.
Histoire de la tyrannie du Gouvernement Anglais exercée envers le célèbre Thomas Muir, Ecossais, etc. Paris, 1798.
Historical Records of Australia.
Historical Records of New South Wales.
HOLDSWORTH, W., *History of English Law.*
HOLT, J., *Memoirs of Joseph Holt, General of the Irish Rebels in 1798.* London, 1838.
HOWELL, T. B., *State Trials.*

JAMES, W., *Naval History of Great Britain.* 1822.
JOHNSTONE, J., *The Works of Samuel Parr.*

LA PEROUSE, J. F. DE GALAUP, Comte de, *A Voyage Round the World.* Paris, 1797.
LOCKERBY, W., *Journal of William Lockerby, 1808–1809.* Hakluyt Society, 1925.

MACKENZIE, P., *The Life of Thomas Muir, Esquire, Advocate.* Glasgow, 1821.
MARGAROT, M., *The Story of the Trial of Maurice Margarot.*
MATHIESON, W. L., *England in Transition.*
MEIKLE, H. W., "The Death of Thomas Muir", *Scottish Historical Review*, vol. xxvii.
——, "Two Glasgow Merchants in the French Revolution", *Scottish Historical Review*, vol. ix.
MILLINGTON, F. H., *History of Thetford.*

NEWMAN, C. E. T., *The Spirit of Wharf House.* Sydney, 1961.
NORRIE, —, *Dundee Celebrities.*

OMAN, C. W. C., "Historical Development of England from 1792 to 1815", *Historians' History of the World*, vol. xxi, book 6, ch. 1. London 1908.
OMOND, G. W. T., *The Lord Advocates of Scotland.*

PAINE, T., *Common Sense.* 1776.
——, *The Age of Reason.* 1793.
——, *A Declaration of Rights.*
——, *A Dialogue Between the Governors and the Governed.*
——, *Prospects on the Rubicon.* 1787.
——, *Public Good.* 1780.
——, *The Rights of Man.* 1791–2.
PALMER, T. F., and SKIRVING, W., *A Narrative of the Sufferings of T. F. Palmer and W. Skirving during a Voyage to Botany Bay in 1794.* London, 1797.
PAUL, C. KEGAN, *William Godwin: His Friends and Contemporaries.*
PERON, P. F., *Mémoires du Capitaine Péron sur ses Voyages.* Paris, 1824.
PHILLIP, A., *The Voyage of Governor Phillip to Botany Bay.* London, 1789.
POWERS, L. B., *Old Monterey.*
PRESCOTT, W. H., *History of the Conquest of Mexico.* 1843.

ROE, M., "Maurice Margarot: A Radical in Two Hemispheres, 1792–1815", *Bulletin of the Institute of Historical Research*, May 1958. London.
ROSEBERY, Lord, *Pitt.* 1891.
Royal Admiral, Log and Journal. Alexander Turnbull Library, Wellington.
RUMSEY, H. J., *Pioneers of Sydney Cove.*
RUSDEN, G. W., *Curiosities of Colonization.* 1874.

Scotsman, 24th August 1844.
SHORT, B., Article, *Unitarian*, October 1964.
SMITH, A., *An Enquiry into the Nature and Causes of the Wealth of Nations*. 1776.
SMITH, S., *Wit and Wisdom of the Reverend Sydney Smith*. 1860.
SMITH, W., *Journal of a Voyage in the Missionary Ship Duff*. 1813.
Sydney Gazette, 1804–6. Various Articles.

TONE, W., *Journal of General Theobald Wolfe Tone*.

VANCOUVER, G., *A Voyage of Discovery to the Pacific Ocean*. London, 1801.
VEITCH, G. S., *The Genesis of Parliamentary Reform*.

WALTER, R., *A Voyage Round the World*. 1748.
WARD, W. R., *Georgian Oxford*.
WATSON, J. H., "Notes on Some Suburbs of Sydney", *Journal of the Royal Australian Historical Society*, vol. xiii.
WHITE, J., *Journal of a Voyage to New South Wales*. London, 1790.
WOODWARD, W. G., *Tom Paine, America's Godfather*.